State College

at

Framingham

10-68-948217

AMERICAN INDIAN AND WHITE CHILDREN

AMERICAN INDIAN AND WHITE CHILDREN

A Sociopsychological Investigation

By
ROBERT J. HAVIGHURST
and
BERNICE L. NEUGARTEN

THE UNIVERSITY OF CHICAGO PRESS
CHICAGO AND LONDON

Library of Congress Catalog Card Number: 54-11208

THE UNIVERSITY OF CHICAGO PRESS, CHICAGO 60637
The University of Chicago Press, Ltd., London W.C. 1

Published 1955. New Impression 1969
Printed in the United States of America

PREFACE

The studies to be reported in this monograph were undertaken as part of the Indian Education Research Project of the Committee on Human Development of the University of Chicago and the United States Office of Indian Affairs.

The general purpose of the Project was to study the development of Indian children in six American Indian tribes—their moral, emotional, and intellectual development—so as to derive implications for the education of Indian children. The field program involved studies of about a thousand children, six to eighteen years old, selected to represent one or more communities in each of the following tribes: Hopi, Navaho, Papago, Sioux, Zia, and Zuni. Thus the results comprise data on five Southwest Indian tribes and a Plains tribe.

The research was planned in 1941. It was decided to enlist Indian Service personnel, mainly teachers, nurses, and school administrators, to do most of the field work. This personnel was to be supplemented by a small group of specialists working in the field—psychiatrists and psychologists. In order to train the Indian Service personnel for field work, a two-week training seminar was held at Santa Fe, New Mexico, early in 1942. Collection of data was made in the field from July, 1942, to July, 1943, and the data were first analyzed by a research staff in Chicago in 1943 and 1944.

Publications of three types have appeared. The first type is the tribal monograph, which reports the findings of the research on a single tribe.[1] A second group of publications includes technical analyses of the data from various instruments and practical recommendations for

1. Monographs already published are: Laura Thompson and Alice Joseph, The Hopi Way (Chicago: University of Chicago Press, 1944); Gordon Macgregor, Warriors without Weapons: A Study of the Pine Ridge Sioux (Chicago: University of Chicago Press, 1945); Dorothea C. Leighton and Clyde Kluckhohn, The Navaho and Children of the People (Cambridge, Mass.: Harvard University Press, 1944 and 1947); Alice Joseph, Rosamond B. Spicer, and Jane Chesky, The Desert People: A Study of the Papago Indians (Chicago: University of Chicago Press, 1949).

administration of Indian Affairs.[2] The third type of publication is one which compares children from the various tribes in one or another aspect of development.[3] The present publication belongs to this third type and presents in comparative form the results of five sociopsychological techniques which were used to study the moral and emotional development of the Indian children. For comparison and contrast, similar studies were made of white children in a typical midwestern community which will be called "Midwest,"[4] and the data on the Midwest children are included in the text of this publication. More recently, in 1953, one of the authors collected data from New Zealand children on two of the tests used here, and these data are included as Appendix F of this monograph.

Specialists from several disciplines have worked together in the Indian Education Research Project—chiefly specialists in anthropology, sociology, psychology, psychiatry, medicine, linguistics, education, and administration. The methods of sociopsychological analysis that provide the content for the present monograph emerged from this collaboration.

Robert J. Havighurst

Bernice L. Neugarten

University of Chicago

2. Laura Thompson, Culture in Crisis (New York: Harper & Bros., 1950). Dr. Thompson has also written a number of technical articles which will be referred to at appropriate points in this monograph.

3. Two articles have been published comparing the intellectual development of the various Indian groups and of white children: Robert J. Havighurst and Rhea R. Hilkevitch, "The Intelligence of Indian Children as Measured by a Performance Scale," Journal of Abnormal and Social Psychology, XXXIX (1944), 419-33; Robert J. Havighurst, Minna Korol, and Inez E. Pratt, "Environment and the Draw-a-Man Test: The Performance of Indian Children," Journal of Abnormal and Social Psychology, XL (1946), 50-63. William E. Henry has published a monograph reporting comparative results on the Thematic Apperception Test, The Thematic Apperception Technique in the Study of Culture-Personality Relations ("Genetic Psychology Monographs," Vol. XXXV [1947]), pp. 3-135. A monograph entitled "American Indian Rorschach Studies," by Hallowell, Hassrick, Henry, Joseph, Klopfer, and Leighton, is now in preparation.

4. The Midwest data were collected in 1942-45 as part of a long-term study of child development being carried on by the Committee on Human Development, University of Chicago. The Midwest community is described fully in W. L. Warner and Associates, Democracy in Jonesville (New York: Harper & Bros., 1949). The moral and intellectual characteristics of its youth are described in Robert J. Havighurst and Hilda Taba, Adolescent Character and Personality (New York: John Wiley & Sons, 1949).

ACKNOWLEDGMENTS

The general planning of the Indian Education Research was guided by a joint committee from the United States Office of Indian Affairs (Commissioner John Collier, Willard W. Beatty, René d'Harnoncourt, Joseph McCaskill) and the University of Chicago (W. Lloyd Warner, Ralph W. Tyler, Robert J. Havighurst), with Dr. Laura Thompson as co-ordinator.

The planning of the sociopsychological aspects of the study was initiated by W. Lloyd Warner and Robert J. Havighurst and was carried forward with the valuable assistance of Professor Eugene Lerner, of Sarah Lawrence College.

When the time came to do the testing in the field, this work was organized and directed by Dr. Thompson, with the assistance of supervisors in the several tribes and communities. While the names of the many supervisors and their field workers, given in the books on the several tribes, are omitted here for lack of space, these persons were the ones who actually interviewed and tested the children, and the quality of the whole study owes much to their interest and their intelligent field work. The testing in Midwest was done by Bernice L. Neugarten and Eleanor Volberding.

In the analysis of data the following people made substantial contributions:

Emotional Response Test—Jean Hall, Iva Osanai Schmitt, Nora Loeb Weckler
Moral Ideology Test—Jeanette Murstine, Irene Goldblatt
Free Drawings Test—Brooke Mordy, Lisbeth Eubank, Edward Rannells, Inger Olson Klumpner
Rules of Games—Lisbeth Eubank

When the preliminary reports on these tests were given to the writers of tribal monographs and to others in the research, these persons supplied valuable criticisms and supplementary information which we have used in this monograph. For this assistance we wish especially to thank Jane Chesky, Florence Hawley Ellis, Dr. Alice Joseph, Clyde Kluckhohn, Dr. Dorothea Leighton, Gordon Macgregor, Laura Thompson, and W. Lloyd Warner.

TABLE OF CONTENTS

APPENDIX

LIST OF TABLES

INTRODUCTION

In this study of the moral and emotional development of Indian children, there were two major purposes: first, to find out as much as possible about the development of the children in the study; second, to devise a battery of tests which might be used by others in researches on child development in various cultures.

Methods for studying moral and emotional development are much less advanced than methods for studying mental development. They are less refined as measuring instruments, and they have as yet found almost no use in comparative studies of child development. Consequently, it was necessary to work out new techniques, to make new adaptations of methods which had been tried before, and to work out ways of quantifying results. Certain quiding questions were kept in mind as the questions to be answered by the new tests: They were:

1. What are the sources of reward and punishment in the life of the child?
2. How do the child's ideas of right and wrong develop?
3. How do the child's concepts of justice and moral law develop?
4. What are the principal emotional experiences in the child's life?
5. What are the child's principal values and aversions?
6. What attitudes does the child develop toward people in his life—toward parents, grandparents, siblings, strangers, other people?
7. What attitudes does the child develop about property?
8. What concepts and attitudes does the child develop toward the supernatural?
9. What age changes are there in the foregoing attitudes and concepts?
10. What sex differences are there in the foregoing attitudes and concepts?

There were a few techniques already worked out which promised to be useful in a cross-cultural study of this kind. Principally these were the methods used by Jean Piaget in studying the child's developing concepts of the moral and physical world.[1] Piaget's methods were simple

1. Jean Piaget, The Moral Judgment of the Child (New York: Harcourt, Brace & Co., 1932).

and adaptable to our purposes. Some of them had already been used in America, and one of them had already been used with Indian children.[2]

The other techniques had been recently employed in tentative, exploratory form by American psychologists or anthropologists and stood ready for further development. One of them, the Emotional Response Test, had not been described in any publication but had been mentioned in a manuscript by Margaret Mead where she referred to some unpublished work by Kilton Stewart.[3]

The Moral Ideology Test had been devised by Alex Bavelas at the State University of Iowa and used by Joan Kalhorn.[4] This test had been adapted by the writers for the Midwest studies and could be immediately applied to the Indian research.

Several varieties of Free Drawing Tests had been tried by persons interested in the development of children's artistic ability, as well as by persons interested in exploring art production as a means of studying personality.

It was with these crude instruments and ideas for instruments that the Indian Study staff started to work. Fortunately, there was opportunity to try them out on Indian children before putting them into final form. At the Santa Fe Seminar for Training Field Workers in 1942, the new tests were tried with Indian children of various ages and revised in the light of this experience. Since most of the tests consisted of questions, it was essential to find the "right" English expressions to convey the meanings that were intended, as well as to make clear to Indian field workers who would use the tests in their own language just what the questions meant.

Thus a battery of tests was devised and placed in a "Manual for Field Workers" (Appendix A). At the same time, a test booklet was created for use with the individual child, containing the following tests:

2. W. Dennis and R. W. Russell, "Piaget's Questions Applied to Zuni Children," Child Development, XI (1940), 181-87.

3. Margaret Mead, unpublished manuscript, later rewritten and published as chapter xiii in the Manual of Child Psychology, ed. Leonard Carmichael (New York: John Wiley & Sons, 1946).

4. A. Bavelas, "A Method for Investigating Individual and Group Ideology," Sociometry, V (1942), 199-212; Joan Kalhorn, "Ideological Differences among Rural Children" (unpublished Master's thesis, State University of Iowa, 1941).

Tests of Moral Judgment (Piaget type)
1. Belief in Immanent Justice and Animism
2. Attitudes toward Rules of Games
The Emotional Response Test
The Moral Ideology Test

These tests are analyzed and their results discussed in this monograph. (In addition, there were several other tests of the Piaget type in the Moral Judgment battery, but, because we have not succeeded in working out a method of dealing quantitatively with the results, they are not reported in this monograph.)

The free drawings have also been analyzed as a source of information concerning the children's interests and their degree of acculturation to the white culture.

The studies collected here were first written up in preliminary form in 1943 and 1944 by Mr. Havighurst and colleagues and were used by the writers of the tribal monographs in preparing their publications. Those preliminary reports were then revised on the basis of further study and of criticism by those writers; the Midwest data were added for purposes of comparison; and all the data were subjected to new and more extensive analyses.

The present monograph is organized in the following manner: After a brief description of the cultures included in the Study and of the sampling procedures used, chapters iii through vii deal, respectively, with the data obtained from each of the sociopsychological techniques utilized in the Study. The two longest chapters, iii and iv, are devoted to the Emotional Response and the Moral Ideology tests. Because these two instruments proved, on the whole, to be the most successful in our battery and are most likely to be used by future investigators and because there has appeared elsewhere in the literature no extended exposition of either method, the first sections of chapters iii and iv constitute a somewhat detailed description of the respective instrument and of the problems involved in the quantification, statistical treatment, and reliability of the data.

In each of chapters iii through vii the data are presented in summary tables for all the cultural groups studied; and there is a brief discussion of our results in terms of cross-cultural comparisons, sex differences, and age trends. Since the data themselves are expected to be of con-

siderable value to anthropologists who are especially interested in one or another culture and who may wish to make more refined analyses of their own, the data are presented in greater detail in a series of appendixes. It is hoped that in this way the monograph will serve as a useful sourcebook for students interested in child development in various cultures.

Having dealt with each technique individually, we have then, in chapter viii, drawn together data from the several tests: (1) to see to what extent various measures agree or disagree in the information they yield regarding moral and emotional development and (2) to obtain a certain over-all description of moral and emotional development of children in each culture. Here, as elsewhere in the monograph, we have proceeded cautiously, knowing that these techniques are of a somewhat different nature from those ordinarily employed by students of culture and leaving it to the anthropologist to expand upon and to make final judgment as to the validity of such generalizations as we have drawn.

In chapter ix we have summarized very briefly what we consider our successes and failures in these studies, and we make certain recommendations concerning the use of these techniques in future research.

In a final Appendix we present, for comparison with the Midwest material, the data from New Zealand children on the Emotional Response and Moral Ideology tests.

CHAPTER I

THE CULTURAL SETTINGS

There are seven principal groups of people involved as subjects of these studies: the Pueblo Indians, represented by three tribes—Hopi, Zuni, and Zia; two other southwestern tribes—the Navaho and the Papago; the Sioux of the Great Plains; and the white American children of the community called "Midwest." We shall describe these seven cultural groups very briefly here, as background for the material to follow. For fuller descriptions the reader may consult the tribal monographs already referred to, as well as the wide literature available on each of the Indian tribes here studied.

The Hopi

For centuries the Hopi have lived in their stone cities on three mesas which extend out from a broad table-like formation in northern Arizona called "Black Mesa." The Hopi, who number nearly 3,500, are the westernmost representatives of the Pueblo Indians. They have managed through the ages to wring a precarious existence from the desert on which they live, and, in so doing, they have managed to keep their culture intact in the face of aggressive Spaniards, Navaho Indians, and Americans. They have maintained their traditional religion with its complex and absorbing ritual, their social structure, and much of their old technology. They have preserved more of their ancestral heritage than any other Indian tribe in the United States, and they show practically no admixture with whites.

The Hopi raise corn, beans, chili, melons, and peaches, and they herd sheep. They have been skilled craftsmen since prehistoric times. Many of the young men earn good wages as stonemasons in the cities of the Southwest for a few years before returning to their homeland to marry and settle down.

Their houses are one- and two-story stone buildings crowded closely together, with a plaza near the center and two or three narrow streets leading into it. In their villages, hugging the tops of the high steep mesa, these people lead a hard existence. Water is scarce and must either be

carried up the steep path from the springs at the foot of the mesa or drawn from shallow cisterns alive with tadpoles and other forms of aquatic life.

Food is grown in fields at the base of the mesa, fields which are flooded by occasional rains or are moistened by seepage from the sandstone of the mesa. Each family has several plots of about an acre apiece, on which they plant corn and beans and squash and melons; and they usually have a small orchard with peaches, apricots, pears, and apples.

The crops depend on summer rains. While there are many sudden light showers which serve to settle the dust on the plaza, only a few times a season is there a downpour sufficient for the water to reach the deep roots of the corn. Then water runs in muddy streamlets down the sides of the mesa and channels into the dry washes, which become raging torrents within a few minutes. The Hopi pray for such downpours. If they have chosen their fields with care, enough water will sink in to nurture the crop; but if the poeple are unlucky, their crop will be washed out or covered with silt. Every three or four years there is so little rain that the corn crop fails to mature.

The Hopi, like most of the Pueblo Indians, are relatively short and thickset, with broad faces. By middle age, many Hopi men are barrel-chested, and most of the women are well-rounded. They are friendly with strangers, and the children will look into a stranger's face and smile. The children wear Navaho jewelry, which their parents have purchased from the Navaho, giving melons, peaches, and corn in exchange. Children and adults wear ordinary farmers' clothes, but many of the older men allow their hair to grow long and bind it with a headband.

Clan membership is the most important social fact about a Hopi individual, and he belongs to the clan of his mother. Land also belongs to the women, and a young man when he marries generally goes to live with his wife's family and to work her land. The clan is the religious unit.

Religion is the center of life for the Hopi. They conceive of the world—including man, the animals, the plants, the land, and the supernatural—as an absolute, ordered system functioning under a definite set of rules which are known to them. In accordance with these rules, they believe they can exercise a measure of control over their environment through regulating their behavior, emotions, and thoughts in a prescribed manner.

The child is early made acquainted with this view of life and the universe. His two religious initiations, at about six and fourteen, teach him what the rules of life are and give him roles to play in the rituals. These he believes to be essential to the well-being of himself, his family, his clan, and his tribe.

Although government schools now enrol all the children, these schools are more a supplement to the Hopi way of life than a center for the learning of a new way. Few Hopis are Christians. The schools adjust their schedules to the religious schedules of clan rituals, as well as to the economic demands made upon the boys of sheepherding and agriculture.

Two of the three Hopi mesas are represented in this study. First Mesa, with its three villages of Walpi, Sichomovi, and Polacca, and Third Mesa, with its villages of Old Oraibi and New Oraibi. Old Oraibi is one of the most conservative and ancient of the Hopi pueblos and, indeed, is probably the oldest continuously inhabited town in the United States, while New Oraibi is one which has been most influenced by modern Western civilization. First Mesa has held to its traditions without much internal stress and is less self-conscious about its religious and other customs than is Third Mesa.

The Zuni

The Zuni tribe live in their pueblo on high ground overlooking the Zuni River in west-central New Mexico. They are a substantial, conservative, and relatively prosperous people, borrowing a good deal from the white culture but retaining many of the satisfactions of their traditional religion and way of life. Most Zunis have fields of land down along the river, where they live in the growing season of spring and summer. They return to their adobe homes for the autumn and winter, when they turn their attention to a ceremonial life which is the center of Zuni existence.

With 2,200 residents, Zuni is the largest of the pueblos. The population is not changing rapidly. Zuni is an island of Pueblo culture which is large and solid enough to withstand successfully the waves of American culture that might threaten a smaller group. The Zuni people have relatively

fertile land, the men own herds of sheep, and the making of Zuni pottery brings cash to many families.

In spite of the fact that there are active Christian missions in Zuni and a good many people are nominal members of Christian churches, the tribal Zuni religion flourishes and gives a richness to the lives of the people, whether pagan or Christian. Autumn—the ceremonial season—is the culmination of the year. In the words of an eighteen-year-old Zuni boy who wrote his autobiography—"During the summertime the families move out to the different farming villages and we do all the farming. By the month of August or September the families start moving back to Zuni where winter is spent with great pleasure of dancing while the children attend the schools."

Ruth Benedict says:

> The Zuni are a ceremonious people, a people who value sobriety and inoffensiveness above all other virtues. Their interest is centered upon their rich and complex ceremonial life. Their cults of the masked gods, of healing, of the sun, of the sacred fetishes, of war, of the dead, are formal established bodies of ritual with priestly officials and calendric observances. No field of activity competes with ritual for foremost place in their attention. Probably most grown men among the western Pueblos give to it the greater part of their waking life. It requires the memorizing of an amount of word-perfect ritual that our less trained minds find staggering, and the performance of neatly dovetailed ceremonies that are charted by the calendar and complexly interlock all the different cults and the governing body in endless formal procedures.
>
> The ceremonial life not only demands their time; it preoccupies their attention. Not only those who are responsible for the ritual and those who take part in it, but all the people of the pueblo, women and families who "have nothing," that is, that have no ritual possession, centre their daily conversation about it. While it is in progress, they stand all day as spectators.[1]

Zuni religion is similar to that of the Hopi, with intricate ceremonies linking the Zuni to their environment. The children know the katcinas as gift-givers and punishers; the children have their initiation ceremonies, as in Hopi pueblos; and they fear witches and witchcraft. In general, the Zuni seem to enjoy their religious life more than the Hopi.

Zuni social structure is traditionally matrilineal, and residence is matrilocal, as with the Hopi; but the Zuni have departed more freely from tradition when practical advantages are to be gained from a married

---

1. Ruth Benedict, Patterns of Culture (Boston and New York: Houghton Mifflin Co., 1934), pp. 59-60.

son's staying in his mother's house, working her land, and so on.

Custom and public opinion are the governing moral forces of Zuni, even more than with the Hopi. Children are controlled by the phrase, "What will people think of our family, that it has a naughty child?" Young men have committed suicide rather than face public disapproval when they have been discovered in some misdemeanor.

Although they maintain business relations with the whites, the Zuni keep to themselves in most ways. They have not intermarried appreciably with whites, and they do not migrate for long periods of time from their home grounds.

The children who participated in the study were a sample from the government day school. About half of the children attend this school, while the other half attend the two mission schools—one Catholic and the other Christian Reformed. There appears to be no perceptible difference between the children in the different schools, and a given child may transfer from one school to another.

Zia

Zia pueblo is a small group which jealously guards against encroachment from without. With 37 families and some 235 residents, it is constantly in danger of being engulfed by the aggressive culture which surrounds it. Perhaps in consequence of this fact, Zia people are more jealous of their cultural integrity, more secretive about their religion, and more negative toward white people than are the other two pueblos in the Study.

Located on the crest of a volcanic hill beside the Jemez River, Zia is 40 miles northwest of Albuquerque, New Mexico. The pueblo is reached by a sandy road, which leaves the traveled highway and traverses the plain of the river. Though the river is dry in August, there is sufficient water in spring and early summer to fill an irrigation reservoir and to grow crops, which are somewhat better and certainly easier to produce than those of the Hopi. Sheep are pastured in the river valley, though only the "wealthy" families possess sheep.

After crossing the river, the road winds up the low hill into the village of small adobe houses. Most of the houses are old two- and three-room structures, though a few new two-story houses give a suggestion of prosperity.

The Zia people are not unfriendly, but they are shy. They do not meet strangers as easily as do the Hopi. Their social structure and religion are similar to those of Hopi and Zuni, except that the public ritual dances of these larger groups play a smaller part in Zia social life. Zia rituals are jealously guarded from the eyes of whites, and visitors are not permitted at the dances, whereas the Hopi dances attract whites and Navahos from a hundred miles away. The patrilineal and matrilineal systems are equally strong at Zia, a fact which differentiates this pueblo from the matrilineal systems of Hopi and Zuni.

The Zia children all go to school, at first to a two-room day school located outside the pueblo at the foot of the hill. Thus the school is "outside" their culture. If the teachers have difficulty with the youngsters, they ask help from the head man of the village, who walks down to the school, talks things over with the teachers, and then admonishes the children. At about the age of fourteen, some Zia children go away to Indian boarding schools, usually to Santa Fe. Thus the school life of the child is physically divorced from his home and community.

The Navaho

Largest of the American Indian tribes, the Navaho occupy the barren lands of northeastern Arizona and northwestern New Mexico. They raise sheep and supplement this source of income with farming, silversmithing, and weaving. Their population has grown rapidly to 62,000 in the present century; and their herds have become so plentiful that overgrazing and soil erosion have become serious problems for them.

In many respects the isolated Navaho life contrasts with that of the village-dwelling Pueblo people. Whereas the Pueblo Indians partake of close-knit communal life, the Navaho live in small family groups and are alone much of the time.

In appearance the average Navaho is rather tall and slender, in contrast to the short, chunky Pueblo tribesman. Colorful clothes and an abundance of silver jewelry, for which the Navaho silversmiths are famous, make the Navaho "attractive" in the eyes of visiting whites. But the Navaho are dignified, aloof, and shy. They will not easily enter into a conversation. If a visitor comes near a Navaho child who is out in the desert watching sheep, the child will run and hide.

Most Navahos live in small family groups of two or three closely related households. Their hogans, which are six-sided houses made of logs and earth, are seldom more than three in number, placed near their cornfields. But they are not tied to their fields, and agriculture is not so imporatnt to them as it is to the Pueblo tribes. Instead, they "follow the sheep" from summer to winter pastures and move about freely in wagons or pickup trucks. The Navaho could not get along without his horses.

While some Navaho have grown wealthy from sheep-raising, most Navaho families are only a few steps ahead of famine, and they maintain this precarious position by continual efforts at farming and herding, in which the children help as soon as they can be trusted to go out and watch the sheep.

Clan relationship is important to the Navaho. The Navaho traveler may expect to be put up for the night by his clan brothers wherever he may travel over the broad and barren area which is the home of his tribe. Clan membership is inherited through the mother, and marriage between clan members is taboo. Polygamy was common in former days and is still practiced in out-of-the-way places.

Public religion for the Navaho centers around "Sings," which may include dances. The "Sings" are ceremonials which may be short and simple or long and complex. While aimed at controlling illness—a source of deep anxiety to the Navaho—the "Sings" also serve the same function that church or lodge attendance may for a white man or that participation in the ceremonial dances does for the Pueblo Indians.

The Navaho believe that their religious practices (together with instructions for weaving, planting, and social conduct) have come down to them from the Holy People. Although a number of Navahos take part in Christian mission services, they tend to add aspects of Christianity to the traditional beliefs they already have rather than to replace one with the other.

Relations with the whites have been peaceful since the Navaho were liberated from their captivity of 1864-68 at Fort Sumner. Still the Navaho feel that they have been pushed out of their most fertile lands by white settlers, and they tend to be suspicious of such government policies as herd-reduction, adopted to prevent ruin of the land through overgrazing.

For this study three Navaho communities were chosen, one with a maximum of contact with whites, one with an intermediate degree, and the

third with almost none. The Shiprock area is a high barren plateau where the states of Arizona, New Mexico, Colorado, and Utah meet. The plateau is dominated by the great volcanic rock which gave its name to this region. The main highway north from Gallup to Mesa Verde National Park brings tourists through the settlement of Shiprock, where are located a boarding school, a day school, a hospital, missions, and trading posts.

Shiprock is an area of maximum contact between Indian and white man, with a good deal of tension and resultant hostility on the part of the Indian. This is the center of antiwhite feeling and of resistance to government programs of stock-reduction and immigration. Yet Shiprock is also closer to the white culture than any other part of the reservation. The single biological family is the most common unit in this area, and polygamous families are extremely rare.

The Ramah area is some 50 miles southeast of Gallup, a 7,000-foot plateau outside the Navaho Reservation. There are about 500 Navahos in this area and a larger number of white people. Since this group of Navaho was outside the Reservation, they had been left more to themselves by the Indian Service than were those in the Shiprock area. Although a few of the children went away to boarding school, most of them had no schooling before a day school was opened by the Indian Service in 1943.

Navaho Mountain is the most isolated, inaccessible area of the reservation. The mountain itself is a huge dome-shaped mass on the Utah-Arizona line just south of the junction of the San Juan and Colorado rivers. Standing alone on the Rainbow Plateau, it serves as a landmark over thousands of square miles but is seldom seen by white people except those who fly by on their way from Denver to Los Angeles. Since the mountain is very holy, it is also fearsome, and no Navahos dwell upon it. But the sagebrush flats and the deep canyons to the south of Navaho Mountain have been occupied since 1898, when a man called "First Settler," with his three wives, children, and one son-in-law, began to come there for winter range for their stock, and later made this their year-round residence. Most of the present population, numbering about 200, is descended from this one extended family.

Navaho Mountain is a peaceful, conservative, "backwoodsy" place, where Navaho traditions are fairly well preserved. For example, the children are more familiar with traditional Navaho games than with the games they are taught in school. There is little hostility toward the whites, who are known to the people through the trader and the schoolteacher. The school was built in 1936 and enrols somewhat less than half the children.

The Papago

The Papago call themselves "the Desert People." They live on a 65-mile-square reservation, west of Tucson, Arizona, and bordering on Mexico. Some 6,000 people live on lonely dry farms or in scattered sprawling villages. It is an arid land, one of the hottest and driest on the continent, with miles of cholla cactus and creosote brush on the valley floor. Where the valleys rise to foothills and then to mountains, there are good forage grasses and oak and scrub pine trees. The Baboquivari Mountains, forming the eastern boundary of the reservation, culminate in Baboquivari Peak, 7,740 feet high and 1 mile above the desert floor.

The Desert People have farmed small fields and raised livestock for centuries, but now they depend increasingly on wage work in cotton fields, near-by mines, and ranches. They are broad-faced, fairly large people, and inclined to grow fat. Women and girls wear cotton or rayon dresses, with more than the usual somber color at fiesta time. Boys and men wear denim or khaki pants and work shirts. The people are quiet, self-contained, slow-moving, and they seem shy to strangers.

Almost all the Papago belong to a Catholic or a Presbyterian church. The first Catholic missionary, Father Kino, came in 1698 and was followed at intervals by other Spanish missionaries. Out of these missionary efforts developed the Sonora Catholic Church, a sect without organization or official Catholic connections. The people combined many of their earlier religious beliefs with some of the Catholic teachings into a religion which is now gradually being regularized by Roman Catholic priests who have recently come to the reservation.

The Presbyterians have been active as missionaries since 1910 and have a following in the eastern, more acculturated part of the reservation. Their adherents include many of the tribal leaders.

Traditionally, the Papago family unit consists of parents, unmarried sons and daughters, and married sons with their wives and children. Though a young couple may wander about in search of employment, the husband's father's house is always home. The Papago are patrilineal and patrilocal by tradition, but in this characteristically flexible society

a man may, for practical reasons, join his wife's family.

The Papago home is a cluster of small adobe or wattle-and-daub buildings with a ramada or arbor roofed with dry grass, where the family cook, eat, and work in the hot weather. Beds are placed out in the open or under the veranda. A large olla (pottery jar) holds water for the household, and water must be hauled by wagon from a well which may be several miles away.

Though the family is the chief social unit, the village exerts a good deal of influence on the Papago child. The village is less influential than the pueblo, but it has a place in Papago life which differentiates the Papago from the Navaho.

The Papago have always been a peaceful, adaptable people. They have adapted recently to American white people; earlier to the Spaniard; and always to the desert land, with its extremes of cold and heat, drought and flood, want and plenty. Although on the surface they seem more nearly assimilated to the white culture than the Pueblos and Navaho to the north, they still retain attitudes and habits of past generations which mark them as a group apart.

Two districts were chosen for this study. Baboquivari district is the more acculturated, having the reservation headquarters at Sells and four related villages: Topawa, Komelik, Supi Oidak, and Choulic. These villages contain 76 households with 129 school children attending government and mission day schools. A few of the older children are in government boarding schools at Tucson and Phoenix. This Baboquivari district is called "Topawa" in this study, after the principal village in the district.

To the west and in less contact with white culture is the Hickiwan — Gu Vo district, with the villages of Hickiwan, Emika, Stoa Pitk, Hotason Vo, Tatia Took, Vaya Chic, Gu Vo, and Kuakatch. These villages contain 38 households with 119 school-age children, about half of whom were in school.

The Sioux

The Sioux are the typical Indians, in the eyes of most Americans. They hunted buffalo, lived in tepees, dressed in eagle-feather war-bonnets, and fought savagely against the whites. The Western or Teton-Dakota, with whom these studies deal, are descendants of several of the hunting bands who led the resistance of the Northern Plains Indians. The Sioux were finally defeated and put on reservations in 1876. Their last great buffalo hunt was held in 1882. In 1881 the reservation superintendent forbade the continuance of the Sun Dance, the great tribal religious ceremony. Thus frustrated and hemmed in, their bitterness grew and sought outlet. In 1889 the Sioux learned of the Ghost Dance which had appeared among the Indians to the west of them. This dance celebrated the belief that a messiah would appear, to destroy the white race and to bring back the buffalo and the Indian dead. Soon the Sioux were dancing the Ghost Dance in a frenzy. In 1890 one great dance brought many bands together, to the terror of the white settlers and the reservation superintendent, who mistook the ritual for a war dance and called for troops. Near Wounded Knee a calvary troop, part of General Custer's former regiment, came upon the Big Foot band of Indians and disarmed them. A shot was fired, and the soldiers attacked, killing 128 warriors and massacring many women and children who were fleeing from the scene.

This event, sometimes called the "Battle of Wounded Knee" and sometimes called the "Massacre of Wounded Knee," "took the heart" out of the Sioux. Then began a period of passive acceptance of white culture. Missionaries came, chiefly Episcopal and Catholic. Children were taken from their families, sometimes forcibly, and sent away to government boarding schools. The Indians were encouraged to raise grain and cattle, to build permanent homes, and to adopt white ways in general. Considerable intermarriage took place, so that today only 40 per cent of the Sioux in the Pine Ridge Reservation are full-blooded Indians.

Gradually the old bands broke up into individual families and settled along the creeks. Individual tracts of land were allotted to all Indians, on which they raised cattle. Eventually they became fairly prosperous, and the issuance of government rations became unnecessary by 1914. Then the high cattle prices of World War I tempted the Indians to sell their herds. To this was added pressure from white stockmen to have the Indians dispose of their cattle and leave their range land to white interests.

In the 1920's the Sioux began selling their land to white settlers and to indulge in an orgy of spending their cash. They bought automobiles and other gadgets and soon ran through their money. While they stayed on, raising chickens and milk cows on small plots of land, the drought

and depression of the 1930's wiped out most of their stock, and they became dependent on government charity.

Since 1935 the government has been aiding Indians to acquire land again for cattle-raising, and there has been a slow return to a self-supporting economy. But many of the young people go to neighboring towns and cities to work as laborers and domestic servants.

Thus the Sioux Indians have little left of their earlier life but bitter memories and a most precarious present and future ahead of them. Their old ways have been shattered by the impact of white culture, and they have not worked out a viable new culture. The men have little to live for, and the children have little to which to look ahead.

The Pine Ridge Reservation, on which 8,500 Sioux now live, is located on the southern boundary of South Dakota and is watered by the White River. Two communities were chosen for the study. Kyle is a village and school center for several farming communities. The Indians are all farmers and represent the rural people of the reservation fairly well in their way of life.

Pine Ridge town, the other community chosen for testing, is the reservation headquarters. Here the majority of Indians are mixed-bloods, and there is much white influence.

A third community, Wanblee, is a rural town composed of people like those at Kyle. Some data were collected on Wanblee children, but the study was not carried out systematically there.

Midwest

The community which is taken to represent American white culture is a small midwestern city with its surrounding rural trading territory. Midwest is the county seat of a county whose working force is between 25 and 50 per cent engaged in agricultural work, with the remainder employed in commerce, industry, and the professions. The population of Midwest is about 6,000. There are two or three small factories and the usual business establishments of a county-seat town. In practically every aspect of its civic and industrial life, Midwest is representative of the kind of community most frequently found in the middle-western part of the United States.[2]

2. See W. L. Warner and Associates, Democracy in Jonesville (New York: Harper & Bros., 1949).

Midwest is somewhat more stratified into social classes than are any of the Indian communities considered in the study. Midwest has five social classes, each class having certain cultural ways and values of its own besides those it shares with the other four classes as part of the general American culture. In number the two highest classes contain about 10 per cent of the population, while the lowest class contains about 15-20 per cent, leaving 70-75 per cent of the population in the two largest classes, known as the "lower-middle" and "upper-lower" classes. These two largest classes are enough alike to permit their being combined conceptually in what Warner has called the "common-man" level. They contain at least three-fourths of the children of Midwest. In any comparison with a quite different culture, these two classes tend to represent the American culture, since they form so much of it by bulk. In occupation the members of these two classes are white-collar workers or manual workers, employed in business or industry.

The Midwest family normally consists of father, mother, and two to four children. This family lives in a house by itself, even though grandparents and other relatives also live in the community. In a few cases, grandparents live with the family. Dominance in the home is usually held by the person who supports the family, nearly always the husband and father. Property is generally held in the name of the man, the wife seldom holding any property in her own name, unless she is in the upper social class. When a young couple marry, they attempt to set up their own home as soon as possible, but sometimes they live with the parents of one or the other spouse for a time.

Although religion is not so important in the lives of Midwest people as it is in the lives of the Southwest Indians, most of the people of Midwest belong to Protestant or Catholic churches and bring up their children in this way. While religious ceremonials, such as Christmas and Easter, are important in their lives, these are only one of many centers of interest for children and adults. Other important events include national holidays, such as Memorial Day and Fourth of July. Social organizations, such as lodges and clubs, and economic organizations, such as labor unions and business associations, are important in the lives of Midwest people.

School is highly important in the lives of all children from the ages of six to fourteen. Social life for children centers about the school, and

to a considerable extent their vocational preparation is received in the school. From fourteen to eighteen most children intensify their interest and activity in school, although a group (growing in number during these years from about 10 to about 50 per cent) drop out of school to go to work or to get married.

CHAPTER II

THE SAMPLES OF CHILDREN

The aim in these studies was to get information on a representative group of children in each culture in the age range six to eighteen. All the children in this age range in a given community were included in the study if their number totaled 150 or less. If the number was larger than this, a representative sample was taken. In general, it can be said that the groups included in these studies were more representative of the groups from which they came than has been the case in any other study of American Indian children. However, the sampling obtained still left much to be desired, especially for the ages over fifteen.

There are two points at which the question of sampling should be considered. First, at the point of selection of the children to represent the group and, second, at the point of administration of a given test to the children selected (seldom were all the children on the list actually tested). The first step in the sampling procedure will be described at this point, while the second step will be discussed separately in the discussions of the various tests.

Table 1 summarizes the data concerning the numbers of children in the sample for each group and community studied. The study group was defined as the children reaching the ages six to eighteen, inclusive, during the calendar year 1942. Summary statements follow concerning the sampling procedure and its accuracy:

Hopi

At both Third Mesa and First Mesa, all the children from six through about fifteen are on the list. Those aged sixteen to eighteen are not all on the list, fewer boys than girls being included. Some of the older children were away at boarding school; others had quit school, and their names were not readily available.

Zuni

As already indicated, about half the children attend the government school, the remainder going to mission schools. Teachers and others

TABLE 1

NUMBERS OF CHILDREN IN THE STUDY

Age Group	Community																					
	Papago				Hopi				Zuni		Zia		Navaho				Sioux				Midwest	
	Topawa		Hickiwan		Third Mesa		First Mesa						Navaho Mountain		Shiprock		Pine Ridge		Kyle			
	M	F	M	F	M	F	M	F	M	F	M	F	M	F	M	F	M	F	M	F	M	F
6-7[a]	12	12	11·	12	11	10	11	7	6	10	6	5	12	6	2	17	3	3	5	5	—	—
8-10	16	15	18	14	13	8	9	16	12	13	10	9	7	5	15	14	7	9	12	12	44	59[b]
11-13	13	13	11	12	14	19	8	13	12	16	10	8	6	7	22	10	4	6	11	10	100	120
14-18	26	22	19	22	16	18	6	11	21	13	11	8	9	9	8	11	9	5	13	22	180	230
Total	67	62	59	60	54	55	34	47	51	52	37	30	34	27	47	52	23	23	41	49	324	409
Grand Total	129		119		109		81		103		67		61		99		46		90		733	

a. These numbers include a few five-year-olds who were in school.

b. These are all ten-year-olds; children under ten were not tested in Midwest.

(including missionaries) at Zuni say that there is no important difference between these two groups. Every sixth child on the government-school list was taken for the sample, together with his brothers and sisters. This procedure yielded 103 names. Some older girls had quit school, and consequently this older group is not adequately represented.

Zia

All 67 children in the pueblo were listed. A few older children were away at boarding school and consequently were not included in the testing.

Navaho

In the Shiprock area there are probably about 2,000 children in the age group six to eighteen. Some of these come by bus to the day school at Shiprock; others come from a wider radius to the boarding school; and many were not attending school in 1942-43. There were 108 day pupils in the Shiprock schools, 99 of whom were put on the list to be studied. This group probably is not representative of the Shiprock area. Probably it represents the more acculturated of the population living in that area.

At Navaho Mountain all the children living in the nine hogan groups nearest the Navaho Mountain Trading Post, 61 in all, were put on the list. While about half the children were not in school, efforts were made to test all of them.

In the Ramah area there were 49 children altogether. Relatively few took the Emotional Response and Moral Ideology Tests, but 70 per cent produced free drawings. Consequently we have included Ramah children only in the study of free drawings (chap. vii).

Papago

All children six to eighteen in the four villages in the Topawa area were listed. The group numbered 129. They attended three kinds of schools—government, Catholic, and Presbyterian. The age group fourteen to eighteen was quite fully represented on this list.

In the Hickiwan—Gu Vo region, all children six to eighteen were listed. Though the list, numbering 119, was quite complete, numbers of children were not in school or in their homes during the testing period, but were away with their families picking cotton or living in the mining towns. The maximum number tested on any of the research instruments was 54. Probably those who were tested were the least acculturated of the group.

Sioux

The Little Wound School at Kyle enrolled about 210 pupils, from the rural communities of Kyle, Thunder Bull, American Horse, and No Flesh. A few of the older children attended boarding school at Pine Ridge. A random sampling of 90 names was taken, with attention given to getting a group which represented the community in degree of admixture of white blood. The 90 on the list probably represented the Kyle community quite well.

At Pine Ridge there were some 300 school children. From this group, 46 children were selected according to a random procedure modified so as to get a representative group on the basis of white-blood admixture. This group probably represents fairly well the more acculturated section of the population.

Midwest

All the children in Grades V through XII, representing ages ten to eighteen and numbering 733 in all, were put on the list. The sample was complete for the years ten to fourteen, when school attendance is compulsory. For ages fourteen to eighteen, progressively more children drop out of school, leaving about 60 per cent of the seventeen- and eighteen-year-olds in schools. The sample is not adequately representative of lower-class youth older than sixteen.

Conclusion

On the whole, it appears that the samples selected for the study were adequately representative of their communities and tribes in the age range six to fifteen or sixteen, and not adequately representative for the years sixteen to eighteen. In the Hopi, Papago, Navaho Mountain, Zia, and Midwest groups the entire age group was included in the sample to be studied. At Shiprock, Zuni, and the two Sioux communities only a portion of the age group was taken, but efforts were made to draw a representative sample from the larger population. Probably the least representative samples in actual practice are those of Shiprock (Navaho) and Hickiwan (Papago). Since the actual testing was more complete in some areas than in others, conclusions as to the adequacy of the sampling must be postponed until the actual record of numbers tested is considered for each test and each community.

CHAPTER III

THE EMOTIONAL RESPONSES OF INDIAN AND WHITE CHILDREN

Section 1. THE EMOTIONAL RESPONSE TEST

The Emotional Response Test[1] was used to get information on a variety of social and personal attitudes held by children of different ages in the various cultures. In the test the subject is asked to describe situations in which he was happy, sad, afraid, angry, ashamed, and to tell what are the best and the worst things that could happen to him. Responses to this test give information about attitudes toward other people in various interpersonal relations, attitudes toward a variety of objects and situations, and attitudes toward the supernatural. The test also gives information regarding the cultural expectations which surround the child—e.g., who punishes, who rewards, what is desirable, what is dangerous, what is threatening, and so on.

Certain important types of information will not, of course, be forthcoming: these include unconscious or repressed material which will not be given directly (but which may be given symbolically) and material about which it is taboo to talk, such as certain sexual practices and fantasies in our own culture or attitudes toward death and the dead in Navaho culture.

Administration of the Test

The Emotional Response Test was given to Indian children as part of a battery of psychological tests. The battery was administered individually, usually by a teacher who knew the subject. In a few cases the test was administered by a field worker who was a stranger to the child. English was generally used, though an interpreter was often called in to help with younger children.[2] The tester asked the questions verbally and wrote down the subject's responses:

1. The test was devised by Kilton R. Stewart for work with Negritos and other nonliterate peoples.

2. At Navaho Mountain and at Hickiwan (Papago) an interpreter was used throughout.

Question: Sometimes people are very happy. Have you ever been very happy?

Answer:

Question: Can you remember when you were very happy? Tell me about it.

Answer:

Question: Can you remember another time when you were very happy? Tell me about it.

Answer:

Question: Can you remember another time when you were very happy? Tell me about it.

Answer:

Similar questions were asked for sadness, fear, anger, and shame. Then the subject was asked, "Tell me, what is the best thing that could happen to you?" Finally, the subject was asked, "What is the worst thing that could happen to you?"

This procedure was changed for the white children in Midwest. There the subjects were tested in classroom groups, and they wrote their own responses. The administrator made the following statement:

> We are interested in learning more about the lives of boys and girls, or young people, so as to compare their experiences with the experiences of people in other cities or other countries. Therefore, we would like to have you tell us a little about your experience. Will you please take a piece of paper and write down on it three things that have made you happy? You can write anything you please. These things might have happened a long time ago or they might have happened recently.
>
> Now write the word "Sadness" on your paper, and under it tell about three times when you were sad. Tell what it was that made you sad.
>
> Now write the word "Fear" on your paper and tell about three times when you were afraid.
>
> Now write the word "Anger" on your paper and tell about three times when you were angry.
>
> Now write the word "Shame" on your paper and tell about three times when you were ashamed.
>
> Now write the words "Best Thing" and tell what is the best thing that could happen to you—not the best thing that has happened to you in the past, but the best thing that could happen to you in the future.
>
> Now write the words "Worst Thing" and tell what is the worst thing that could happen to you.

As would be expected, responses to any given question of the test varied greatly from age to age, and from culture to culture.

The following responses are illustrative of those given by Indian children to the question "Have you ever been afraid? Tell me about it."

One time some of the katcinas chased us at Second Mesa—chased us up on top. We got away.

Yeibichai. They whip little children and put you in a bag.

In the hospital—I thought he was going to take my teeth out.

When my mother is going to spank me.

I'm afraid of cars.

When the war is coming.

The Problem of Language

From the very beginning of this Study we have been concerned with the problem of language in conveying the meanings of the tests to children with various cultural backgrounds, children who had learned a native language at home and who learned and spoke English mainly in school. In trying out the tests at the training seminar at Santa Fe, we searched for the simplest and least ambiguous English words to use.

We then conducted two "language experiments," one with Hopi and one with Papago children. In both cases a group of children was tested in the English language by one of the white teachers, and again in their native language by a teacher or native interpreter. The two testings occurred within a few weeks of each other.

There were 13 Hopi children tested, ranging in age from six to sixteen. The one six-year-old seemed not to understand the test in English, although he responded readily to it when it was given in Hopi. One eight- and one nine-year-old gave only two or three responses in the English form but responded fairly fully when the test was given in Hopi. One other eight- and two nine-year-olds responded fully both in English and in Hopi administrations. The ten children who responded fairly well to both tests gave a total of 133 responses to the Hopi form and 118 to the English form. When the content of responses from the two administrations was compared, there was a considerable degree of identity (see p. 32 for a discussion of the reliability of these responses).

From this experience we concluded that the test could be given in English without much sacrifice for Hopi children over eight. The major language problem seemed to center on the question about shame, which is discussed in a later section (see Sec. 5 of this chapter).

There were 17 Papago children aged six to sixteen tested both in Papago and in English. These children were in the day school at Topawa

and were presumably more familiar with English than were the Hickiwan children. Responses to the Emotional Response Test were fuller in the English version in ten cases, about the same as in Papago in five cases, and fuller in the Papago version in two cases. One possible reason for the greater responsiveness in English is that the children were better acquainted with the white teachers than with the Papago interpreter. This experience seemed to justify giving the test in English to most Papago Topawa children except the very youngest.

The native language was used systematically in some places where the Indian children were known to use English almost never outside of school. At Navaho Mountain an interpreter worked with the teacher who administered the test, and the teacher herself knew some Navaho. At Shiprock, the teacher who gave the test was herself a Navaho, and she used the Navaho language whenever she thought it necessary. She used a standard translation.[3] At Hickiwan, a Papago interpreter was used to give the tests.

The Samples

The question of the adequacy of the samples of Indian children has been dealt with in chapter ii. Since most of the children who took any tests at all took the Emotional Response Test, the samples are at their best for this test.

Table 2 reports the number of children who took the test, by age group, sex, and tribal group. The Midwest sample needs further description. The test was given to all the children in Grades V, VII, IX, and XI of the schools of Midwest. Consequently, we have relatively few children aged eleven, thirteen, fifteen, and seventeen in the Midwest sample, and none at all aged eighteen. The Midwest age groups, therefore, are not strictly comparable to the Indian age groups. The Indian eight to ten group is compared with the Midwest ten to eleven group; the Indian eleven to thirteen group is compared with the Midwest twelve to thirteen group; the Indian fourteen to eighteen group is compared with the Midwest fourteen to seventeen group.

Undoubtedly, the Midwest sample represents the community of

---

3. For a description of the testing conditions of the Navaho see Dorothea C. Leighton and Clyde Kluckhohn, Children of the People (Cambridge: Harvard University Press, 1947), pp. 126-27 and 144-45.

TABLE 2

NUMBERS OF CHILDREN TAKING THE EMOTIONAL RESPONSE TEST

Tribal Group	Age Group and Sex								Total
	8-10		11-13		14-18		8-18		
	M	F	M	F	M	F	M	F	
Papago	22	18	15	17	19	22	56	57	113
Hopi	19	21	18	30	22	26	59	77	136
Zuni	12	13	12	16	20	11	44	40	84
Zia	12	6	7	5	5	6	24	17	41
Navaho Mt.	7	5	9	5	9	9	25	19	44
Shiprock	14	15	18	10	7	10	39	35	74
Sioux	21	21	14	17	25	29	60	67	127
Midwest[a]	44	59	32	41	83	109	159	209	368

a. Ages groups were ten to eleven, twelve to thirteen, and fourteen to seventeen.

Midwest adequately, for all the children of the specified grades are included except a small number who were absent from the school when the test was given and a number of sixteen- and seventeen-year-olds who had dropped out of school. Children aged ten to thirteen in the Catholic parochial school in the city were included in the group.

Responsiveness to the Test

The average numbers of responses to the questions about each emotion are given in Table 3. It will be seen at once that there are considerable differences in responsiveness between groups. These differences may depend upon two factors.

a) A general responsiveness factor which causes the children in some societies to respond more readily than those in other societies. While there may be such a factor operating, it hardly seems likely that Zuni, Zia, Navaho Mountain, and Midwest would have such a factor in common—yet they are the most responsive groups.

b) Peculiarities in the administration of the test. The test administrator may have obtained better rapport in some places than in others. This might explain the higher frequency at Navaho Mountain than at Shiprock, but it hardly seems an adequate explanation of the relative paucity of responses at Hopi, where the testing was done by four different people whose rapport with the children was judged by Indian Service supervisors to be fully as good as that which the Zuni administrators had. Still we know from the language experiment at Hopi that a Hopi teacher, employing the Hopi language, obtained more responses than a white teacher employing English. Thus there seems to be no single explanation of the differences in responsiveness among the various groups.

Differences in responsiveness concerning the various emotions also occur. Responses were most frequent to questions concerning happiness, fear, and "best thing," and least frequent to questions on shame and anger. These differences could probably have been predicted. Children generally are perhaps more willing to talk about pleasant than unpleasant things; and among unpleasant things they may be more ready to talk about fear than about anger and shame, since these latter may be less acceptable emotions. It will be observed in Table 3 that girls are slightly more ready to speak about sadness and fear, while boys are more ready to speak of anger.

Quantification of the Data

As is true of any free-response material, quantification of the data becomes a major problem. A system of categorization was necessary which would be appropriate for the responses of younger as well as older children, which would be appropriate for children of various cultures, and which, at the same time, would yield a maximum degree of reliability in scoring the test protocols.

Categorizing Responses

It was decided that a system of categories should be devised on an inductive basis; that is, that categories of responses should be devised from the data themselves rather than from any a priori frame of reference. Accordingly, verbatim responses of a number of subjects from various tribes were copied onto cards, and members of the research committee grouped those cards that obviously belonged together. As far as possible, interpretation of responses was avoided. That is, the question "What does the subject really mean?" was avoided by creating a new category for a response which did not obviously fit one of the existing categories.

Categories were also devised for the "persons involved" in the responses. For example, if a child said he was happy when he received a gift from his father, "receiving a gift" was recorded in its proper category under "happiness," and "father" in its category among "persons involved."

In this way, a large number of empirical categories was created. There was a total of over 200 categories, the number of categories for a single emotion varying from 25 to 70. There were 47 categories of "persons involved."

Agreement among Scorers

When the categories had been established, the responses for successive sets of protocols were scored independently by either two or three persons who had worked together on the derivation of the categories.[4]

4. The following persons co-operated in devising the categories and in scoring the test protocols: Mildred Dorr, Aracelis Burgos Fernandez, Jean Hall, Robert J. Havighurst, Inez Ellis Pratt, and Iva O. Schmitt.

TABLE 3 [a]

AVERAGE NUMBER OF RESPONSES PER CHILD ON THE EMOTIONAL RESPONSE TEST

	Tribe																	
	Papago		Hopi		Zuni		Zia		Navaho Mt.		Shiprock		Sioux		Midwest[b]		Average	
	Boys	Girls	Boys	Girls	Boys	Girls	Boys	Girls	Boys	Girls	Boys	Girls	Boys	Girls	Boys	Girls	Boys	Girls
No. of subjects	56	57	59	77	44	40	24	17	25	19	39	35	60	67	159	209	466	521
Emotion:																		
Happiness	2.4	2.7	2.5	2.2	3.2	3.3	3.1	3.4	3.1	3.0	2.4	3.0	2.8	2.6	2.7	3.2	2.8	2.9
Sadness	1.6	1.4	1.4	1.9	2.6	2.5	2.4	2.4	2.0	1.7	1.4	2.0	1.8	2.1	2.0	2.6	1.9	2.1
Fear	1.8	1.9	1.3	2.0	3.0	2.7	2.8	3.0	3.4	3.3	2.3	2.4	2.2	1.9	2.0	2.5	2.3	2.5
Anger	1.3	1.1	1.7	1.3	2.6	2.5	2.5	2.6	0.9	0.6	1.6	1.6	1.9	1.6	2.2	2.4	1.9	1.7
Shame	0.9	1.0	1.1	1.5	2.6	2.6	1.0	0.5	2.4	1.8	0.4	0.6	1.5	1.2	1.6	2.2	1.4	1.4
Best thing	0.9	0.9	0.9	0.8	1.0	1.0	1.0	1.0	1.1	1.2	0.6	0.8	0.9	0.9	1.1	1.1	0.94	0.96
Worst thing	0.9	0.7	0.9	0.5	1.0	1.0	0.9	1.0	1.0	0.9	0.5	0.6	0.9	0.8	0.7	1.0	0.85	0.81
Total	9.8	9.7	9.8	10.2	16.0	15.6	13.7	13.9	13.9	12.5	9.2	11.0	12.0	11.1	12.3	15.0	12.1	12.4

a. Ages eight to eighteen.

b. Ages ten to seventeen.

The score sheets for each set of protocols were then compared, item by item, and the number of disagreements between scorers was noted. The initial disagreements varied from about 8 to about 20 per cent, depending upon the tribal group and the emotion being considered.

The principal source of disagreement was uncertainty as to whether a response belonged in one or another of two or three very closely related categories. For example, "When I got a new pair of shoes" as a happiness response could be placed in the category "receiving materials," in the category "having nice things, clothes, etc.," or in the category "owning property, horses, clothes, toys, etc." In other words, had the original categories been less finely drawn, agreement among scorers on the preliminary scoring of protocols would have been even higher than was actually obtained.

In any case, each disagreement was discussed, and an agreement was usually reached as to the proper category for the response in question. "Residual" disagreements were counted and found to exist for 1-2 per cent of the responses.

Combining Categories

After the preliminary scoring was completed, tables were drawn up for each emotion, showing the percentage of responses in each category by tribal group, sex, and age group. It was evident at once that for each emotion a small number of categories contained the majority of the responses, a half-dozen categories usually accounting for half to three-quarters of the responses.

To gain economy in describing the data, the original categories were then grouped into combinations on the basis of psychological similarity. For example, under happiness, the following ten categories were grouped together to make the combination called "Amusement, parties, games":

1. Playing, playing games, with pets, toys
2. Playing competitive sports
3. Winning games or sports (the team or school)
4. Personal achievement in games or sports
5. Watching sports
6. Riding horses, roping calves
7. Singing, hiking, going for a walk, hunting, fishing, swimming
8. Going to rodeo, circus, movie, fair
9. Going to or having parties, picnics, dances (not tribal)
10. Having a good time, something going on

For the various emotions the number of combinations varies from 13 to 22. Usually 3 or 4 combinations account for three-fourths of the responses for any given emotion. The list of combinations for each emotion, together with the original categories contained in each combination, will be found in Appendixes B-1 through B-7. After the categories had been grouped into these combinations, disagreement among scorers as to the combination in which a given response belongs was very rare.

Reliability of the Instrument

Two tests of the statistical reliability of the Emotional Response Test have been made. One was in the nature of a test-retest experiment. Five Hopi boys and five Hopi girls aged eight to fifteen were given the test twice, once in English and the other time in the Hopi language at intervals of 2-16 weeks. While the main purpose was to test the effect of language on the administration of the test,[5] this procedure may also be regarded as a test-retest procedure for determining reliability—and a test of special rigor, since the administrator and the language were both changed from one testing to the other.

The entire test was treated as a unit, and the numbers of responses counted in each category of the combinations. A total of 53 combinations had one or more responses in one or the other testing. The product-moment coefficient of correlation was computed, using the frequencies of response in a given combination as the pair of scores to be correlated. The product-moment correlation is not ideal for measurement of degree of association in this case, since the distributions are so highly skewed (the extreme or zero score has the highest or next to highest frequency). Nevertheless, using the product-moment correlation procedure for what it is worth, we find a coefficient of correlation of $.62 \pm .06$ for the 10 children in the experiment. If we assume that the differences between these two sets of tests are primarily due to fluctuations which would disappear in large enough populations, we would need 30-50 children taking the test before we could expect the frequencies to possess a high degree of stability. Since we have at least this many children in every group, the tribal averages, even broken down by sex, may be expected to be fairly reliable.[6]

5. See p. 25.

6. Another way of studying reliability is to find out what proportion of times these same children mention the same category combination in both

For the other test of reliability the Midwest children's responses were studied. It was assumed that if two groups of children of the same age, same educational background, and same community gave similar responses, it would attest to the reliability of the instrument for studying group differences. Accordingly, a comparison was made of the responses of two groups of twelve- to thirteen-year-old boys and girls in Midwest—41 girls and 32 boys who were twelve to thirteen years old when tested in 1943; and 49 girls and 35 boys who were twelve to thirteen years old when tested in 1945. (These comprised all the children of this age in the seventh grade who were present in school on the days the test was given.) The responses were tabulated under category combinations, and the product-moment correlation coefficient was computed between frequencies in the various combinations for the 1943 group against the 1945 group. Responses under happiness, sadness, and anger (because these had the highest frequencies) were compared. Coefficients of correlation were as follows:

Happiness:	.95 ± .02 for boys;	.93 ± .02 for girls
Sadness:	.63 ± .10 for boys;	.86 ± .04 for girls
Anger:	.59 ± .12 for boys;	.66 ± .10 for girls

Here we are dealing with groups numbering 30 to 50, and we might expect reliability coefficients of at least .90, if our inferences from the Hopi experiment are correct. But half of the six correlation coefficients are well below this level. The relatively low coefficients from boys on sadness and anger are due to large differences in one or two or three categories. The 1943 group mentions sadness and anger caused by loss or theft of property very much more frequently than the 1945 group does. We can see no obvious reason for this difference, but it indicates clearly that if we had used a split-half method of testing reliability in either the 1943 or the 1945 group, we would have found higher reliability coefficients for these particular emotions. Furthermore, the 1943 group (boys) gave about 50 per cent more responses per person on anger and

---

testings. There were 98 pairs of responses (98 responses in one testing were complemented by responses in the other testing) which therefore might have been identical as to combination. The number of possible combinations varied from 13 to 23 for any given emotion, and thus the chance of accidental coincidence of combinations was rather small, even though certain combinations were much more popular than others. Actually, there were 43 out of a possible 98 identical pairs, about 50 per cent. For the separate parts of the test the proportion varied from 5 out of 7 for "best thing" to 0 out of 8 for "worst thing."

sadness (but not on happiness) than the 1945 group did, and the same was true for girls on anger. This suggests that when there are gross differences in numbers of responses per person, comparisons may not be justified between groups.

These tests of reliability of the instrument suggest that we are justified in generalizing from groups of 40 or more children and in comparing groups of this size, provided that they have roughly the same average number of responses per person. Generalizations for smaller groups, comparisons of smaller groups, and comparisons of groups showing large differences in number of responses per person should be made only with great caution. We have selected a cautious method in comparing groups—the method of comparing proportions or percentages of responses. This method requires that very large differences be present before reliable conclusions can be drawn about groups as small in number as 40 or fewer.

Method of Scoring

In scoring the Emotional Response Test, we have been concerned throughout only with group scores. The responses were tabulated for each age, sex, and tribal group by categories; then grouped according to the category combinations. The percentage of responses in a given combination was the significant datum. Another possible method of scoring—namely, the percentage of individuals mentioning a given category—was considered but not used, for reasons indicated in the report on the Moral Ideology Test (see p. 92, n. 7).

Validity of the Test

In studying and interpreting the results of the Emotional Response Test, certain general considerations should be kept in mind. Some of them are the following:

Since he is asked for only three responses to a particular emotion, the subject must select from a variety of emotion-arousing events. It is likely, therefore, that recent events will be preferred; that traumatic or exciting events will be preferred; and that taboos on talking about certain subjects will operate. If a given type of event does not appear in the data, it cannot be concluded that this event is not emotion-arousing. It is safe to say only that, in competing with other events to be reported, this event did not occur first, second, or third in the child's mind.

The test administrator will also have some influence on the responses given. When the test is given orally and individually, the child will surely respond to some extent to the personality of the tester. For the Indian children, the tester was usually a teacher, usually white, and occasionally a stranger. These facts must have exerted a selective influence over what was reported by the child.

It may be asked whether the Emotional Response Test is valid (a) in the sense that it represents the most significant emotional experiences of the child reporting or (b) in the sense that it elicits a representative sample of emotion-arousing experiences from the culture to which the child belongs. While, with the qualifications mentioned above, there is evidence that the test possesses considerable validity in both senses, it is the second that concerns us most, and it is the second in which we feel most confidence.

For instance, evidence on the validity of the test as a report of the emotion-arousing experiences of the culture is given by Hilda Davis in her doctoral dissertation.[7] She studied the ethnological reports on the Hopi, Papago, and Navaho published between 1900 and 1940 and systematically drew inferences which could be tested by the data from the Emotional Response and Moral Ideology tests. She found that the majority of her inferences were supported by data from the Emotional Response Test and that, in general, the test has sufficient validity to justify its use as a method of investigating the emotional experiences of groups of children.

Section 2. PRINCIPAL SOURCES OF THE VARIOUS EMOTIONS

The data from the Emotional Response Test were first analyzed for each of the various emotions separately, our questions being "What are the principal sources of happiness for children in each culture?" "The principal sources of sadness?" "Of fear?" and so on. These data are summarized in Tables 4-10, which follow.

To acquaint himself with the original data and our methods of quantification, the reader may wish to study these tables in relation to Appendixes B-1 to B-7. In those appendixes will be found, for each emotion, the list of

7. Hilda A. Davis, "A Study of Moral Ideology and Emotionalized Attitudes of Children of Three Southwestern Indian Tribes" (unpublished Ph.D. dissertation, University of Chicago Library, 1953).

TABLE 4[a]

PRINCIPAL SOURCES OF HAPPINESS OF INDIAN AND MIDWEST CHILDREN (PERCENTAGES)

Nature of Experience	Sex	Papago	Hopi	Zuni	Zia	Navaho Mt.	Shiprock	Sioux	Midwest[b]
I. Amusements, parties, games	M	27	16	32	15	8	27	26	21
	F	25	14	16	4	0	15	20	12
II. Holidays, birthdays, ceremonials	M	23	28	15	6	11	8	10	13
	F	20	26	22	14	6	6	11	11
III. Tribal ceremonials, fiestas[c]	M	14	12	11	3	9	3	0	0
	F	16	13	18	7	2	5	1	0
IV. Receiving food, gifts, money	M	17	30	16	41	49	36	33	29
	F	14	19	9	42	46	21	18	25
VI. Work, earning money	M	8	6	4	2	9	6	5	4
	F	1	3	7	0	11	5	1	1
VII. Travel, going to town	M	13	5	10	20	3	4	4	11
	F	14	7	11	20	2	10	7	14
VIII. Going to school	M	6	7	6	0	8	5	6	3
	F	10	11	9	3	2	11	9	6
IX. No school	M	1	1	2	2	2	0	0	3
	F	1	1	5	0	0	1	0	1
X. Family solidarity	M	3	2	5	10	5	3	5	4
	F	6	10	11	13	27	8	17	16
XI. Good relations with peers	M	1	1	2	0	0	2	0	3
	F	3	1	2	0	0	3	2	3
XIII. Individual achievement	M	1	3	2	1	3	5	2	12
	F	2	2	3	3	16	2	3	8
XXI. Being grown up	M	0	0	0	2	1	0	0	2
	F	0	0	2	0	6	0	0	1
No. of responses as base for percentages	M	137	148	142	76	77	92	167	426
	F	152	172	134	58	57	104	172	671

a. Ages eight to eighteen.
b. Ages ten to seventeen.
c. III is also included in II.

TABLE 5[a]

THE BEST THING THAT COULD HAPPEN TO INDIAN AND MIDWEST CHILDREN (PERCENTAGES)

Nature of Experience	Sex	Papago	Hopi	Zuni	Zia	Navaho Mt.	Shiprock	Sioux	Midwest[b]
I. Personal achievement	M	18	20	10	0	7	12	18	27
	F	12	16	3	6	7	7	19	25
II. Personal pleasure and comfort	M	20	22	23	26	25	18	18	20
	F	19	24	21	35	3	13	11	24
III. Meeting social expectations	M	6	11	21	16	11	8	4	5
	F	11	17	17	0	0	14	14	3
IV. Family or group solidarity	M	0	0	0	0	5	0	2	3
	F	0	4	5	0	0	11	5	13
V. Good social relations	M	0	2	0	0	0	0	0	3
	F	6	5	2	6	15	0	2	5
XII. Reticence about "best thing"	M	2	0	0	0	0	0	0	0
	F	2	6	0	0	7	11	0	0
XV. Receiving clothes, property	M	36	20	37	50	49	48	38	28
	F	22	24	42	47	55	41	32	20
No. of responses as base for percentages	M	50	50	45	24	26	25	53	181
	F	45	59	40	17	23	29	58	244

a. Ages eight to eighteen.

b. Ages ten to seventeen.

TABLE 6[a]

PRINCIPAL SOURCES OF SADNESS OF INDIAN AND MIDWEST CHILDREN (PERCENTAGES)

Nature of Experience	Sex	Papago	Hopi	Zuni	Zia	Navaho Mt.	Shiprock	Sioux	Midwest[b]
I. Death of someone	M	21	19	21	10	21	7	23	20
	F	27	28	25	14	15	15	20	21
II. Death of a pet	M	1	2	0	8	5	7	3	13
	F	0	1	0	0	6	0	1	10
III. Illness or injury of others	M	12	16	21	10	8	7	4	10
	F	9	13	15	13	8	6	9	13
IV. Being punished	M	7	8	8	0	9	3	5	3
	F	12	14	2	4	5	1	1	2
VI. Personal failure, inability	M	3	1	0	0	2	3	4	5
	F	2	2	2	0	3	4	3	2
IX. Disappointment due to others	M	4	3	2	2	0	6	8	15
	F	1	2	4	9	0	1	12	14
X. Disappointment due to circumstances	M	6	2	4	0	2	0	24	6
	F	4	2	4	0	0	7	4	10
XI. Loss of property	M	8	13	5	12	13	44	10	12
	F	2	6	3	21	11	28	5	5
XII. Absence of friends and family	M	4	7	5	18	25	17	10	4
	F	8	6	16	19	29	18	19	10
XIII. Being bad	M	8	1	1	5	0	0	6	1
	F	11	2	4	0	3	4	4	2
XIV. Badness of others	M	3	6	9	7	5	6	6	1
	F	16	22	12	6	0	7	6	3
XVII. Bad weather	M	0	0	2	0	10	0	0	1
	F	2	0	0	0	13	0	0	0
XX. Illness or injury of self	M	16	15	19	22	4	0	9	8
	F	3	6	6	12	0	4	5	3
No. of responses as base of percentages	M	87	81	116	57	50	53	109	321
	F	77	143	102	42	33	71	138	360

a. Ages eight to eighteen.

b. Ages ten to seventeen.

TABLE 7[a]

PRINCIPAL SOURCES OF FEAR OF INDIAN AND MIDWEST CHILDREN (PERCENTAGES)

Nature of Experience	Sex	Papago	Hopi	Zuni	Zia	Navaho Mt.	Shiprock	Sioux	Midwest[b]
I. Supernatural beings	M	8	28	13	10	45	23	13	1
	F	12	23	10	6	40	31	4	1
II. Subjective danger	M	5	25	9	21	19	12	21	10
	F	13	16	6	4	29	14	11	18
III. Danger from animals	M	52	14	41	49	14	22	33	21
	F	37	18	36	54	0	32	38	14
IV. Danger from natural elements	M	13	1	6	5	14	17	14	35
	F	16	4	4	4	29	0	15	32
VII. Personal delinquency	M	3	7	2	2	0	0	1	9
	F	1	8	6	5	0	3	3	4
VIII. Being punished	M	5	5	6	3	1	3	5	3
	F	1	3	6	5	0	0	3	2
IX. Aggression by others	M	6	8	9	9	2	16	8	9
	F	9	7	14	12	1	11	14	8
No. of responses as base of percentages	M	99	79	133	68	85	88	131	324
	F	107	151	108	52	66	90	129	534

a. Ages eight to eighteen.

b. Ages ten to seventeen.

TABLE 8[a]

PRINCIPAL SOURCES OF ANGER OF INDIAN AND MIDWEST CHILDREN (PERCENTAGES)

Nature of Experience	Sex	Papago	Hopi	Zuni	Zia	Navaho Mt.	Shiprock	Sioux	Midwest[b]
I. Loss of property	M	8	21	5	23	0	44	26	16
	F	16	23	13	18	0	30	11	13
III. Restrictions on desires	M	2	6	6	0	3	3	6	15
	F	19	15	4	7	0	9	10	16
V. Inconsiderateness of others	M	20	8	16	19	0	13	12	17
	F	18	18	20	21	11	15	7	25
VI. Being disciplined	M	11	12	13	16	16	5	4	7
	F	9	12	12	17	6	12	8	8
VII. Aggression by others	M	30	30	35	35	43	25	24	21
	F	23	18	42	49	39	42	36	21
VIII. Fighting	M	8	9	0	4	6	2	4	4
	F	11	0	0	2	0	0	4	1
IX. Misdeeds of others	M	1	7	5	3	0	1	3	4
	F	1	6	3	0	33	11	1	6
X. Perversity of animals	M	18	6	17	13	21	5	25	5
	F	4	10	1	0	6	0	9	2
XII. Personal inadequacy	M	1	2	3	0	6	0	5	7
	F	3	3	4	0	0	0	3	4
No. of responses as base for percentages	M	70	99	118	62	22	62	113	358
	F	63	97	103	45	11	55	106	518

a. Ages eight to eighteen.

b. Ages ten to seventeen.

TABLE 9[a]

PRINCIPAL SOURCES OF SHAME OF INDIAN AND MIDWEST CHILDREN (PERCENTAGES)

Nature of Experience	Sex	Papago	Hopi	Zuni	Zia	Navaho Mt.	Shiprock	Sioux	Midwest[b]
I. Making a poor appearance	M	13	8	7	20	25	8	19	10
	F	16	7	7	8	18	49	14	9
II. Embarrassment before others	M	36	25	55	12	30	25	6	2
	F	24	23	53	17	52	7	8	2
V. Personal failure, inadequacy	M	6	7	9	3	10	0	1	22
	F	3	10	6	0	13	7	9	21
VII. Bad behavior, aggression	M	14	33	11	47	10	25	47	46
	F	33	27	11	64	0	17	41	50
X. Being disciplined	M	7	7	2	5	7	13	6	4
	F	2	9	4	11	0	3	6	3
XI. Aggression by others	M	8	7	11	3	8	13	6	2
	F	9	14	3	0	10	0	4	2
No. of responses as base for percentages	M	52	64	118	24	61	16	88	260
	F	55	114	107	9	36	21	80	478

a. Ages eight to eighteen.

b. Ages ten to seventeen.

TABLE 10[a]

THE WORST THING THAT COULD HAPPEN TO INDIAN AND MIDWEST CHILDREN (PERCENTAGES)

Nature of Experience	Sex	Papago	Hopi	Zuni	Zia	Navaho Mt.	Shiprock	Sioux	Midwest[b]
I. Death of self	M	6	16	5	10	4	6	16	15
	F	13	12	6	11	0	3	16	3
II. Death of relative or friend	M	0	0	0	0	0	0	0	7
	F	0	1	0	6	0	3	2	16
III. Accident or illness of self	M	35	39	20	54	11	25	35	11
	F	40	26	12	53	29	11	21	7
V. Frightening experience	M	6	10	9	0	78	3	1	0
	F	3	10	7	0	56	0	3	1
VI. Being punished	M	0	16	15	0	0	0	1	3
	F	7	19	27	6	0	0	10	3
VII. Aggression by others	M	3	2	9	3	0	0	9	1
	F	10	6	17	7	0	11	14	3
VIII. Bad behavior, aggression	M	19	12	19	18	4	10	19	1
	F	13	9	6	0	16	19	13	8
IX. Personal inadequacy, failure	M	8	1	2	0	4	11	0	19
	F	0	1	5	0	0	0	2	18
X. Misfortune, discomfort	M	17	4	4	8	0	10	9	15
	F	5	7	12	12	0	26	9	16
XI. Loss of family or friends	M	0	0	0	0	0	0	0	5
	F	3	2	0	6	0	0	4	8
XII. To lose the war	M	0	0	0	0	0	0	0	9
	F	0	2	0	0	0	0	0	6
No. of responses as base for percentages	M	49	50	46	22	25	20	57	127
	F	42	35	40	17	17	21	55	228

a. Ages eight to eighteen.

b. Ages ten to seventeen.

the original categories; the category combinations; and illustrative responses taken from the protocols.

Tables 4-10 can be examined for cross-cultural comparisons, one culture with another. Thus, for example, happiness resulting from "Receiving food, gifts, money" is especially high among Zia, Navaho Mountain, and Shiprock children (Table 4).

We may also regard Papago, Hopi, Zuni, Zia, and Navaho (Navaho Mountain and Shiprock) as a group of Southwest Indian cultures roughly similar to one another—as compared with the Plains culture of the Sioux or with the modern white culture of Midwest. Thus, for example, Table 4 shows a striking difference between Midwest and the Southwest Indians in happiness resulting from "Individual achievement."

Midwest Compared with Southwest Indians

While the reader will wish to make comparisons of his own, we shall simply comment here upon some of the most salient differences between Midwest and Southwest Indian children, as shown in Tables 4-10.

We have already mentioned the difference in happiness resulting from "Individual achievement." The situation is similar on "best thing" (Table 5), where Midwest children give more responses dealing with "Personal achievement" than do Southwest Indian children.

As regards sadness, Table 6 shows a striking difference between Midwest and Southwest Indian children in "Disappointment due to others." The Indian children seldom mention this but mention, instead, "Badness of others." It is as though the Midwest children were more self-centered and felt a personal sadness when not given their own way in such matters as going to a movie or getting new clothes, while the Indian children were more group-centered, feeling sad when people were aggressive or bad, even though the aggression may not have been directed against them personally.

As seen from Table 7, "Supernatural beings" is a major source of fear in Indian children but is almost never mentioned by Midwest children. Another big difference is in "Danger from animals," which is mentioned much more frequently by Indian children. This is probably due to the greater amount of contact of Indian children with mean dogs, angry cattle, and so on. In these comparisons, animals usually explicitly associated with the supernatural are excluded from the category combina-

tion entitled "Danger from animals" and are included under "Supernatural beings." However, there is probably a tendency for some of the Indian children to think of all animals as having certain supernatural characteristics which make them fearsome. This is quite likely among the Papago, who give the highest frequency of mentions to "Danger from animals."[8]

The most marked contrast of Indian and Midwest children in anger (Table 8) appears in the proportions of responses on "Restrictions on desires," which the Midwest children mention much more frequently. Examples are:

> When my folks wouldn't give me the car (Midwest M14).
> When my mother wouldn't buy me a pair of shoes I wanted (Midwest F14).
> When I had my mind set on going to a party and had to stay home (Midwest F14).

This is probably similar to the higher frequency of mention by Midwest children of sadness caused by "Disappointment due to others." Again this might be interpreted as due to greater self-centeredness and personal initiative on the part of Midwest children. They "want what they want when they want it," and they feel keenly when other people prevent them from satisfying their wants. The Southwest Indian children, on the other hand, have a more passive attitude and become angry only when other people are directly aggressive or punitive toward them.

Children's responses regarding shame suggest a basic distinction between shame as embarrassment and shame as sense of guilt. Contrasts of Southwest Indians with Midwest on sources of shame are considered at length in the section on "Conscience and Self-consciousness" (see pp. 74-83). Indian children feel shame most frequently when they appear in a bad light in the presence of other people. Midwest children, on the other hand, mention shame much more frequently than Indian children in connection with "Personal failure and inadequacy" and "Bad behavior and aggression" (Table 9).

Indian children often mention "Accident or illness of self" or "Frightening experience" as the worst thing that could happen to them. (Table 10). Most of the Indian responses describe things which might

8. See Alice Joseph, Rosamond B. Spicer, and Jane Chesky, The Desert People: A Study of the Papago Indians (Chicago: University of Chicago Press, 1949), p. 205.

happen to the child and cause him physical suffering. At the same time, there is a number of Indian responses dealing with "Bad behavior or aggression" which imply that the child might lose control of himself and get into trouble. The Midwest pattern of "worst thing" responses is quite different. It consists more of mental suffering than of physical suffering. Thus the most frequent category is that of "Personal inadequacy or failure."

Section 3. PREDOMINANT VALUE-THEMES AND AVERSIONS

Children express their values and aversions on the Emotional Response Test. They do this within the limits set by taboos, on the one hand, and by commonplace expectations, on the other hand. For example, some groups, such as the Navaho, do not mention death, while other groups speak of it freely. A commonplace value such as fresh air is not expressed at all. Food is seldom mentioned except by Hopi children, who live in a society which has suffered food scarcity and experiences food anxiety.

The principal values and aversions actually stated by the children can be discovered by looking for themes that run through the responses concerning the several emotions. For instance, Individual Achievement is a value-theme which is expressed in certain responses concerning happiness, sadness, fear, anger, shame, "best thing," and "worst thing." A boy may say he was happy when he made good school grades, sad when he lost a job because of carelessness, angry when he failed to make the team, ashamed when he missed an easy shot in a basketball game, the "best thing" for him would be the become an Eagle Scout, and the "worst thing" to be expelled from high school. These responses all deal with the theme of individual achievement.

Data on the principal values and aversions are presented in Tables 11 and 12.[9] (The themes we have selected as values and aversions are

9. The procedure for computing Tables 11 and 12 will be illustrated: For "Individual achievement" among the Papago, tabulations were made by age group and by sex. The number of responses in a relevant category combination was expressed as the percentage of the total number of responses given by the age-sex group for the particular emotion under which the category combination occurred. These percentages for the category combinations included under "Individual achievement" were then averaged, yielding a single percentage for each age-sex group on "Individual achievement" (the results of these operations are shown in Table 43 in Appendix B-10). The average of the three percentages for

listed in Appendix B-9, together with the category conbinations which contribute to them.)

In Tables 11 and 12 the several Indian groups can be compared with one another and with Midwest. In addition, the average of the five Southwest Indian tribes is shown for comparison with Midwest.[10] The Indian tribes will be compared with one another and with Midwest by taking up one theme at a time.[11]

Value-Themes

Individual Achievement

This theme includes all responses that reported a positive emotion in connection with an achievement in work or play that depended on individ-

the three age groups was then taken to represent the relative frequency for a given sex. For example, the Papago boys gave frequencies of 4.7, 2.0, and 5.5 per cent for the three age groups (see Table 43). These average to 4.1, which is the figure given in Table 11 for Papago boys on "Individual achievement."

The percentages have a base of at least 100 responses for the smaller groups (Navaho Mountain and Zia) and over 1,000 responses for Midwest. The only exceptions are the themes which refer to only one emotion (Death of self, Fear of supernatural, Objective danger) where the base is small and small percentage differences are unreliable. In Tables 11 and 12 a difference of three percentage points or less is not statistically reliable. Even greater differences are unreliable in the cases of Zia and Navaho Mountain. (Table 43 gives the number of responses used as a base in determining percentages. Hence the actual reliability of any percentage in Tables 11 and 12 can be determined by reference to Table 43.)

10. The average for the Southwest Indians was obtained by adding together the percentages for each tribal group and dividing by 6 (the two Navaho groups were left separate because of the relatively wide cultural differences between them), yielding a mean percentage to be compared with Midwest. All six groups were thus given equal weights, although there were more children in some groups than in others. The comparisons then are made between about 500 Southwest Indian children aged eight to eighteen and about 370 Midwest white children aged ten to seventeen. These comparisons will show reliable differences if the percentage frequencies differ by only two or three points, since the number of responses are relatively large.

11. Certain of these themes have been studied in terms of how they correlate with one another from one society to the next. The reader is referred to Table 47 in Appendix E-1. In the upper left quadrant of that table are shown the correlations between variables taken from the Emotional Response Test ("variables" are certain of the principal values and aversions). The table is to be read as follows: For all eight societies studied, "Individual achievement" is negatively related to "Smooth personal relations." That is, a society which gives a high proportion of responses to "Individual achievement" gives a low proportion of responses to "Smooth personal relations"; and vice versa. "Individual achievement" is also negatively related to "Aggression by others." It is not significantly related, either positively or negatively, to the other ERT variables listed in that table.

ual initiative or that singled out the individual for special attention. It also includes responses of negative emotions over failure to achieve. Examples are the following:

To be a good auto mechanic (B.T.,[12] Hopi M17).
When I play football. If I could make a touchdown (B.T., Hopi M12).
Be a good medicine man (B.T., Navaho Mt. M17).
When I learned my first chant perfectly (B.T., Navaho Mt. M17).
When I wove my first good blanket [i.e., one that could be sold] (H., Navaho Mt. F17).
When I first went out alone to herd the sheep (H., Navaho Mt. M11).
To graduate from high school (B.T., Navaho Mt. M14).
To be a success in all my work and have other pleasures, too (B.T., Midwest F14).
To become an Eagle Scout (B.T., Midwest M13).

As might well have been anticipated, Midwest boys and girls give two or three times as many responses on this theme as do the Indian children. Among the several Indian groups there is not much difference, except that Zia is definitely below the others.

Property and Possessions

Having property and receiving gifts is a value reported most frequently by Navaho and Zia children. The particular kinds of possessions which are most treasured vary from the sheep and cowboy hats of the Navaho to the bicycles of Midwest. (The Navaho children appear to desire both the solid material values of sheep and silver jewelry and the flashier individual values of clothing, guns, and decorated saddles.)

The Indian children, compared to Midwest, give definitely more mention of the securing of property, food, clothing, and other possessions as sources of pleasant emotion and the loss or damage or absence of these things as sources of unpleasant emotions. With the exception of Zuni and Papago, the Indian children all appear to be more property-conscious than those of Midwest. The relatively wealthy Zuni are definitely below the other groups.

Self-gratification

In this theme were included responses that indicated a kind of hedonistic attitude. Games and amusements figure heavily, as well as

12. In these examples the first initials of the emotions are given, e.g., "B.T." stands for "best thing," "H." for happiness, etc. The sex and age of the child are also indicated, e.g., Hopi M12 means a Hopi male aged twelve.

TABLE 11[a]

EMOTIONAL RESPONSE TEST: COMPARISON OF CULTURAL GROUPS ON VALUE-THEMES (PERCENTAGES)

Value-Theme[b]	Sex	Papago	Hopi	Zuni	Zia	Navaho Mt.	Shiprock	Sioux	Midwest[c]	Southwest Indians[d]
Individual achievement	M	4.1	4.8	3.1	0.7	3.8	4.4	3.2	11.1	3.3
	F	2.6	3.5	3.7	1.2	5.4	2.0	4.1	9.2	3.1
Property and possessions	M	12.2	17.7	7.1	20.6	17.9	29.5	16.3	14.9	17.2
	F	10.7	11.5	7.6	22.2	19.6	22.4	10.6	10.9	15.7
Self-gratification	M	29.2	22.7	23.9	22.8	16.1	21.6	25.9	29.6	22.7
	F	30.4	22.7	19.8	25.6	8.6	21.7	25.3	32.5	21.5
Smooth personal relations	M	14.9	15.3	19.5	17.4	8.3	14.6	13.0	12.2	15.0
	F	16.5	17.4	20.7	21.0	7.6	16.3	17.3	13.9	16.6
Family-centered-ness	M	2.1	1.3	3.0	6.3	3.6	2.0	3.7	3.6	3.1
	F	4.2	5.6	6.5	9.4	13.4	7.8	11.8	12.6	7.8
Work	M	8.2	9.0	6.6	4.8	8.2	5.3	5.0	6.5	7.0
	F	2.5	5.3	8.9	1.2	7.9	6.8	2.9	3.0	5.4
Ceremonials, fiestas	M	9.2	8.5	8.5	2.3	6.8	2.2	0.3	0	6.3
	F	8.0	9.9	14.6	5.3	1.6	3.4	0.9	0	7.1

a. Ages eight to eighteen.

b. Comparison should not be made between value-themes, since the absolute sizes of the percentages depend on factors in the tabulation that distort the relations between the various themes. Thus Midwest and Papago can be compared on "Individual achievement," but "Individual achievement" cannot be compared with "Property and possessions" for any tribal group.

c. Ages ten to seventeen.

d. Average of the six Southwest Indian groups.

TABLE 12[a]

EMOTIONAL RESPONSE TEST: COMPARISON OF CULTURAL GROUPS ON AVERSIONS (PERCENTAGES)

Aversion[b]	Sex	Papago	Hopi	Zuni	Zia	Navaho Mt.	Shiprock	Sioux	Midwest[c]	Southwest Indians[d]
Aggression by others	M	10.2	11.5	15.2	14.5	7.6	14.6	10.8	8.2	12.3
	F	14.0	11.7	18.1	17.8	4.9	15.4	15.8	8.1	13.7
Discipline and authority of others	M	6.6	7.9	8.1	5.5	5.5	3.7	4.5	4.0	6.2
	F	6.2	9.7	7.7	8.5	1.5	3.2	4.8	3.9	6.1
Illness and danger of others	M	4.4	7.8	10.4	4.0	1.7	2.5	3.1	4.4	5.1
	F	3.1	7.6	9.0	6.7	2.3	1.6	5.3	9.3	5.1
Death of others	M	10.9	11.3	15.1	6.8	8.2	4.7	15.6	16.2	9.5
	F	16.7	19.5	17.2	11.5	10.0	12.7	17.4	19.5	14.6
Death of self	M	8.2	17.9	5.3	10.0	3.7	6.0	16	15.3	8.5
	F	11.7	11.7	6.0	11.3	0	3.7	16	2.6	7.4
Illness, accidents to self	M	20.8	21.6	19.6	33.6	8.1	6.1	18.2	9.4	18.3
	F	16.3	14.0	7.5	24.1	11.3	6.3	9.7	3.8	13.5
Fear of supernatural	M	7.6	28.4	12.7	10.0	43.3	23.4	13.3	1.2	20.9
	F	11.9	22.7	10.1	5.9	39.6	31.1	4.5	0.9	20.2
Objective danger	M	62	18	47	53	28	39	47	56	41.1
	F	52	22	40	57	29	32	52	46	38.7

a. Ages eight to eighteen.

b. Comparison should not be made between aversions, since the absolute sizes of the percentages depend on factors in the tabulation that distort the relations between the various aversions.

c. Ages ten to seventeen.

d. Average of the six Southwest Indian groups.

travel, freedom from school and other routines, freedom from restriction and discipline, and personal pleasures and comforts.

Papago and Midwest lead the series, with Navaho Mountain at the other extreme. Midwest children are definitely higher than Indian children in responses mentioning pleasure in doing what one pleases.

Smooth Personal Relations

Getting along without friction in interpersonal relations (with both peers and adults) seems to be most highly valued by Zuni, Zia, and Hopi, with Navaho Mountain far below every other group. These relative standings are probably related to differences between the tribes in the closeness of living arrangements. Children in the three Pueblo village cultures grow up with a maximum of interpersonal contact. These societies put a premium on smooth interpersonal relations, at the same time that the child encounters a maximum of opportunities for friction. Thus the Pueblo child is happy when he gets along smoothly, and unhappy when he is involved in conflict with others; and he is aware all the time of the emotion-arousing interpersonal situation.

Papago parents emphasize and reward pleasant interpersonal relations perhaps as much as do Pueblo parents, but the Papago child has more elbowroom and consequently is not so keenly aware of and sensitive to the quality of his interpersonal relations.

The low frequency provided by Navaho Mountain is probably based primarily on geography. Only among the Navaho Mountain children do we find repeated references to happiness at being alone—out with the herds, watching the clouds. We have no reason to suppose that the quality of interpersonal relations at Navaho Mountain is different from that to be found in the pueblo cities—but the quantity is different. This probably causes the Navaho Mountain children to think less frequently of times when they were happy or angry over an incident of interpersonal relations.

Family-Centeredness

This theme consists of responses indicating happiness at being with the family, at having a new baby in the family, at returning to the family, and sadness at being away from the family or losing family members.

Examples are:

That I be going back home from school: I get anxious to see my family again (B.T., Navaho Mt. M8).
My mother and father would go back together (B.T., Midwest F13).
When my father comes home to us in the evenings (H., Hopi F8).
When I became an uncle (H., Midwest M15).
To take my father or mother away (W.T., Midwest F12).

As might be expected, the girls of all groups give expression to this value more frequently than the boys do. Among the girls, those of Navaho Mountain, Midwest, and Sioux mention this theme most frequently.

The paucity of responses for Hopi and Papago boys and girls on this theme can hardly be taken to mean that Papago and Hopi have less family solidarity than the other groups. It is possible that the families of these two groups are less frequently broken by absence of family members than is the case in the other groups. Thus Hopi and Papago children may be taking Family-Centeredness for granted while children in other communities are more frequently stimulated emotionally by absences and returns of family members.

Work

Work as a value is certainly inculcated in the children of all of these groups, with Midwest about midway in the series.

Getting jobs and earning money is presented as a value especially for boys. Boys are higher than girls except for Zuni and Shiprock, and about equal to girls at Navaho Mountain. Since girls' work and boys' work are not highly differentiated in the Navaho community, the Navaho results are not surprising. But the emphasis on work among Zuni girls needs further study.

Ceremonials, Fiestas

This theme deals with feelings of happiness at the ceremonials and fiestas which characterize the Southwest Indian communities. (These are distinguished from holidays and celebrations of the American culture, such as Christmas and Fourth of July.) They consist of ceremonial dances, especially at Hopi and Zuni, fiestas at Papago, squaw dances and sings with the Navaho. Examples of such responses are:

When the katcinas come to dance because they bring nice things to children (H., Hopi F7).

The Buffalo Dance (H., Hopi F15).
When I go to a squaw dance (H., Shiprock M14).
When I go to sing with the others (H., Navaho Mt. M15).
Shalako comes (B.T., Zuni M10).

Such responses are, of course, nonexistent in Midwest and practically so with the Sioux. The highest frequencies of responses are given by Zuni, Hopi, and Papago. A striking fact is that Zia responses are almost as low as the Navaho responses, although Zia is reported to have a considerable set of tribal ceremonies. The Zia ceremonies, however, are not reported with such evident pleasure as are the Zuni and Hopi ceremonies. They may be guarded more jealously, and the children accordingly may not talk so freely about them at Zia. The Navaho experiences most frequently mentioned are squaw dances, which appeal particularly to the older boys and girls.

Aversions

Aggression by Others

The frequency with which children mention aggression by others as sources of sadness, fear, anger, shame, and the worst thing is highest at Zuni, Zia, and Shiprock, and lowest in Midwest and Navaho Mountain. Examples of the responses are:

When the big boys fight me (F., Zuni M13).
The big boy chase me (F., Zia M11).
Boy tell lie on me (A., Zia M9).
I was angry at Marietta because she scold me (A., Zuni F14).
When boys make names for the girls (A., Shiprock F16).
A little girl fight me and I cried and was ashamed (Sh., Zuni F6).
A man chased me (Sh., Zia M14).
Crazy man come and get you and kill you. He could come to the door and grab you and bring you out (W.T., Sioux F14).

The high figures for Zuni, Zia, and Shiprock are probably not related to the actual amount of aggression present in those communities. There is probably more open and violent aggression among the Sioux than among any other group, and a good deal of it in Midwest. As is the case with other aversions, the frequency of response is probably based on two factors which are related in complex ways — the actual amount of fighting, quarreling, and gossiping in the community and the attitudes taught the children about aggression. Comparing Midwest with the average of Southwest Indians, the inference would seem to be that the Indian cultures make children more sensitive to, and probably more concerned about, aggressive behavior.

Discipline and Authority of Others

Related to the preceding aversion is this aversion toward being disciplined or ordered about by other people; and here, too, Indian children mention this theme, on the average, more frequently than do Midwest children. Zuni, Zia, and Hopi lead in responses on this theme. The high mentions of Zuni and Zia may be related to their high mentions of the theme "Aggression by Others." The children may interpret instances of control and discipline as aggression.

Examples of responses in this area are:

Last week when my mother scolded me (Sad., Zia F18).
I was afraid that the policeman was going to get my brother (F., Papago M14).
When I stole something and the man sent someone to punish me (F., Zuni M17).
I am late to school and teacher tell me to stay in at recess (A., Zia M8).
Sometimes I get mad when my father or mother tell me to do some thing (A., Zuni M17).
When sometimes my mother gets after me in front of a crowd of people (Sh., Papago F15).
In a school show I shot paper wads with rubber bands. Somebody caught me and gave me a talking. That was the worst punishment I ever had. I was sure ashamed (Sh., Sioux M15).
To get kicked out of school (W.T., Hopi M18).
My father spanks me (Sad., Hopi M8).

Illness and Danger of Others

Zuni and Hopi give much higher response than the other groups on this theme. "Others" are usually other members of the family, as:

When my grandmother get sick (Sad., Hopi M9).
The baby get sick (Sad., Zia F10).
When my father was sick (Sad., Midwest F12).
When my mother, father, and sister were out in a boat on a lake and a storm came up (F., Midwest F12).

Extremely low are the two Navaho groups. All the Indian groups have known much illness, the Navaho groups as much as the others. In fact, a measles epidemic killed most of the one-year-old children at Zia a year before this research was undertaken. Yet Zia children fail to mention illness and danger of others as often as do Hopi and Zuni.

Death of Others

The mentions of death of others show a pattern somewhat different from that of "Illness and Danger of Others." Midwest is highest, followed

by Sioux, Zuni, and Hopi; and Midwest is significantly higher than the average for the Southwest Indians.

The low frequencies of mention of death by Navaho may be ascribed to the fear of talking about death, although the same does not apply in the case of Zia. Among the Sioux the funeral is a great social ritual; and thus death, as associated with funerals, may take on added drama.

Upon further analysis, it appears that there is very little difference between Midwest and Indians on mentions of "Death of Others" as a cause of sadness, but a considerable difference on mentions of "Death of Others" as the "worst thing." The latter is not mentioned at all by Indian boys and rarely by Indian girls.

Death of Self

A striking thing about the responses on "Death of Self" is that there are very large and irregular sex differences. Among the Papago the girls mention Death of Self more frequently than do boys; while Hopi, Navaho, and Midwest boys all mention this more frequently than do the girls as the worst thing that could happen to them.

As compared with other cultures, the Sioux lead in this category, another evidence of the important place that death has in the Sioux scheme of things.

Illness and Accidents of Self

This category is the favorite male category, the only exception being the Navaho, who often reverse the sex differences against the common pattern. Zia leads with a relatively high frequency in this category, followed by Papago, Hopi, and Sioux. The Navaho experience illness fully as much as the other Indian children, however, and their infrequent mention of this theme may perhaps be related to their unwillingness to talk about death.

The marked difference between Midwest and Southwest Indians on this theme may be a realistic reaction to the greater incidence of illness and danger in the lives of Indian children. Midwest children are not ill so often as Indian children, and illness is not so dreadful for them.

Fear of the Supernatural

This category deals with fear of supernatural beings, witches, ghosts, and animals associated with the dead. The two Navaho groups and the Hopi lead on this theme, where a fourth to a third of their fear responses are of the following type:

Sometimes I afraid of owls (F., Hopi M12).
When the adashlay ran after me (F., Zuni F14).
Afraid of ghosts; they come in the night (F., Papago F10).
I thought I heard a witch outside: I wouldn't go to the toilet (F., Navaho Mt. M10).
When I first saw the yei they frightened me with their masks (F., Navaho Mt. M18).
Tchindis. Maybe one will curse me (F., Navaho Mt. F17).
I'm afraid of a Navaho wolf (F., Shiprock F6).

As would be expected, Midwest is at the low extreme on this theme, far below the nearest Indian group. The high Shiprock totals, though not so high as Navaho Mountain, are evidence of a very strong holdover of such beliefs in a group that has largely adopted white customs and beliefs. Perhaps the belief in evil supernatural forces is one of the last things to die out during the process of acculturation.

Objective Danger

At the opposite pole from fear of the supernatural stands "Objective Danger" as a source of fear. Such responses as the following were common:

I am afraid of wild animals (F., Zuni M10).
I'm afraid of bulls. Some of them are mean (F., Shiprock F16).
I'm afraid of mean dogs (F., Shiprock F12).
When we had a runaway I was afraid (F., Sioux M12).
Riding in a car on a slippery road (F., Sioux M15).
When I was thrown from a horse (F., Midwest M13).
When I tipped over on the bicycle (F., Midwest F12).

Zia and Papago, together with Midwest, are at the top on this theme. Mentions of "Objective Danger" are least where fear of the supernatural and subjective danger are highest, namely, in Hopi and Navaho responses.

Midwest children mention "Objective Danger" more frequently than the average of Southwest Indians. This does not mean that Midwest children are more exposed to objective danger, but rather that Indian children have two main sources of danger, the supernatural and the objective reality, whereas the Midwest children recognize only one, the objective forms of danger.

Sex Differences

Studying the differences between boys and girls in their emotional responses, we may look first for general differences true of all or nearly all the societies investigated, and then for differences characteristic of one or another society.

General Sex Patterns

The special male pattern consists of pleasure in work and sadness over illness and accidents to one's self. The female pattern is characterized by happiness over family solidarity and smooth personal relations, combined with fear and sadness over aggression by others and death of others. These minimal patterns are supplemented in some, but not all, of the societies by other values and aversions which make the boys appear self-centered and the girls other-centered. That is, the boys seem more concerned about what happens to them, while the girls are more concerned with what happens to others or is done by others.

Societal Sex Patterns

The general sex patterns just mentioned are a basis for further similarities among boys of Midwest, Shiprock, and Papago, who exceed girls in pleasure over individual achievement, in gaining property and possessions, and in fear of objective danger. These boys may be characterized as object-oriented as well as self-centered. They are active in seeking what they want from the environment and realistic about the dangers of the environment. The girls in these societies are more timid and more afraid of the supernatural.

Opposite in some ways to the typical sex patterns are the Navaho Mountain boys and girls. Here the girls have the more usual masculine pattern of pleasure in individual achievement and in property and possessions, while they are equal to the boys on pleasure in work, and they have some of the masculine sadness over illness and accidents to the self. The boys, on the other hand, have relatively more of the usual feminine fear and sadness over aggression by others and pleasure at smooth personal relations. Navaho Mountain boys are the only boys that stand out over the girls in their concern over discipline and authority of others.

The three Pueblo tribes show very little in common for either sex beyond the minimum general sex patterns already described. One thing the Pueblo boys have in common is a greater fear of the supernatural than do the girls. The girls report more happiness over ceremonials and fiestas than do the boys.

In general, the sexes are more nearly alike among the Indians than among the whites. On nearly all the values and aversions the Indian boys and girls are closer together than are the white boys and girls.

Age Trends

Age trends, as would be anticipated, vary from theme to theme. For some values and aversions there are no striking age changes; for others there are fairly steady increases or decreases in frequency of mention with age; for still others there is no change from age eight to thirteen, but a change after thirteen; and so on. And the pattern differs from one cultural group to another.

Since the data on age trends are too complex to be easily summarized here, the reader is referred to Table 43 in Appendix B-10, where the data on values and aversions are given by age-sex breakdowns for each cultural group.

Speaking quite generally of Midwest as compared with Southwest Indian children, both groups grow from a simple, naïve, and limited emotional sphere to one which is much more complex, more sophisticated, and far more comprehensive. There is a general downward trend with age in the frequency of the following types of responses: having and receiving property and possessions; getting gifts and food, playing games, having excitement and other forms of self-gratification; feelings of sadness and apprehension about illness, accidents, and death of one's self; fear of the supernatural. These may all be interpreted as egocentric responses. In contrast is the increase with age of such more complex and sociocentric responses as pleasure in tribal ceremonials; value in individual achievement (which means that the person feels more responsible for his own behavior and more self-direction, and thus moves from simple constraint toward a more complex autonomy of moral life); a corresponding increase at adolescence of the value of work (which is a social rather than an individual value); and concern over the death of others.

Section 4. PERSONS INVOLVED IN CHILDREN'S EMOTIONS

Emotional experiences may involve persons, animals, inanimate objects such as food and clothing and property, institutions such as school and government, and supernatural beings. When children tell what makes them happy, sad, or fearful, they are free to mention persons involved in the experiences they report. Hence it is possible to see how often children's emotional experiences involve people and also how children regard the various kinds of people around them, whether as bringers of happiness or bringers of sadness.

The catalogue of "persons involved" in the responses of these children is a long one. While we originally tallied such responses under 47 different categories (see Appendix B-8), only certain of these original categories appeared frequently enough to justify statistical treatment. The responses were consequently recombined, and comparisons between groups were made on the basis of the following categories:

Family in general (including relatives, parents, folks, aunt, uncle, grandmother, grandfather, cousin)
Father
Mother
Siblings of the same sex
Siblings of the opposite sex
Peers of the same sex
Peers of the opposite sex
Peers in general, friends
Teacher and school (mentions of school were categorized as "persons involved")
Tramps, drunk men, strange men or women
"They," somebody (a general term for a person or persons indefinitely named)
Supernatural beings (real persons who appear to the child in the guise of supernatural beings: katcinas, yeibichai, adashlay, but not witches or ghosts)

References to one's self occur frequently ("when I fell and broke my leg," "the worst thing would be to die") but are not included in this analysis.

Which Emotions Most Often Involve Other Persons?

Children are more likely to mention persons in connection with experiences of anger and sadness than with the other emotions. This is shown in Table 13 and is true of all the groups studied. On the other hand, fear, happiness, "best thing," and "worst thing" involve other people much less frequently. The latter experiences and expectations are more object-related and more self-centered.

Emotional experiences may be said to be object-related if the child thinks primarily of possessing or gaining something, such as clothing, food, or gifts. Many of the emotional responses on the test indicate that the children are hardly aware that "the gift without the giver is bare," for they are wrapped up in the possession and enjoyment of things.

Emotional experiences may be said to be self-centered if they refer to what the experience does to the self. Children giving self-centered responses say the worst thing that could happen is to die or be sick; the best thing is to receive a gift or to own property; they are sad when they are sick; they are happy when they receive a present or go to a party.

Anger seems to be mainly an experience in interpersonal relations, since nearly all anger responses involve other persons. Occasionally anger responses involve the perverse behavior of animals, and very seldom did a person report that he was angry because of some purely impersonal circumstance—for instance, the Hopi girl who was "Angry at my dress: it was tight, and I took it off and tore it with my teeth."

Sadness also often results from an interpersonal situation: from illness or death or absence of family members or from being disciplined or being the subject of another person's aggression.

It should be pointed out that there is one complication in interpreting the data on persons involved in sadness which does not occur with the other emotions. With the exception of sadness, all the emotions represented in the test call forth unambiguous responses. That is, in reporting on sources of happiness and "best thing," a child reports on things which caused pleasant emotion. His reactions to the experiences are positive, as are his reactions to the persons involved in these experiences. A child says, "I was happy when my father gave me bow and arrows." Everything is positive. In reporting on fear, anger, shame, and "worst thing," a child reports on things which caused unpleasant emotion. His reactions to these experiences and to the people involved are negative. A child says, "I was angry when my father spanked me." Everything is negative.

But reports on sources of sadness are ambiguous. Sadness itself is unpleasant, but the people involved may be seen either positively or negatively. Thus a child may say, "I was sad when my mother was sick," or, differently, "I was sad when my mother scolded me."

TABLE 13[a]

EMOTIONAL RESPONSE TEST: AVERAGE NUMBER OF "PERSONS INVOLVED" PER RESPONSE

Emotion	Tribe															
	Papago		Hopi		Zuni		Zia		Navaho Mt.		Shiprock		Sioux		Midwest[b]	
	Boys	Girls	Boys	Girls	Boys	Girls	Boys	Girls	Boys	Girls	Boys	Girls	Boys	Girls	Boys	Girls
Happiness	0.15	0.15	0.26	0.34	0.14	0.22	0.15	0.43	0.46	0.51	0.27	0.26	0.22	0.29	0.17	0.24
Sadness	.56	.69	.58	0.82	.56	.69	.39	0.71	.66	.61	.36	.68	.50	.63	.51	.53
Fear	.12	.09	.24	0.30	.18	.26	.06	0.19	.02	.00	.13	.12	.09	.19	.11	.20
Anger	.66	.76	.50	1.09	.70	.81	.84	0.87	.36	.73	.76	.80	.57	.74	.53	.61
Shame	.35	.38	.31	0.48	.40	.43	.33	1.00	.15	.11	.38	.33	.49	.23	.43	.51
"Best thing"	.08	.04	.10	0.15	.31	.48	.08	0.18	.07	.00	.08	.24	.23	.17	.11	.20
"Worst thing"	0.04	0.10	0.04	0.34	0.20	0.40	0.05	0.18	0.00	0.00	0.05	0.05	0.07	0.18	0.16	0.29
Average	0.28	0.30	0.32	0.51	0.36	0.46	0.30	0.50	0.26	0.25	0.31	0.37	0.32	0.37	0.31	0.38
No. of responses	544	541	571	781	718	634	333	240	348	243	356	391	718	738	1,997	3,233
No. of persons involved	151	161	181	405	261	293	100	119	89	61	111	145	226	276	612	1,237

a. Ages eight to eighteen.

b. Ages ten to seventeen.

For this reason the responses on persons involved in sadness cannot be combined with those of the other negative emotions (as in Table 20) when we want to draw conclusions about those people toward whom the child reacts unfavorably.

Shame is nearly always the result of some interpersonal relation, but the person or persons involved are not always mentioned. Thus a child may say, "I was ashamed when I fell down and got dirty," which implies that this put the child in a poor light in the eyes of other people. Shame may also be the result of some wrongdoing which troubles the conscience of the child—"I was ashamed when I stole some candy."

Happiness may involve persons who make the child happy by giving him things or by being with him, but, in general, the responses reporting happiness are object-centered or self-centered.

Fear usually involves danger, either objective or subjective. When subjective, the response may include a mention of specific supernatural beings, who appear in reality to the child because they are humans dressed as supernatural beings; or the subjective fear response may deal with "scary" conditions, such as darkness, strange noises, strange shapes, animals associated with the supernatural. Aside from supernatural beings, there is not much mention of persons in connection with fear unless they are strangers or unless the child is fearful that some harm may befall a friend or family member.

Sex Differences

Girls are, generally speaking, more involved with persons in their emotional experiences than boys are, according to Table 13. In only two groups, Papago and Navaho Mountain, do the boys mention persons as frequently as do the girls.

Cultural Differences

The Pueblo villages, with their physical and social compactness, give the highest number of "persons involved" responses. Then come Midwest, Sioux, and Shiprock, where people are less closely associated both physically and socially. Finally, Papago and Navaho Mountain have the smallest number of "persons involved," probably reflecting the relative physical isolation in which these children live.

The variation among the groups in numbers of "persons involved" is much greater for girls than for boys. In fact, practically all the differences between groups is produced by the girls' differences.

Probably the observed differences in the numbers of persons mentioned can be accounted for in part, as suggested above, by simple facts of geographical and social compactness or isolation. Nevertheless, these differences may be due partly to differences in feelings about interpersonal contacts. Certainly, such different feelings underlie individual differences in the numbers of persons mentioned: but we cannot say whether or not there are group differences of this sort.

Comparisons of Various Societies on Types of "Persons Involved"

In Tables 14-20 the various societies are compared with respect to the principal categories of "persons involved."[13]

---

13. In these tables the boys or girls of all ages from eight to eighteen are grouped together. There was a problem of arriving at a percentage frequency of response which would adequately represent the total group. This problem was handled for the Indian groups by counting the number of "persons involved" in a given category and dividing by the total number of "persons involved." This was done separately for boys and girls, and the percentages for the two sexes were then averaged, to get a figure for the total tribal group. This procedure has the effect of weighting the more populous age groups more heavily: for instance, if there are twice as many persons mentioned by twelve-year-olds as by seventeen-year-olds, the twelve-year-old frequency has twice the weight of the seventeen-year-old frequency in determining the final figure. But the numbers of responses mentioning "persons involved" were so small in many cases that if the group had been divided into three age groups and the percentages computed for each age group, some percentages would be computed on as few as 10 or 20 responses and thus would be subject to very high chance error.

For Midwest a more accurate procedure was used, since there were larger numbers of responses. The Midwest responses were divided into four age groups: ten to eleven, twelve to thirteen, fourteen to fifteen, sixteen to seventeen. The percentages of "persons involved" in the various categories were computed for each group, and the four percentages averaged to give a figure representing the total age group. This gave each age group equal weight, even though the number of children varied from one group to another. Exceptions to this rule were made in the cases of fear, "best thing," and "worst thing," where responses were fewer, and where the method used for the Indian tribes was followed.

In getting an average percentage for the negative emotions (fear, anger, shame), the numbers of responses for "persons involved" in the various categories were added for the three emotions, and new percentages were computed. Thus each emotion was weighted according to the number of responses it drew.

TABLE 14[a]

EMOTIONAL RESPONSE TEST: PERSONS INVOLVED IN HAPPINESS (PERCENTAGES)

Persons	Papago			Hopi			Zuni			Zia			Navaho Mt.			Shiprock			Sioux			Midwest[b]		
Involved	B	G	T	B	G	T	B	G	T	B	G	T	B	G	T	B	G	T	B	G	T	B	G	T
Family (except father, mother, sibs)	0	17	9	13	26	24	15	17	16	20	13	16	23	14	18	8	15	12	17	30	24	25	33	29
Father	35	4	19	34	24	29	30	10	20	40	22	31	40	10	25	56	22	39	14	6	11	10	8	9
Mother	5	30	17	5	11	8	10	10	10	0	26	13	3	28	15	8	30	19	17	22	19	22	14	18
Sibs, same sex	5	9	7	3	5	4	10	0	5	20	0	10	17	35	26	4	4	4	28	8	18	12	10	11
Sibs, opposite sex	5	9	6	5	5	5	0	7	3	0	17	9	3	10	6	0	7	4	3	8	6	2	14	8
Peers, same sex	10	4	7	3	0	1	10	13	11	10	4	7	3	0	2	8	0	4	0	12	6	1	5	3
Peers, opposite sex	0	0	0	0	0	0	10	0	5	0	4	3	0	0	0	0	0	0	3	2	3	12	7	10
Peers in general	15	22	18	3	10	7	10	10	10	0	0	0	6	3	4	0	7	4	3	2	3	6	6	6
School and teacher	0	0	0	0	2	1	0	7	3	0	4	3	3	0	2	0	0	0	0	0	0	8	2	5
Tramps, drunks	0	0	0	0	0	0	0	0	0	0	0	0	0	0	0	0	0	0	0	0	0	0	0	0
They, somebody	20	4	12	13	10	11	5	17	11	10	8	9	3	0	2	16	19	18	17	10	13	2	3	3
Supernatural	5	0	2	21	10	15	0	10	5	0	0	0	0	0	0	0	0	0	0	0	0	0	0	0
Total no. of persons involved	20	23	43	38	62	100	20	30	50	10	23	33	35	29	64	25	27	52	36	50	86	73	158	231

a. Ages eight to eighteen.

b. Ages ten to seventeen.

TABLE 15[a]

EMOTIONAL RESPONSE TEST: PERSONS INVOLVED IN SADNESS (PERCENTAGES)

Persons	Papago			Hopi			Zuni			Zia			Navaho Mt.			Shiprock			Sioux			Midwest[b]		
Involved	B	G	T	B	G	T	B	G	T	B	G	T	B	G	T	B	G	T	B	G	T	B	G	T
Family (except father, mother, sibs)	27	19	23	13	15	14	20	27	24	18	10	14	21	20	20	32	25	29	37	33	35	39	42	41
Father	14	13	13	13	9	11	8	7	7	0	3	2	15	5	10	16	0	8	2	6	4	17	9	13
Mother	8	17	13	17	19	18	15	12	23	9	13	11	21	25	23	11	15	13	11	18	14	10	20	15
Sibs, same sex	16	2	9	9	11	10	15	9	12	27	10	14	18	35	27	16	15	16	18	13	15	11	5	8
Sibs, opposite sex	4	12	8	11	16	14	12	14	13	9	17	13	12	15	14	0	21	11	17	15	16	4	9	7
Peers, same sex	4	11	7	6	3	4	2	9	5	5	0	2	0	0	0	5	2	4	6	5	5	3	1	2
Peers, opposite sex	4	4	4	0	3	2	3	0	2	0	3	2	0	0	0	0	0	0	0	1	1	3	6	5
Peers in general	2	2	2	0	3	2	3	0	2	5	3	4	0	0	0	0	0	0	0	0	0	6	5	6
School and teacher	2	2	2	0	0	0	0	3	2	0	7	3	6	0	3	0	2	1	6	0	3	3	2	3
Tramps, drunks	2	0	1	0	0	0	0	0	0	0	0	0	0	0	0	0	0	0	0	0	0	0	0	0
They, somebody	14	21	18	30	20	26	22	19	20	27	33	30	6	0	3	21	21	21	4	9	6	1	2	2
Supernatural	0	0	0	2	1	1	0	0	0	0	0	0	0	0	0	0	0	0	0	0	0	0	0	0
Total no. of persons involved	49	53	102	47	117	164	65	70	135	22	30	52	33	20	53	19	48	67	54	87	141	164	297	361

a. Ages eight to eighteen.

b. Ages ten to seventeen.

TABLE 16[a]

EMOTIONAL RESPONSE TEST: PERSONS INVOLVED IN FEAR (PERCENTAGES)

Persons	Papago			Hopi			Zuni			Zia			Navaho Mt.			Shiprock			Sioux			Midwest[b]		
Involved	B	G	T	B	G	T	B	G	T	B	G	T	B	G	T	B	G	T	B	G	T	B	G	T
Family (except father, mother, sibs)	25	10	17	11	4	7	17	8	12							0	22	11	0	8	4	14	15	15
Father	8	0	4	5	4	5	8	0	4							22	0	11	0	0	0	6	8	7
Mother	8	10	9	5	7	6	4	11	7							0	9	5	8	13	10	11	21	16
Sibs, same sex	17	0	9	5	2	3	0	8	4							9	0	4	8	8	8	11	8	10
Sibs, opposite sex	0	0	0	0	2	1	0	8	4							0	9	5	0	4	2	0	15	8
Peers, same sex	0	0	0	11	7	9	8	21	15							0	0	0	16	8	12	29	4	17
Peers, opposite sex	0	0	0	0	11	6	0	8	4							0	0	0	0	17	9	0	4	2
Peers in general	0	0	0	5	2	3	4	0	2							0	0	0	8	0	4	3	1	2
School and teacher	8	10	9	5	4	5	4	8	6							0	9	5	0	0	0	6	3	5
Tramps, drunks	17	50	33	0	0	0	8	0	4							54	33	43	16	8	12	3	9	6
They, somebody	17	20	19	37	33	35	25	21	23							9	33	21	42	33	37	17	12	15
Supernatural	0	0	0	21	22	22	21	11	16							9	0	4	0	0	0	0	0	0
Total no. of persons involved.	12	10	22	19	45	64	24	28	52	4	10	14	2	0	2	11	11	22	12	24	36	35	106	141

a. Ages eight to eighteen.

b. Ages ten to seventeen.

TABLE 17[a]

EMOTIONAL RESPONSE TEST: PERSONS INVOLVED IN ANGER (PERCENTAGES)

Persons	Papago			Hopi			Zuni			Zia			Navaho Mt.			Shiprock			Sioux			Midwest[b]		
Involved	B	G	T	B	G	T	B	G	T	B	G	T	B	G	T	B	G	T	B	G	T	B	G	T
Family (except father, mother, sibs)	9	2	5	0	5	3	9	7	8	0	3	1	0	0	0	4	2	3	3	8	6	3	9	6
Father	0	2	2	10	7	8	6	0	3	15	3	9	0	0	0	2	0	1	2	6	4	2	2	2
Mother	4	4	4	14	8	11	7	8	8	0	8	4	0	0	0	0	2	1	9	6	8	7	8	8
Sibs, same sex	17	15	16	8	12	10	6	12	9	17	5	11	12	50	31	11	11	10	9	21	15	12	21	17
Sibs, opposite sex	7	2	4	2	14	8	6	2	4	0	3	1	12	38	25	2	11	7	8	5	6	5	10	8
Peers, same sex	13	21	17	24	9	16	32	29	30	31	10	20	38	12	25	17	18	17	25	9	17	19	8	14
Peers, opposite sex	4	0	2	0	10	5	3	10	6	4	5	5	0	0	0	2	2	2	9	14	11	2	7	5
Peers in general	4	8	6	2	6	4	1	2	2	10	24	17	0	0	0	0	0	0	2	3	2	4	4	4
School and teacher	2	2	2	2	0	1	1	4	2	4	5	5	12	0	6	0	0	0	2	0	1	9	5	7
Tramps, drunks	2	4	3	0	0	0	0	0	0	0	0	0	0	0	0	0	0	0	0	0	0	0	0	0
They, somebody	37	40	39	38	30	34	29	26	28	19	36	28	25	0	12	62	52	57	32	28	30	39	26	33
Supernatural	0	0	0	0	0	0	0	0	0	0	0	0	0	0	0	0	0	0	0	0	0	0	0	0
Total no. of persons involved	46	48	94	50	105	155	82	84	166	52	39	91	8	8	16	47	44	91	65	78	143	189	317	506

a. Ages eight to eighteen.

b. Ages ten to seventeen.

TABLE 18[a]

EMOTIONAL RESPONSE TEST: PERSONS INVOLVED IN SHAME (PERCENTAGES)

Persons	Papago			Hopi			Zuni			Zia			Navaho Mt.			Shiprock			Sioux			Midwest[b]		
Involved	B	G	T	B	G	T	B	G	T	B	G	T	B	G	T	B	G	T	B	G	T	B	G	T
Family (except father, mother, sibs)	11	10	10	0	4	2	9	4	6	12	0	6							2	11	6	9	10	9
Father	11	0	5	5	7	6	4	0	2	12	0	6							9	0	4	5	2	4
Mother	0	14	7	5	18	12	4	7	5	63	11	37							21	28	24	20	30	25
Sibs, same sex	0	10	5	0	7	4	2	0	1	0	22	11							9	6	7	2	11	7
Sibs, opposite sex	0	0	0	0	5	3	2	2	2	0	0	0							2	6	4	10	7	9
Peers, same sex	6	0	3	25	2	13	23	28	26	0	33	17							8	6	7	13	6	10
Peers, opposite sex	22	5	13	5	9	7	11	4	7	0	11	5							21	6	13	13	5	9
Peers in general	0	5	2	0	4	2	6	4	5	0	11	5							0	6	3	5	5	5
School and teacher	0	5	2	15	9	12	9	11	10	0	11	5							16	0	8	9	10	10
Tramps, drunks	6	5	5	0	0	0	0	0	0	0	0	0							0	0	0	0	0	0
They, somebody	44	48	46	40	35	37	30	37	33	12	0	6							9	33	21	17	17	17
Supernatural	0	0	0	5	0	2	0	2	1	0	0	0							0	0	0	0	0	0
Total no. of persons involved	18	21	39	20	55	75	47	46	93	8	9	17	9	4	13	6	7	13	43	18	61	111	244	355

a. Ages eight to eighteen.

b. Ages ten to seventeen.

TABLE 19[a]

EMOTIONAL RESPONSE TEST: PERSONS INVOLVED IN POSITIVE EMOTIONS (HAPPINESS AND "BEST THING") (PERCENTAGES)

Persons	Papago			Hopi			Zuni			Zia			Navaho Mt.			Shiprock			Sioux			Midwest[b]		
Involved	B	G	T	B	G	T	B	G	T	B	G	T	B	G	T	B	G	T	B	G	T	B	G	T
Family (except father, mother, sibs)	0	16	8	12	22	17	9	14	12	20	13	17	24	14	19	7	18	13	15	27	21	27	30	28
Father	37	8	23	35	21	28	41	20	30	40	21	30	40	10	25	56	18	37	15	5	10	10	9	10
Mother	4	28	16	5	14	10	6	12	9	0	25	12	3	28	16	7	24	16	19	25	22	15	14	15
Sibs, same sex	4	12	8	5	4	4	9	0	4	20	0	10	16	35	26	4	12	8	21	7	14	15	9	12
Sibs, opposite sex	4	8	6	5	4	4	0	6	3	0	17	8	3	10	6	0	3	2	2	8	5	2	14	8
Peers, same sex	8	4	6	2	0	1	6	8	7	10	4	7	3	0	1	7	0	4	0	11	6	2	4	3
Peers, opposite sex	4	0	2	0	0	0	9	0	4	0	4	2	0	0	0	0	0	0	4	2	3	11	9	10
Peers in general	12	20	16	2	8	5	6	10	8	0	0	0	5	3	4	0	3	2	2	2	2	4	5	5
School and teacher	0	0	0	0	1	1	0	6	3	0	4	2	3	1	2	0	0	0	2	0	1	11	2	6
Tramps, drunks	0	0	0	0	0	0	0	0	0	0	0	0	0	0	0	0	0	0	0	0	0	0	0	0
They, somebody	21	4	12	16	13	14	15	14	14	10	13	12	3	0	1	18	24	21	21	13	17	3	4	4
Supernatural	4	0	2	19	13	16	0	8	4	0	0	0	0	0	0	0	0	0	0	0	0	0	0	0
Total no. of persons involved.	24	25	49	43	72	115	34	49	83	10	24	34	37	29	66	27	34	61	48	60	108	93	208	301

a. Ages eight to eighteen.

b. Ages ten to seventeen.

TABLE 20[a]

EMOTIONAL RESPONSE TEST: PERSONS INVOLVED IN NEGATIVE EMOTIONS (FEAR, ANGER, AND SHAME) (PERCENTAGES)

Persons	Papago			Hopi			Zuni			Zia			Navaho Mt.			Shiprock			Sioux			Midwest[b]		
Involved	B	G	T	B	G	T	B	G	T	B	G	T	B	G	T	B	G	T	B	G	T	B	G	T
Family (except father, mother, sibs)	12	5	9	2	4	3	10	6	8	2	2	1	5	8	7	3	6	5	3	8	5	5	10	8
Father	4	1	2	8	6	7	6	0	3	16	3	9	0	0	0	5	0	2	4	4	4	4	3	4
Mother	4	8	6	10	10	10	6	9	7	8	9	8	11	0	5	2	8	5	13	11	12	12	17	15
Sibs, same sex	13	11	12	6	9	8	4	8	6	14	7	10	11	33	22	9	10	9	9	16	12	8	14	11
Sibs, opposite sex	4	1	2	1	9	5	4	3	3	0	3	2	11	33	22	2	10	6	4	5	4	5	9	7
Peers, same sex	9	13	11	21	6	13	22	27	25	26	13	20	16	8	12	17	13	15	18	8	13	18	6	12
Peers, opposite sex	8	1	4	1	10	6	5	8	6	3	7	5	0	0	0	2	2	2	13	13	13	4	6	5
Peers in general	3	6	4	1	4	3	3	3	3	10	17	13	0	0	0	0	0	0	2	3	2	5	4	4
School and teacher	3	4	3	6	3	4	4	6	5	3	9	6	31	8	19	0	5	3	7	0	3	9	6	8
Tramps, drunks	5	10	8	0	0	0	1	0	1	2	2	2	0	0	0	9	5	7	2	2	2	0	2	1
They, somebody	36	40	38	38	32	35	29	28	28	19	28	23	11	8	9	50	42	46	25	30	28	29	22	25
Supernatural	0	0	0	6	5	5	3	3	3	0	0	0	5	0	2	2	0	1	0	0	0	0	0	0
Total no. of persons involved.	76	79	155	89	205	294	153	158	311	62	58	120	19	12	31	64	62	126	120	120	240	335	667	1,002

a. Ages eight to eighteen.

b. Ages ten to seventeen.

Father and Mother as "Persons Involved"[14]

What parts do fathers and mothers have in the emotional experiences of children? Considering boys and girls together, it is seen from Table 19 that the order of the groups for fathers as persons involved in happiness and "best thing" is (figures given in parentheses refer to percentages): Shiprock (37), Zuni (30), Zia (30), Hopi (28), Navaho Mountain (25), Papago (23), Sioux (10), Midwest (10). The difference between the Southwest Indians and Midwest and Sioux is striking.

This order is partially reversed when we rank the groups for mothers as persons involved in happiness and "best thing": Sioux (22), Papago (16), Shiprock (16), Navaho Mountain (16), Midwest (15), Zia (12), Hopi (10), Zuni (9).

Family versus Nonfamily as "Persons Involved"

Comparison of family members with people outside the family as persons involved in happiness and "best thing" reveals the following order, where the numbers in parentheses indicate the percentage of responses involving family members. Navaho Mountain (92), Zia (77), Shiprock (76), Midwest (74), Sioux (72), Hopi (63), Papago (61), Zuni (58) (see Table 19; "family members" represents the total of the first five rows of the table).

In the case of the negative emotions, fear, anger, and shame, the order is: Navaho Mountain (56), Midwest (45), Sioux (37), Hopi (33), Papago (31), Zia (30), Shiprock (27), Zuni (27) (see Table 20).

Navaho Mountain children experience very little social interaction outside their own extended families. Therefore, we might have anticipated this finding that Navaho Mountain mentions members of the extended family more frequently than any other society. Nor is it surprising to find the three Pueblo villages toward the bottom of the series, indicating that they have the greatest amount of emotionally tinged social interaction with people outside the family. It is, however, somewhat of a surprise to find Midwest following the Navaho as the more family-centered group, since we do not usually think of the

14. Incidentally, the traditional role of the mother's brother as punisher among the Hopi is not mentioned in the Emotional Response Test. Throughout the Study the only reference to the uncle as punisher was made by a half-dozen younger Hopi children, who, when told a story of a boy stealing a saddle and asked what should be done to him, said that he should be punished by his uncle.

white American society as being especially family-centered.

Age-Mates as "Persons Involved"

When we consider age-mates or peers as persons involved in emotional experiences (Table 19, when the sixth, seventh, and eighth rows are totaled), we find the following order for positive emotions: Papago (24), Zuni (19), Midwest (18), Sioux (11), Zia (9), Hopi (6), Shiprock (6), Navaho Mountain (5).

For the negative emotions (Table 20) the order is not entirely similar: Zia (38), Zuni (34), Sioux (28), Hopi (22), Midwest (21), Papago (19), Shiprock (17), Navaho Mountain (12). But it is clear that Zuni shows the greatest amount of peer interaction (if these data are taken as a measure) and the Navaho groups the least.

Community Members as "Persons Involved"

The indefinite "they" or "somebody" was used by children to refer to the community members generally, either as bringers of happiness or as bringers of negative emotions (more often the latter). As seen in Table 19, the order for happiness and "best thing" was: Shiprock (21), Sioux (17), Hopi (14), Zuni (14), Papago (12), Zia (12), Midwest (4), Navaho Mountain (1).

For the negative emotions (Table 20) the order was: Shiprock (46), Papago (38), Hopi (35), Zuni (28), Sioux (28), Midwest (25), Zia (23), Navaho Mountain (9).

The infrequency of such responses at Navaho Mountain is probably the result of isolation: but the other Navaho community leads the list, while Midwest is low. There seems to be no one explanation to account for the order of societies in this case, probably because the indefinite "they" actually means different kinds of people for different societies. It may mean "neighbors" in one community and "strangers" in another.

Comparison of Southwest Indians with Midwest

It is not too useful, perhaps, to combine the responses of Southwest Indians on "persons involved" because of the relative isolation of Navaho Mountain and Papago families, which tends to restrict their children's mentions of people to the child's own family. Nevertheless, by com-

bining the frequencies of "persons involved" for the Indian groups, we get large enough numbers to permit us to draw reliable conclusions about some of the differences suggested by the intertribal comparisons drawn from Tables 14-20.

Table 21 shows a comparison of Midwest with Southwest Indian children on "persons involved" in the positive emotions (happiness and "best thing") and the negative emotions (fear, anger, and shame). The inferences previously suggested about the greater significance of the father in producing happiness for Indian boys and girls is fully borne out. The Midwest mother appears to be as closely related to her sons as to her daughters in the producing of happiness, while the Indian mother is much more closely related to her daughters in this way. The Midwest father seems to have less of a role as a reward-giver for his sons and daughters than does the Midwest mother, and also less of a role as punisher.

Community members play a greater part in producing both pleasant and unpleasant emotions in the Indian children than in Midwest children. This difference, as shown in Table 21, is reduced by the fact that Navaho Mountain children have very few community contacts and consequently do not mention community members as often as any other group.

When all family members are considered together, they are more frequently associated with negative emotions in Midwest than among Southwest Indians, and more frequently associated with positive emotions in Midwest than in any Indian groups except the Navaho. This indicates two things: (1) The greater power of the people in the Indian community outside the family to influence the emotions of children (especially in the Pueblo villages); (2) the greater use of the family for disapproval and discipline of children in Midwest.[15]

Summary

The differences in frequency of various categories of "persons involved" in emotional experiences of children reflect considerable

15. As with the values and aversions themes, certain categories of "persons involved" were studied in terms of how they correlate with one another from one society to the next. The reader is referred to the upper quadrant of Table 48 in Appendix E-2. To interpret that table, see n. 11, p. 46.

TABLE 21[a]

EMOTIONAL RESPONSE TEST: COMPARISON OF SOUTHWEST INDIANS WITH MIDWEST ON "PERSONS INVOLVED" (PERCENTAGES)

Persons Involved	Happiness and "Best Thing"						Fear, Anger, and Shame					
	Southwest Indians			Midwest[b]			Southwest Indians			Midwest		
	Male	Female	Total	Male	Female	Total	Male	Female	Total	Male	Female	Total
Total Family	67	73	70	69	76	74	32	37	34	34	53	45
Father	42	16	29	10	9	10	6	2	4	4	3	4
Mother	4	22	13	15	14	15	6	7	7	12	17	15
Peers	12	11	12	17	18	18	26	23	24	27	16	21
Community members	14	11	12	3	4	4	31	30	30	29	22	25
School and teachers	1	2	1	11	2	7	8	6	7	9	6	8
Supernaturals	4	4	4	0	0	0	3	1	2	0	0	0
No. on which percentages are based	175	233	408	93	208	301	463	574	1,037	335	667	1,002

a. Ages eight to eighteen.

b. Ages ten to seventeen.

differences in the actual social environment of the children and also differences in the attitudes of children toward various categories of people.

Children at Navaho Mountain are physically isolated and see very few people outside their immediate and extended families. Hopi, Zuni, and Zia children, by contrast, grow up in small crowded villages. Mothers and fathers in the several societies vary in their roles as gift-giver and punishment-giver. While the matrilineal, matrilocal societies (Hopi, Zuni, Zia, Navaho) tend to place the father in the gift-giver and happiness-bringer roles, there are some exceptions, such as Zia, where the father is also the chief bringer of negative emotions to boys. The mother's roles in Midwest appear to be more emotion-laden than the father's, both positive and negative, as is also true of the Sioux.

Section 5. CONSCIENCE AND SELF-CONSCIOUSNESS

When a child is asked, "Have you ever been ashamed?" what does the question mean to him? A Midwest boy of fifteen says, "I am ashamed when I have been copying in school." A girl of fourteen was ashamed "when I have gotten angry or falsely accused someone." Another fourteen-year-old girl was ashamed "when I acted selfish and another girl wasn't and taught me a lesson." A nine-year-old Hopi boy says he is ashamed "when I hit little boys." An eleven-year-old Hopi girl was ashamed "when I stole something." In all these cases it appears that the child feels guilty, or his "conscience hurts him," over something he knows he should not do. He accuses himself.

Contrast these responses with the following: A nine-year-old Hopi girl says: "When I play and talk with my dolls and somebody comes near me and hears me, then I get ashamed." A Zuni girl of seven is ashamed "when the wind blow my dress up." Another Zuni girl of seven is ashamed "when the neighbors come to visit my house." A Zia boy of twelve is ashamed "when I wear my school suit to town." Another Zia boy of seven says he is ashamed "when my uncle cut my hair. He don't know how and he make me funny." A fourteen-year-old Midwest boy is ashamed "when I was to address a large crowd and forgot the things I was to say." In these cases the emotion is one of embarrassment because one makes a poor showing in front of others. The shame is caused by the presence of other people.

Thus we find two meanings of shame being employed by the children —

sense of guilt, on the one hand, and embarrassment, on the other hand.

The shame responses were analyzed to discover the relative frequencies of embarrassment and of guilt. Some children gave shame responses that were entirely of the guilt variety, some gave nothing but embarrassment responses, some gave responses that were not clearly one or the other, and some gave responses of both kinds.

Not all answers were easy to classify. A ten-year-old boy says, "When I shot a sparrow out of a tree." We cannot tell whether he was guilty about this, or whether someone scolded him for it and made him feel embarrassed; similarly, when a child writes, "I am ashamed when I break something," or "not going to church," or "sassing mother or teacher," or "not getting work done."

Whenever it was clear that the child's discomfort was due to the presence of others and his feeling that he would be laughed at or scolded or punished, the response was classified as embarrassment. When it was clear that the child's discomfort was due to some inner sense of guilt and that the presence of people was not a necessary aspect of the feeling, it was classified as guilt. Where the response was ambiguous, it was classified as questionable.

The results of analysis of the responses of children in five tribal groups are given in Table 22. Only the protocols from children aged ten, fourteen, and sixteen in Midwest were analyzed.

The Language Problem

Before discussing the significance of Table 22, we should examine the possible ambiguity of the test question, "Have you ever been ashamed?" Did this question have the same meaning to the children of the various tribes, many of whom understood English poorly? And when the question was translated to some of the Papago, Hopi, and Navaho children, how was it translated?

For Midwest and Sioux children there was no ambiguity caused by failure to understand the word "ashamed," since both groups use English all or most of the time. For Zuni, Zia, and Hopi, the children nearly all learn a native language at home and then learn English when they go to school. Thus most of them become acquainted with the word "shame" only as part of their school experience. If there is a one-to-one correspondence between "shame" and some native word, then children

TABLE 22[a]

EMOTIONAL RESPONSE TEST: ANALYSIS OF SHAME RESPONSES

	Percentage Frequencies									No. of Responses		
	Guilt			Embarrassment			Questionable					
	Male	Female	Total	Male	Female	Total	Male	Female	Total	Male	Female	Total
Hopi[b]	30	23	26	57	61	59	13	16	15	60	132	192
Zuni	12	12	12	83	80	81	5	8	7	77	94	171
Navaho Mt.	0	6	3	99	94	96	1	0	1	67	35	102
Sioux	37	24	30	54	71	63	9	5	7	70	76	146
Midwest[c]	43	48	46	48	39	42	9	13	12	182	261	443

a. Ages eight to eighteen. The Indian data include a few responses from six- and seven-year-old children.

b. This analysis was not performed on Papago, Shiprock, and Zia responses.

c. Ages ten, fourteen, and sixteen.

might be expected to make the translation easily and to understand the word clearly. But it is doubtful that there is such a close correspondence of words. In fact, a white teacher at Zuni stated that she believed there was no Zuni word for "shame."

Thus we may suppose that the children of these tribes had to interpret "shame" without having a direct unequivocal synonym for it in their native languages. Most of the white teachers who gave this test to the Southwest Indians reported to us that the "Indian children misunderstood the question about shame." This we infer was their interpretation of the fact that so many Indian children gave instances of embarrassment, which was not what the white teachers expected. We may also suppose that the teachers by their own unspoken attitudes encouraged the children to give guilt rather than embarrassment responses.

In this connection the language experiment conducted with Hopi children may throw some light on the problem. As described earlier (see p. 25), a group of children in the age range eight to sixteen were given the Emotional Response Test in Hopi by a Hopi teacher, and a few weeks before or after this they were given the same test in English by a white teacher. In general, the only striking difference was that the Hopi language test secured more answers and longer answers from the children (whether this was due to the difference in language or the difference in test administrators is not known). The proportions of embarrassment to guilt to questionable responses was quite similar for the two language situations, with slightly more embarrassment responses when the test was given in Hopi. For example, among girls aged eight to eighteen, there were 17 shame responses in the Hopi administration, of which 16 were in the embarrassment category and 1 in the questionable category. The same group of girls gave 14 shame responses when tested in English, 10 of them in the embarrassment category, 2 questionable, and 2 guilt. Among the boys there were 11 responses in the Hopi administration, all embarrassment; and 5 responses in the English administration, 4 embarrassment and 1 questionable.

The test was given to many of the Papago children in their native tongue, to all of the Navaho Mountain children in Navaho, and to the younger Shiprock children in Navaho.

If we had been aware of the probable ambiguity of meanings of the

word "shame" and its equivalents in the several Indian languages, we would have asked each person who gave the test in a native language to tell us what word or words were used for "shame," and we would then have consulted experts in linguistics. But when we eventually realized the usefulness of having this information, the testers were difficult to locate, and most of them had forgotten just how they had translated the question,"Have you ever been ashamed?"

Child-rearing and Conscience

It will be seen that Table 22, in general, supports the conclusion that Midwest children give many more guilt responses than do the Southwest Indians, who give mainly embarrassment responses.

The evidence from language experts that Navaho and Zuni and perhaps the Hopi, Zia, and Papago languages do not contain a word for the sense of inner guilt or remorse; the evidence from the Indian children's responses to the question about shame, which are overwhelmingly embarrassment rather than guilt responses; the contrast of the Midwest with the Southwest Indian responses—all these combine to support the hypothesis that the Southwest Indian children have much less conscience or superego function than do the Midwest children. Where conscience operates to control behavior in Midwest children, self-consciousness or sense of shame or public disapproval seems to operate in the Southwest Indian children.[16]

From our findings it appears that Midwest and Sioux have more highly developed feelings of inner, personal responsibility for moral

---

16. We may look at Table 9, "Principal Sources of Shame in Indian and Midwest Children," for evidence which confirms this hypothesis and supplements Table 22.

Among the category combinations of Table 9, the first two belong clearly in the embarrassment category—"Making a poor appearance" and "Embarrassment before others." So does "Being disciplined."

"Bad behavior and aggression" might at first sight seem to express remorse or sense of guilt, but this is not necessarily so. For instance, the very large proportion of Zia responses under this heading consist mainly of statements such as "I was ashamed when I didn't bring in the wood—didn't wash the dishes." These refer to neglect of duty or obligation, and we cannot tell whether the cause for shame was the scolding or punishment the child received or the pangs of conscience. Probably it was the former; but unless some further clue was given, such responses were placed in the questionable category of Table 22. "Personal failure and inadequacy" is more likely to contain responses of the guilt type; but even here a Navaho Mountain response, "I was ashamed when I let a lamb get cold and die," is ambiguous.

behavior than do the Southwest Indians and that Navaho Mountain and Zuni are at the other extreme in having little of this inner feeling but in having very highly developed feelings of shame in the presence of others. In other words, Midwest children are considerably controlled by the inner voice of conscience, whereas at Zuni and Navaho Mountain the chief moral control is public opinion and social pressure. (This distinction between conscience and self-consciousness as a source of moral control has quite often been made by anthropologists and has been applied to the Zuni and Navaho in comparison with white American children.)

In a community like Midwest, the children are punished by their parents, who love their children and are loved by them. Children eventually internalize the moral voices of their parents and are controlled by this internal voice of conscience. Consequently, they will cite frequent cases of being ashamed when they did something wrong and were punished by their conscience (felt remorse), although nobody else knew what they had done.

Among the Southwest Indians, and particularly at Zuni and Navaho Mountain, children are punished relatively seldom by parents. Instead, they are warned, when they are naughty, that people will talk about them. Or they are warned of punishment by supernatural beings—the katcinas and yeibichai. Also, at Zuni they may be threatened or even whipped by a stranger, who is asked (unknown to the child) to do this when a child is intractable. Thus much of the children's experience of punishment comes from outside the home and comes from persons whom they do not love. Morally controlling forces remain in the outside world, as far as these children are concerned, and they grow up without much inner moral control. This may result in their being excessively bashful as children and exceedingly subject to the pressure of public opinion.[17]

17. Since this was written, the writers have read chapter xi, "The Origins of Guilt," in Child Training and Personality by John W. M. Whiting and Irvin L. Child (New Haven: Yale University Press, 1953). Those authors use the term "guilt" substantially as we are using it, and undertake to measure it for a number of simple "primitive" societies by using as an index of the degree to which guilt feelings characterize the members of a society the extent to which a person who gets sick blames himself for having gotten sick. With this criterion of guilt feelings, they rank four of our six tribes as follows: Navaho (high), Hopi, Papago, Sioux. This is about the reverse of the order we have found by our method. They do not attempt to rank the modern American society. Our methods and theirs are so different that a comparison would require an extensive theoretical discussion. We are impressed by their method, but we do not see how our data can be accounted for by their theory.

Conscience and the Zuni

Anthropologists who have studied the Zuni are quick to point out their relative absence of feelings of personal guilt and responsibility. Ruth Benedict says: "Sin is unfamiliar to them, not only in sex but in any experience. They do not suffer from guilt complexes.[18] Ruth Bunzell points out that, for the Zuni, social behavior is more significant than individual behavior. "No action that is entirely personal and individual receives more than passing interest."[19] Thus individual moral responsibility is not emphasized but rather the accountability of the person to the group.

Irving Goldman, who had access to the research notes of Benedict and Bunzell, says:

> Out of the entire range of human behavior the Zuni have selected the nonaggressive cooperative aspects to stress. It is to this norm that the child, if he is to fit into the cultural framework set for him by his parents, must conform. He is not broken or forcibly coerced into this pattern but is gradually fitted to it under the most subtle stress of social sanction. The Zuni child grows up under little restraint: he faces no stern disciplinarian in the house. Rather, his parents are all kindness to him and humor his wants. He is rarely scolded or spanked. But where the Zuni minimize physical force as a sanction, they strongly emphasize shame.[20]

The comparative lack of conscience developed by Zuni children may perhaps be explained best in terms of the lack of strong identification with any one person and the fact that affection and discipline (or reproof) are divorced from each other by those to whom the child looks for security. From reports of the Zuni it seems likely that the household members do not threaten to withhold affection because of "bad" behavior of the children, and the "bad" behavior is not defined solely by the family but rather by the whole community.[21] There is no need to internalize moral values, because the group works as a unit in reacting to disapproved behavior and hence serves as a restraining influ-

18. Patterns of Culture (Boston: Houghton Mifflin Co., 1934), p. 126.

19. "Introduction to Zuni Ceremonialism," 47th Annual Report of the Bureau of American Ethnology to the Secretary of the Smithsonian Institution (Washington, D.C., 1929-30), pp. 467-1108.

20. "The Zuni Indians of New Mexico," in Cooperation and Competition among Primitive Peoples, ed. Margaret Mead (New York: McGraw-Hill Book Co., 1937), chap. x, pp. 338-39.

21. Yet for contradictory evidence see the data on moral surrogates in chap. iv, Table 26 and p. 120.

ence upon the individual. There is little conflict in values, and the individual himself does not need to serve as judge of his own behavior.

One specific response on shame appeared with great frequency among the Zuni—that of embarrassment at entering someone's house or having someone (not a household member) enter the subject's house. These responses seem to substantiate the remarks of anthropologists on the sanctity of the Zuni home. Parsons says that the house is more than a shelter. "It is a place of manifold and binding associations."[22] She goes on to say that while there is little individual privacy within the home, household privacy is well provided for. "Between households where there are no familial links or other ties, there is scant visiting." There is also evidence of a great deal of animosity between families in Zuni, which would result in children's being warned to stay out of other people's houses.

Conscience and the Navaho

Much of what has been said of child-rearing and the formation of conscience of Zuni is also true of the Navaho, especially when, as with Navaho Mountain, there has been little contact with whites. Leighton and Kluckhohn, writing about Navaho childhood, say:

> Supernatural agencies may be said to provide the ultimate sanctions for all behavior, of children and adults alike, but the effective sanctions of daily life are provided still more by gossip and ridicule. Parents sometimes say flatly that a youngster is "naughty" or call him a dunce or a fool, but they have an insistent propensity for referring the child to what "people" will say. One of the most noticeable peculiarities of Navaho conversation is the tendency to evade personal responsibility for a statement. Any long narrative is full of such qualifications as "he says," "that one says," and especially "they say."
>
> The mother, instead of complaining "If you act like that you'll disgrace me," points out "If you act like that people will make fun of you." Rather than setting themselves up as rewarding and punishing surrogates, parents utilize this essentially impersonal "shame" mechanism. This is meaningful to the child, for he experiences not merely the disapproval of his elders but also the most intangible ridicule of other children when he fails to conform.
>
> Never have the writers known a Navaho parent to demand socially acceptable behavior as the condition of parental love and protection or to say to a child "If you do that, mother won't love you any more." There are occasionally conditional statements,

22. Elsie Clews Parsons, Pueblo Indian Religion (Chicago: University of Chicago Press, 1931), p. 1.

> "If you act like this we won't take you to the trading store this afternoon." Physical punishment is rare, slight, and usually spontaneous.[23]

This kind of training tends to make people extremely sensitive to public disapproval:

> By white standards, adult Navahos are hypersensitive to shame or ridicule. This may be illustrated by incidents from quite varied spheres of life. One of the reasons that The People are often unwilling to be photographed or are indignant when they are snapped without their permission is that they are sensitive about being seen by others in "old clothes." A very common experience is to have an individual or group say that they would like to have their pictures taken but that they must "get ready" first. When they have put on their best clothes and their finest jewelry, they are quite willing to be photographed. The same attitude is exemplified in the unwillingness to attend a festive gathering unless new garments are available.[24]

Shame and shyness or self-consciousness are clearly related in the experience of all people and certainly of the Navaho:

> The line between "shyness" and "respect" is also not the line with which white people are familiar. When they press for an explanation as to why some Navaho has or has not done something, they are often told, "Well, he got ashamed," or "He is too shy." But the Navaho word which English-speakers usually render as "shamed" or "shy" is actually a composite of these two notions with that of respect, and in discussing relationships of respect-avoidance such as that between son-in-law and mother-in-law the same word-root is constantly used. The hesitancy in speaking in front of unknown white persons is thus, in part, the type of embarrassment which whites themselves also often feel before a much more prominent or powerful person than themselves. Where the white person tends to overcompensate for his feeling of inadequacy by braggadocio or overweening behavior, the Navaho stands speechless, with his head down, turning from side to side, twisting his hands. The Navahos are always talking about "shaming," "being ashamed," or "acting ashamed" (to use the translation that they usually choose).
>
> Control of the individual is achieved in Navaho society primarily by "lateral sanctions" rather than by sanctions from above. That is, the Navaho from childhood on is brought into line more by the reactions of all the people around him rather than by orders and threats of punishment from someone who stands above him in a hierarchy. "Shame" is the agony of being found wanting and exposed to the disapproval of others, as opposed to the fear that some single superior person will use his power to deprive one of rewards and privileges if specified tasks are not carried out according to instructions.

23. Leighton and Kluckhohn, op. cit., p. 52.

24. Ibid., p. 104.

> Navaho sensitivity to "shame" likewise largely takes the place that remorse and self-punishment have in preventing antisocial conduct in white society. Navahos do not lie awake nights worrying about the undiscovered "bad" things they have done. Because they have not internalized the standards of their parents and other elders but, rather, accept these standards as part of the external environment to which an adjustment must be made, "divine discontent" is an emotion foreign to the normal Navaho. It is believed by some that "progress" occurs in societies of the Christian tradition largely because each socialized individual is trying to avoid the self-reproach that would be incurred by failing to live up to the ideals inculcated in childhood. Navaho society is (or would be if not under continual pressure from white society) much more static, since "shame" ("I would feel very uncomfortable if anyone saw me deviating from accepted norms") plays the psychological role which "conscience" or "guilt" ("I am unworthy for I am not living up to the high standards represented by my parents") has in the Christian tradition."[25]

Conclusion

It appears that a fundamental difference in moral control exists between the children of Midwest and those of the Southwest Indian tribes. Each method appears to be suited to the conditions of life in the society which employs it. However, there is evidence that some change in the relative effectiveness of conscience and self-consciousness or shame is taking place in the Indian tribes as they become more influenced by the white man's world around them.[26]

25. Ibid., pp. 105-6.

26. For a different interpretation of our data as they relate to shame and guilt in various societies see Gerhart Piers and Milton B. Singer, Shame and Guilt (Springfield, Ill.: Charles C Thomas, 1953), Part II, chap. iii.

CHAPTER IV

THE MORAL IDEOLOGY OF INDIAN AND WHITE CHILDREN

Section 1. THE MORAL IDEOLOGY TEST

The Instrument

A method originally described by Bavelas was employed to study moral ideology.[1] This is a technique in which the child is asked to name specific behaviors which he considers "good" or "bad" and to name the source of authority for each behavior. It yields data on so-called "official," as distinguished from "private," ideology—"official" signifying that set of moral beliefs and values common to most members of a group. The application of this method enables the investigator to discover what behaviors are considered approved or disapproved, what are the sources of approval and disapproval (hereafter referred to as the "surrogates" of behavior), and the ways in which these are related. It is understood that a child's actual behavior may not be accurately represented by his responses on this test; he may do things he says are bad to do and may fail to do things he says are good to do. But, certainly, official moral ideology influences behavior.

The Sample

Among the Indian groups, the children who took this test are practically identical with those who took the Emotional Response Test (see chap. iii, Sec. 1). For the Midwest children, however, the sample is larger (the number is 686 compared with 368 who took the Emotional Response Test). The Moral Ideology Test was given to all the children in Grades V through XII; and our data therefore include boys and girls through age eighteen.

Administration of the Instrument

Questions concerning moral ideology formed one section of the test booklet administered individually to each Indian child. The child was

1. Alex Bavelas, "A Method for Investigating Individual and Group Ideology," Sociometry, V (1942), 371-77.

told by the tester, "I want to find out what boys and girls of your age think are good things to do and bad things to do." Then the following questions were asked, the tester recording the answers on the test booklet:

1. What could a boy (girl) of your age do that would be a good thing to do, so that someone would praise him (her) or be pleased?
2. Who would praise him (her) or be pleased?
3. What is another thing, a very good thing, that a boy (girl) could do so that someone would praise him (her) or be pleased?
4. Who would praise him (her) or be pleased?
5. What is still another thing, a very, very good thing, that a boy (girl) could do so that someone would praise him (her) or be pleased?
6. Who would praise him (her) or be pleased?

These questions regarding "good things to do" and "who would praise" were asked each subject at least three times and more often if the subject talked freely. Then the child was asked:

1. What could a boy (girl) of your age do that would be a bad thing to do so that someone would blame him (her) or think badly of him (her)?
2. Who would blame him (her) or think badly of him (her)?

These questions were asked at least three times of each Indian child; more frequently in cases where the child responded freely. The instructions to the white children in Midwest were as follows:

> Put your name and age at the top of a blank sheet of paper.
>
> We are interested in finding out what boys and girls of different ages consider good things to do, and what they consider bad things to do. This is not a test. Any answer you give is correct, but the best answers are what you <u>really</u> think. A "good thing to do" or a "bad thing to do" might be at school, at home, at work, at play—<u>anywhere</u>.
>
> What is something a boy or girl of your age could do, which would be a good thing to do, and which would be praised or approved?
>
> <u>Who</u> would praise or approve?

Midwest children were asked for nine "good" things and, by rephrasing the question accordingly, for nine "bad things." Thus Midwest children gave a total of eighteen responses as compared with a total of six responses from Indian children.[2]

2. The comparability of six and eighteen responses is discussed later (see p. 94).

So that the reader may gain some acquaintance with the original material, we have selected typical protocols as illustrations.

A Hopi girl, aged fifteen, was more responsive than most Indian children. Her responses to the Moral Ideology Test were:

They would help their mother . . . (Who would praise?) . . . their mother
Grind corn . . . her mother
To cook . . . her mother
To wash the clothes . . . her mother
Clean the house . . . mother
Dress up her sisters . . . mother
To make plaques . . . mother

Steal something . . . mother
To break something . . . mother
She don't know anything . . . mother
Steal money . . . mother
She don't iron her dresses . . . mother
Scold her sisters . . . her sisters
Run away . . . her brother

A Hopi boy, aged ten, says:

Help to get water . . . mother
Chop some wood . . . mother
Help take the horses somewhere . . . my father

Steal something . . . me
Broke something, somebody's things, a box . . . my mother
When mother told him to chop wood, he don't want to chop it . . . his mother

A Navaho Mountain girl, aged ten, says:

To weave a rug . . . mother
Herd sheep well . . . mother and father
Cook the food by myself . . . mother and father

Make other children cry . . . teacher
Taking things that don't belong to her . . . mother, father, teacher
Play, when my mother asks me to do something . . . mother, family

A Navaho Mountain boy, aged thirteen, says:

To be a good sheep herder . . . my mother
To be a good worker . . . my brothers and sisters
To be able to handle wild horses . . . my father, all the people

To be lazy . . . brothers, sisters, father
To steal . . . everyone
To hurt someone badly . . . all the people

A Papago girl, aged ten, says:

To be happy to my mother . . . my mother would praise me
She would be nice to her parents . . . her mother
To be nice to the animals . . . her family

To steal something . . . her father
To fight the little child . . . her mother
To take something away from a little girl . . . her father

A Papago boy, aged fourteen, says:

Work . . . parents
Play football . . . the people
By working for somebody else . . . the one that he is working for

Drunk . . . people
Smoking . . . parents
Stealing . . . parents

A Midwest girl, aged thirteen, says:

Do what you are told . . . her mother and father and other people
Don't get other people angry by saying things that aren't true about them . . . everybody
Obey the patrol in your school . . . everyone
Don't be a wet blanket every time someone forms a club and an idea . . . your classmates
Always be friendly with your school friends and teachers . . . teachers and friends
Help with activities more . . . everyone
Be interested in your friends and games . . . friends
Obey your mother and father . . . they will praise you
Help your mother more and play less . . . everyone

You shouldn't blame your playmates for something you have done . . . your friends
You shouldn't talk at the table when you are eating
Don't holler out loud on the street. People will think your mother hasn't taught any manners and that you don't know any better
Don't be crabby all the time . . . your friends don't like people like that
Don't talk about other people
Don't tell falsehood to your mother . . . mother
Don't stay out of school for no reason . . . teacher
You shouldn't go any place without informing someone first
Don't be a snob around girls and other people . . . everybody

A Midwest boy, aged eleven, says:

Buy U.S.A. war bonds . . . the government
Help old people across the street . . . the person who you helped
Obey the school rules . . . the teachers
Help your mother or father when they want you to . . . your mother and father
Don't poke everybody you see . . . your parents
Go to church and do not swear . . . God
Don't skip school . . . teachers
Don't walk in everybody's yard . . . the people who own the yard
Don't kill birds in the summer . . . the birds

To stick your tongue out at people . . . the people
Do let the poor old blind people walk across the street by themselves . . . the people
Don't obey the school rules . . . the teachers
Don't help your mother or father when they want you to . . . your mother and father
Poke everybody you can . . . the people you poke
Don't go to church . . . God
Skip school . . . teachers
Do walk in everybody's yard . . . the people who own the yard
Kill all the birds . . . the birds

Comments on the Instrument

It is recognized that this technique yields data only on those aspects of moral ideology which the subject is willing to express in a relatively formal situation. Behaviors which the individual has learned are taboo are seldom mentioned. For example, while there is good evidence that masturbation is a common source of conflict in childhood and adolescence in our own society, it was never mentioned by any of the subjects.

Furthermore, there are factors in this question-and-answer situation which probably operate in such a way that the subject avoids mentioning areas of conduct in which he has anxieties. For example, an Indian child who has been taught that he will become ill if he gets angry may hesitate to describe instances in which he was angry—instances in which "anger" was a "bad thing."

For a few individuals the test acts as a projective technique in eliciting personally revealing information. However, the brief, matter-of-fact replies obtained from the large majority of subjects made it clear that what was being expressed was that "official" set of values commonly accepted by the group.

In examining the responses of Midwest children, it was found that boys and girls almost never mentioned as "good" an act which was known to be commonly disapproved; nor as "bad," a commonly approved act. The prevailing American standards were consistent throughout the entire sample of subjects. A child might say that smoking was a bad thing to do or that not smoking was a good thing to do; but no child said smoking was good.

If the same phenomenon is operating in the Indian children (and we have no reason to believe otherwise), this, in a sense, is a validation of the instrument itself. The children are describing the "official" attitude.

On the other hand, it is likely that those behaviors which are so well established as to be taken for granted and which are no longer matters of any concern are also omitted from children's responses. For example, the control of physical aggression, so frequently mentioned by young white children, is almost never mentioned by white adolescents.

In short, the technique yields data on that part of the value-pattern which is, so to speak, in the forefront of consciousness, which is relatively free of emotion, and which is, therefore, readily expressed.

Treatment of the Data

The first problem in dealing with unstructured data of this kind is that of working out a method for quantifying responses. A system of categorization was needed which would fit the responses of younger as well as older children; which would make it possible to categorize responses with a maximum degree of reliability; and which would be applicable to data obtained from children of various cultures.

It will be recalled that each response given by the child contained two parts: that part dealing with good and bad behavior and that part dealing with praisers and blamers, or "surrogates." Since the methodological problems involved in treating the two types of data proved to be somewhat different, they are discussed separately.

Categorizing the Behaviors

Working with the protocols of Midwest children, several systems of categories, developed on an a priori basis, were tried out. These were discarded, one by one, as it became evident that a high degree of interpretation was involved in deciding whether a response fell in one category or another, resulting in lack of agreement between judges.[3]

Finally, it was decided to work out a set of categories derived from the data themselves, without reference to any a priori conceptual scheme. All the responses from a sample set of papers were listed, then grouped on the basis of similarity. Each category thus formed was assigned a number. For example, category 1, "amusements," included such responses as "going to movies," "swimming," "dancing," "sports," "go out and have a good, clean time," "dating," "fishing," "bicycling." Category 4, "achievement in school," included such responses as

3. Four judges were involved in devising the categories: R. J. Havighurst, William E. Henry, Bernice L. Neugarten, and Iva O. Schmitt.

"getting higher grades," "being an industrious student," "take an interest in your studies," "do your school work."

Judges then categorized independently another sample set of papers; and results were checked for agreement. This process was repeated with successive sets of protocols, and categories were refined, until new samples did not add to the number of categories or to the reliability with which responses could be categorized.

While this method resulted in an unwieldy number of categories, it had several distinct advantages. By adding only a few more categories, the system of categorization was directly applicable to the data from Indian children.[4] Second, the first step in quantification—that of categorizing original responses—could be accomplished with relative objectivity.[5] Third, the categories could be grouped in various ways at later stages in the analysis to meet different research interests. Thus certain combinations of categories could be used in studying age and sex differences among Midwest children; certain other combinations in studying intercultural differences.

Categorizing the Surrogates

Devising a system of categories for surrogates proved to be a simpler problem than that for behaviors, since there was less likelihood of ambiguity or misinterpretation of the original response. Category 1, "family," was used when the response was "(praised by). . .my family," "my home," "my relatives." Category 2, "father," was used when the father alone was given as the surrogate; category 3, when the mother alone was given; and so on. Distinctions between such responses as "everybody" and "some people," between "boys and girls" and "my friends," between same-sex and opposite-sex peers, were maintained by creating separate categories; but, by and large, the data on "surrogates" presented few difficulties. There are a total of twenty categories for the white children, to which six additional categories were added for the Indian children (see Appendix C-2 for the total list

4. There were 65 categories of behaviors for the white children; 5 additional categories were created for the Indian children (see Appendix C-1).

5. Employing 62 categories of behavior, each of three judges categorized independently the responses on 180 papers of Midwest children. Disagreement was tallied each time one judge disagreed with one of the other two. Although this constitutes a rigorous method of computing reliability, agreement between the three judges was found to be 96.7 per cent.

of surrogate categories).

Relative Width of Categories

The categories of behavior (as well as the categories of surrogates) are not to be thought of as equally broad in scope. For example, category 24, "smoking," is narrower than category 1, "amusements." A child may mention "smoking" as bad, or "not smoking" as good, but the category will occur a maximum of two times on any protocol. On the other hand, a child may mention "swimming," "hiking," "dancing," "bowling," "riding," as good—all of which fall into category 1. As a result, certain categories have more chances of appearing than certain others, because they are more inclusive in character.

The variation in relative width of categories cannot be avoided with data of this kind. Had the categories been equated, for example, in terms of relative frequency, it would be impossible to study differences between groups. Neither does there seem to be any sound psychological basis for equating the categories.

Consequently, if one category is mentioned more often than another, there are at least two factors which may be responsible: first, that the area of conduct is one of the greater concern to the subjects; second, that the category may be more inclusive than the first and contain more kinds of items from the protocols. These facts should be kept in mind in making any comparisons between categories and later between combinations of categories.

Tabulating the Behaviors

Each response on the child's paper was given one tally under the appropriate behavior category. A single tabulation was made for all behavior items, without differentiating between those mentioned as "good" and those mentioned as "bad." This seemed advisable on the grounds that no psychological distinction was possible between the positive and negative mentions of a category. For instance, it would be difficult to say that "smoking" mentioned as "bad" is psychologically different from "not smoking" mentioned as "good."[6] With the exceptions of categories

6. Some response items might occur in any one of four ways: "minding my mother" as good, "not disobeying my mother" as good; "not minding my mother" as bad and "disobeying my mother" as bad. If any distinction was to be drawn between positive and negative mentions, a four-way distinction would have to be made with an item of this kind. Obviously, any such tabulation would be hopelessly cumbersome.

1 and 2 (where it seemed sound to differentiate between "good" amusements and "bad" amusements) then, all categories of behavior include both "good" and "bad" items as they occurred on the protocols.

The number of tallies in each category (or, later, in each combination of categories) was added up, and this number expressed as a percentage of the total number of responses given by the group of subjects. Thus the importance of a given category of behavior is measured by the number of times it is mentioned by a group of subjects, irrespective of the number of persons who mention the category.[7]

Tabulating the Surrogates

While each response on the child's paper was given only one tally for behavior, it was given one or more tallies for surrogate. For example, if the child had written, "Always say please . . . (praised by) . . .my mother, teacher, everybody," a tally was placed under behavior category 9 and tallies under surrogate categories 3, 11, and 14.

7. The two methods of tabulating the data—number of times mentioned and number of persons mentioning—were both tried on the data from white children, and the methods were compared on a series of different criteria. When the data were analyzed for age and sex differences, neither method showed clear superiority; either method showed definitive age trends, and sex differences were consistent with both methods.

A second consideration in deciding which method of tabulation to use was related to the statistical treatment of the data. When comparison between groups is to be made, a method for describing the significance of differences is necessary. The number-of-individuals method, had it been used, would have made impossible the use of standard methods of estimating the significance of differences between groups. This is due to the fact that when, later, original categories were grouped in combinations, numbers of responses greater than the number of individuals were obtained. For example, if there were 100 subjects, there might be 130 tallies when categories 4, 5, 6, and 7 were combined. This makes impossible the use of formulas based on per cent of N.

A third consideration was related to the fact that comparisons were to be made between protocols of 6 responses and protocols of 18 responses. (It will be recalled that Indian children were asked for 6 responses, whereas Midwest children were asked for 18.) While the comparability of 6 versus 18 responses is discussed later (see p. 94), it should be stated at this point that the total-mentions method yielded fewer differences between the 6- and 18-response protocols than did the method of number of individuals mentioning. Two comparable groups of white children were used for this comparison; one group being asked for 6 responses, the other for 18. When these data were compared, each combination of behavior categories received approximately the same proportion of total mentions, the differences in the percentages in no instance exceeding 3 per cent. When number of individuals mentioning was used as the index, there was considerable fluctuation from combination to combination between the two groups.

With the surrogates, furthermore, separate tabulations were made for positive and negative mentions, or, in other words, for "praisers" and for "blamers." There seems to be a real psychological difference between "praisers" and "blamers"—in certain age, sex, or cultural groups, for example, it might be found that the mother is more often mentioned as a "blamer" than as a "praiser," and so on.

The number of tallies in each surrogate category was added up, and this number was expressed as a percentage of the total number of surrogate responses given by the group of subjects.[8]

Reliability of the Instrument

There were three major aspects of the question of reliability of the Moral Ideology Test. These are as follows:

1. The consistency of response when the test is repeated on the same or comparable groups of subjects. This is the usual problem of the reliability of any test instrument.

2. The degree to which data obtained from 6-response tests, as given to the Indian children, are comparable to data obtained from 18-response tests, as given to the children of Midwest.

3. Inasmuch as the data from the Indian children were to be compared to that from the white children, the question of whether or not the children of Midwest are representative of white culture.

Test-Retest Reliability

While the investigators did not have retest data on Indian children, such data were available for the Midwest children. Sixty boys and 70 girls in the fifth and sixth grades were tested in May, 1942, and again in November, 1942. Coefficients of correlation were computed separately for the boys and the girls on the 65 categories of behavior, the coefficients being .91 ± .02 for the girls and .86 ± .003 for the boys.

Differences which were obtained for certain categories, especially in the case of the boys, seemed to be due to changes in the seasons.

8. There seemed little question, in dealing with surrogates, that the only method of tallying was that of counting the number of times mentioned. Since subjects, especially at older ages, mention several surrogates for each behavior item, many surrogate categories are mentioned at least once by every child. If number of persons mentioning had been used as the index, differences between groups would have been obliterated.

For example, in November boys gave more responses under "sportsmanship" and "leadership" than they did in May, presumably because during the fall, when football and other such sports are on the calendar, boys would indicate as a good thing "to participate in sports," "to be a good sport," or as an activity for which they would be praised, "being a leader."

Another type of test-retest was that of testing two groups in consecutive years who were the same age at the time of testing. This was done by testing one set of 82 girls and 76 boys of the fifth and sixth grades of Midwest in May, 1942, and a second set of 81 girls and 73 boys in the same grades in November of the same year. While seasonal differences again apparently caused some changes in responses, correlation coefficients computed for the 65 categories were .84 ± .02 for boys and .89 ± .02 for girls.

Six versus 18 Responses

To check on the comparability of results obtained from 6-response tests and 18-response tests, children from another white community were used as subjects. A group of boys and girls eleven, twelve, thirteen, and fourteen years of age living in a community comparable to Midwest in size, composition, and culture pattern were given the Moral Ideology Test. Six responses were asked from 64 boys and 56 girls; 18 responses from 49 boys and 61 girls.

Here the 65 categories of behavior were grouped into 22 combinations, and correlations were computed on the basis of these combinations. The coefficients of correlation were .91 ± .01 for boys and .84 ± .01 for girls.

The 22 categories of surrogate responses were grouped into 13 combinations. When these data on surrogates were correlated on this basis, the coefficients of correlation were .95 ± .004 for boys and .96 ± .004 for girls.

In the light of these high coefficients of correlation, it is evident that, using the methods of quantification as described, results will be approximately the same, whether 6 or 18 responses are obtained. We therefore felt confident that a comparison of 6-response data from the Indian children with 18-response data from the white children would be valid.

Midwest as Typical of American Culture

As has already been indicated, children in another white community were tested on the Moral Ideology Test. There were 49 boys and 61 girls, eleven to fourteen years of age, who gave 18 responses to the test. These were compared with 18 responses made by 132 boys and 140 girls, eleven to fourteen years of age, from Midwest. The data were compared for boys and girls separately. While several of the category combinations were not altogether comparable for the two communities and were thus excluded from the comparison, there were very few combinations in which the difference between the data from Midwest and the comparable group was more than 2 per cent.

The coefficients of correlation for these data (computed on the basis of category combinations) were .81 ± .01 for boys and .86 ± .02 for girls. These coefficients are sufficiently high to warrant the conclusion that the responses of Midwest children are typical of American white children in small midwestern communities.

A Note on Reliability

The foregoing tests of reliability were computed on the basis of the original 65 categories of behavior or on 22 combinations of the original categories. When we later turned our attention to studying differences between tribal groups on the Moral Ideology Test, it became evident that the original categories (both for behaviors and for surrogates) were too refined a breakdown of the data to allow either (1) economy in the consideration of results or (2) frequencies large enough for statistical treatment. It also became evident that our first attempt to form combinations of behavior categories (the 22 used to study reliability) needed further revision if we were to draw meaningful comparisons between groups. We therefore formed new combinations, on the basis of which to compare Indian and white children (these combinations will be described in detail in the following sections).

It should be pointed out here, however, that our procedure as we have described it constitutes a rigorous test of reliability. Had we first formed our final combinations and then computed reliability on the basis of those combinations (rather than on the greater number of original categories), the coefficients of correlation would have been even higher than those given above.

Responsiveness to the Test

Table 23 shows the average number of behavior and surrogate responses per subject in each of the tribal groups. It will be seen that, among the Indian groups, Papago and Sioux subjects were least responsive, while Navaho Mountain children averaged the largest number of responses.

Midwest is different from the Indian groups, since Midwest children were asked for 18, rather than 6, responses to the test.

Section 2. THE DATA ON MORAL BEHAVIOR

It will be recalled that responses on the Moral Ideology Test yielded data of two kinds:

1. Items of conduct that the child evaluates as good or bad. These data (which we have called "behaviors") can be used to study the areas of experience in a child's life which, through the process of socialization, have become associated with morality and with concepts of right and wrong. The child is warned against certain kinds of behavior, rebuked for certain acts, praised for certain other acts. Data from the Moral Ideology Test give us information concerning the atmosphere of moral judgment in which children of various cultures live and information regarding the moral values of the culture as experienced and reported on by the child.

2. Persons who praise or blame the child for good or bad conduct (the surrogates). These data give information regarding the agents of society, the persons who implement the moral values held by the society and who, in an operational sense, are the "socializers" of children.

We shall deal, in this section, with the data on "behaviors"; in the section to follow, with the "surrogates."

The Major Themes of Moral Behavior

The behavior categories were first combined into seven major combinations, each dealing with a different "theme" or "area" of moral conduct. These combinations subsume as nearly as possible the total range of the data from all the tribal groups, including Midwest; and thus they represent our attempt to organize the data in their entirety. This pattern was devised in order to analyze in parsimonious fashion similarities and differences between tribal groups, differences between the sexes, and age trends within and between tribes. (As will be seen in the discussion of results, this organization proved more useful in certain of these analyses than in others. For certain intertribal comparisons, for instance, another set of combinations might have proved more meaningful.)

The data, as they will be presented later in Table 24, have been organized to show, first, these seven major themes and, second, certain subsidiary themes. The subsidiary themes have been drawn from the wide range of the data and include only certain of the original categories.

For convenience, the themes have been given abbreviated titles. The seven major themes have been called "Competence," "Self-restraint," "Personal Virtues," "Relations to Authority," "Regard for Others," "Service," and "Sex." The first three of these seven focus attention upon the individual himself, where his conduct does not directly involve other persons; the other four focus upon the individual in relation to the people around him.

Of the subsidiary themes, those entitled "Family," "School," "Church," "Community," and "Property" deal with the child's relations to certain social institutions—institutions which are common to all the cultures studied but which vary in importance in the child's life from one culture to another. Here our analysis has been concerned less with the question "What conduct is approved or disapproved?" and more with the question "Toward what social institutions is the child's moral conduct primarily oriented?"

Because the abbreviated titles for most of the themes may be somewhat ambiguous, each combination will be described, together with the list of the original categories included in each (see Appendix C-1 for examples of the original responses included under each category).

It should be reiterated at this point that included under each of the themes are responses given both as "good" and as "bad" things to do; in other words, both positive and negative items of behavior. Thus the "Competence" theme deals in reality with both competence and incompetence, and "Self-restraint" with both self-restraint and self-indulgence.

"Competence"

This area includes the themes of achievement as excelling over others (in responses such as "be an outstanding athlete" or "win a prize"); the realization of one's potentialities and one's opportunities ("make the best

TABLE 23[a]

MORAL IDEOLOGY TEST: FREQUENCIES OF BEHAVIOR AND SURROGATE RESPONSES PER SUBJECT

	Tribal Group															
	Papago		Hopi		Zuni		Zia		Navaho Mt.		Shiprock		Sioux		Midwest[b]	
	Boys	Girls	Boys	Girls	Boys	Girls	Boys	Girls	Boys	Girls	Boys	Girls	Boys	Girls	Boys	Girls
No. of subjects	56	60	59	79	44	40	24	16	26	19	37	35	58	59	306	382
Average no. of behavior responses per subject	5.4	5.4	5.7	6.4	6.0	6.0	5.7	6.0	6.2	5.7	5.5	5.9	5.4	5.6	14.1	18.6
Average no. of surrogate responses per subject	5.4	5.3	5.6	5.5	5.9	5.8	5.5	5.9	9.0	8.3	8.4	8.8	5.3	5.4	18.7	22.6

a. Ages eight to eighteen.

b. Ages ten to eighteen; each subject was asked for 18, rather than 6, responses.

of yourself," "study to learn," "do your work well"); and competence in the sense of accepting responsibility and attaining maturity ("find yourself a job," "be sensible and act your age"). Competitive behavior is thus merely one part of the behaviors included in this area. This combination includes the following categories:

4. Achievement in school
5. Job (employment)
6. and 6a. Self-improvement; ambition
7. Industry
11. Maturity
17. Initiative; leadership
49. Social skills

"Self-restraint"

Into this combination went all the responses dealing with "fun," "games," and the types of self-indulgence which children listed as approved behavior—those recreational activities which are considered "good" or "all right" for children to engage in. It also includes that wide variety of behaviors which have in common the element of restriction or restraint upon the individual's personal behavior—the behavior which does not directly concern other persons. The authors have thought of this combination as dealing primarily with that part of the socialization process which controls the individual's desires for self-indulgence, when that indulgence does not involve other persons directly. It is as if society says, "You must do this, and you must not do that—not so much because it affects other people, but because of what we expect of you as an individual." The categories subsumed under this heading are as follows:

1. Amusements
2. Bad amusements
3. Hobby
8. "Right" people and "right" places
9. Etiquette
10. Rowdy behavior
23. "General" good and bad behavior
24. Smoking
25. Drinking
26. Swearing
30. Health
31. Keeping regular hours
32, 64. Recklessness of person
50. Curiosity
60. Aggressivity
62. Self-control

The inclusion of the "amusements" and "hobby" categories under this heading perhaps requires a word of explanation. When it first became evident that responses such as "going to movies," "swimming," "sports," "photography," and so on were being given in answer to the question "What would be a good thing. . .to do?" we considered whether or not the children were properly interpreting the question. That is, did they think of "good things" as something morally good or as something that would be fun (having a good time)? Indian children as well as white gave

responses dealing with games and amusements (about 6 per cent of all responses given by Midwest children dealt with amusements and hobbies; 6 per cent of Shiprock responses; and from 1 to 2 per cent of responses from other tribal groups).

Such responses did, however, always carry mention of the persons who would praise or blame (surrogate responses). Furthermore, the child who gave such responses also gave additional ones which fell into other categories of moral behavior—responses such as "keep quiet," "do my work well," "don't pick on younger children"—responses which indicated that the child had not misinterpreted the question.

We concluded, therefore, that amusements, fun, and games were actually being considered within the context of morality and that such activities carried with them, in the eyes of the child, moral implications.

"Personal Virtues"

This theme deals primarily with personal character traits approved by society. The emphasis here is not so much on the restraint of behavior as on the more positive aspect of developing certain consistent patterns of behavior. The categories included are as follows:

7. Industry
15. Sportsmanship
16. Honesty
17. Initiative; leadership
18. Dependability; persistence
19. Punctuality
21. Courage
23. "General" good and bad behavior
27. Gambling
28. Thrift
29. Neatness
51. Modesty
52. Loyalty[9]

"Relations to Authority"

This is the first of the four themes which deal primarily with the interaction of the child with other individuals. This area is concerned with the child's relation to authority in its various forms. The categories included are as follows:

7a. Obedience to employer
12. Running away
40 and 40a. Obedience and respect for parents
42, 42a, and 42b. Conformity to school rules and school expectations
43. Obedience and respect for teachers
45. Religious observance
47. Reverence for Deity
57. Respect for government and community

9. This is not, of course, a complete list of the character traits approved by any society. Others, such as friendliness, co-operativeness, altruism, have not been included because they are primarily concerned with interpersonal relations—they are included in the combinations which follow.

"Regard for Others"

This is a very broad area, including the observance of property rights; the general worth of other persons, both peers and elders; co-operation with others; and the curbing of aggression toward others. Included are the following categories:

13. Verbal aggression
14. Fighting
15. Sportsmanship
22. Stealing
26. Swearing[10]
33 and 33b. Care of property
34 and 65. Courtesy; kindness; tolerance
35 and 63. Pleasant disposition
36. Friendliness
37. Co-operation; generosity
39 and 39a. Regard for family
48. General social participation
50. Curiosity
60. Aggressivity
61. Treatment of animals and pets

The underlying theme here is, of course, the curbing of the individual's impulses and desires as they directly affect the rights of other members of the community.

"Service"

This area includes service to other individuals and to institutions. It contains all the so-called "altruistic" responses given by subjects. The categories included are as follows:

38. Service to others
41. Work at home
44. School activities; school loyalty
46. Church activities
58. Active work for government and community

"Sex"

While, on the whole, responses in this area were few in number, the categories dealing with sex behavior were combined into a separate combination, since they seemingly did not fit into any of the other combinations previously described and since we expected clear age differences on this theme. The categories included here are:

53. "Necking"
54. Marriage
55. Sexual morality
56. Other sex behavior

"Family"

Included in this grouping were the following categories:

10. Swearing is included in this area because so many of the responses in this category involved swearing at somebody.

39 and 39a. Regard for family
40 and 40a. Respect and obedience for parents
41. Work at home

"School"

This combination includes:

42. Conformity to school rules and school expectations
42a. Care of school property
42b. Neatness in school
43. Obedience and respect for teachers
44. School activities

(Category 43 includes responses relating to other school personnel, such as the principal, superintendent, school nurse, school board, etc.)

"Church"

Two categories have been combined:

45. Religious observance
46. Church activities

Category 47, "reverence for Deity," was not included here, since the responses in that category dealt exclusively with personal relations to the Deity, irrespective of the church as an institution.

"Community"

This combination includes two categories:

57 and 57a. Respect for government and community
58. Active work for government and community

"Property"

Included in this combination are six categories:

22. Stealing
27. Gambling
28. Thrift
33, 33a, 33b. Care of property
42a. Care of school property

"Work"

Included here are the following:

5. Job and employment
7. Industry
41. Work at home

"Aggression toward Peers"

This category includes the following:

13. Verbal aggression
14. Fighting
60. Aggressivity

Intertribal Comparisons

Before considering our results, it might be well to repeat a point made earlier—that the test does not tell us what things are done or not done. The child who says stealing is a bad thing may never have been himself involved in stealing. We may suppose that stealing is done by certain people in the society and that the act affects all members of the group, so that children are constantly warned against it.

To take another example, working around the home is the most frequent single response in most tribal groups. This kind of work is probably the subject of much praise, and failure to do this work the subject of much blame. Hence it is "on top of the mind" of the child. We cannot tell from the data whether Sioux children, for example, who give the smallest number of responses in this category, actually do less work around the home. What we can say is that, in the context of this test, this type of behavior is not so much "on the mind" of Sioux children as with other children.

Comparisons between Indian and white subjects must be made with caution for two reasons: First, the age range is ten to eighteen in the case of the white children, and eight to eighteen for the Indians. Second, white children were asked for 18 responses, and the Indian children for only 6. The result of this difference may be to reduce the proportions of certain responses for the whites and to increase others. (In general, any category which can be mentioned at most only twice, once as a good thing and once as a bad thing, will appear less frequently in the results for the whites. For example, stealing could hardly be mentioned more than twice. Thus it could not occur more than 11 per cent of the time for white children, but it might occur 33 per cent of the time for Indian children.)

On the basis of our original 65 categories, over one-third of the responses from Midwest children fell into categories not used by Indian children. This may be due partly to the fact that Midwest children, asked for 18 rather than 6 responses, had perforce to consider areas of experience that might not have occurred to them in their first six responses and that, consequently, we have obtained a wider sampling of the child's moral experiences in Midwest than in the Indian cultures. On the other hand, our study of the comparability of 6 versus 18 responses among children of another white midwestern community, reported earlier

(see p. 94), led to the conclusion that results are approximately the same under both conditions—that, in other words, the areas of experience mentioned on the test are the same and occur in about the same proportion of times, whether the child is asked for 6 responses or for 18.

The fact that Midwest children mention more categories of behavior than do Indian children, then, seems to be less a function of the difference in number of responses than a real difference between the cultures of Indian and white children. The resulting hypothesis would seem to be that, in general, wider areas of child behavior in white culture than in Indian culture are invested with moral values and moral judgments.

Table 24 summarizes the data on the themes of moral ideology (the "behaviors") for all the children in the Study. (These same data are presented in more detail—by age as well as by sex for each tribal group—in Appendix C-3, so that the reader who has special interest in one or more of the Indian tribes will be able to make more refined analyses and interpretations than are relevant to this report.)

For the seven major themes, the totals of the columns shown in Table 24 are greater than 100 per cent. This is due to the fact that a few categories occur in more than one of the seven combinations. For example, category 7, "industry," was included under "Competence" and also under "Personal Virtues."

Where frequencies in the table are of the order of 10-20 per cent, the difference between two frequencies must be at least seven to twelve percentage points, depending upon the number of responses involved, to be statistically reliable. When frequencies are less than 10 per cent, the difference between two frequencies may be as low as three or four percentage points and yet be statistically reliable.

Studying the columns in Table 24 entitled "Average," we shall consider first each theme as it varies from one tribal group to another; then each tribal group as it differs from the next in its patterning of the seven major themes.

"Competence" and "Work"

Table 24 shows striking differences between the tribal groups on the "Competence" theme; differences which range from the Navaho Mountain group (47 per cent) to Midwest (8 per cent). This finding must, however, be interpreted in relation to the "Work" theme.

TABLE 24

THEMES OF MORAL IDEOLOGY FOR INDIAN AND MIDWEST CHILDREN (PERCENTAGES)[a]

	Papago			Hopi			Zuni			Zia		
	Boys	Girls	Average	Boys	Girls	Average	Boys	Girls	Average	Boys	Girls	Average
No. of responses	305	323	628	338	503	841	266	240	506	137	97	234
Major themes:												
Competence	14	12	13	19	12	15	19	12	16[b]	12	13	13
Self-restraint	14	11	13	9	6	8	7	5	6	10	11	10
Personal virtues	12	13	12	12	11	11	8	10	9	8	16	12
Relations to authority	7	10	8	9	10	10	9	10	10	8	7	7
Regard for others	29	23	26	36	38	37	25	23	24	43	35	39
Service	29	27	28	25	27	26	37	38	38	26	32	29
Sex	..	1	1	..	1	1	1	5	3	..	..	..
Subsidiary themes:												
Family	31	38	35	23	32	27	41	48	44	27	38	32
School	3	3	3	5	4	5	4	5	5	2	3	2
Church	..	1	..	..	..	..	..	..	..	1	1	1
Community	..	...	..	1	..	..	2	..	1	2	2	2
Property	23	11	17	20	18	19	15	11	13	14	12	13
Work	39	44	42	34	30	32	50	42	46	32	38	35
Stealing	15	10	12	14	14	14	12	5	8	11	9	10
Drinking	3	2	3	..	..	..	2	..	1	1	..	1
Bad language	1	1	1	..	..	..	..	..	..	4	4	4
Aggression toward peers	4	1	2	10	6	8	7	4	5	12	9	10

a. Indian children are aged eight to eighteen; Midwest, ten to eighteen.

b. These percentages are given in round numbers, as they were rounded after averaging the age subgroups. This accounts for the seeming inconsistencies in the "Average" columns, inconsistencies, of course, which are always within 1 per cent.

TABLE 24—Continued

	Navaho Mountain			Shiprock			Sioux			Midwest		
	Boys	Girls	Average	Boys	Girls	Average	Boys	Girls	Average	Boys	Girls	Average
No. of responses	162	109	271	202	207	409	314	329	643	5,333	7,105	12,488
Major themes:												
Competence	54	40	47	22	23	23	11	6	9	8	8	8
Self-restraint	7	10	9	21	8	14	10	10	10	29	23	26
Personal virtues	37	17	27	19	14	17	7	5	6	13	13	13
Relations to authority	2	2	2	7	8	8	10	19	14	17	23	20
Regard for others	18	13	15	27	24	25	45	33	39	27	26	26
Service	13	10	11	17	33	25	22	21	21	14	14	14
Sex	3	7	5	..	4	2	1	5	3	1	1	1
Subsidiary themes:												
Family	8	13	10	20	36	28	14	21	17	13	15	14
School	3	1	2	4	3	3	6	9	8	9	11	10
Church	..	..	..	..	..	..	..	2	1	1	2	2
Community	1	..	..	..	..	..	3	1	2	5	4	5
Property	10	6	9	15	10	12	25	15	20	9	6	8
Work	53	43	48	37	46	41	19	17	18	11	9	10
Stealing	10	5	8	11	9	10	19	12	15	2	2	2
Drinking	1	..	..	..	..	..	2	2	2	2	2	2
Bad language	..	..	..	..	..	..	1	1	1	2	2	2
Aggression toward peers	4	8	6	10	9	9	12	11	12	8	5	6

The original category 5, "job and employment" is included in both the "Competence" and the "Work" themes. It drew heavy response from Southwest Indian children, less from Sioux children, and very little from white children. It is mainly this difference on category 5 that is reflected here.

Thus we may conclude—not that Indian children attach greater moral value to self-achievement than do white children or that Indian children are under greater pressure than white children to compete and to excel—but that our combination "Competence" has, in this context, proved a less meaningful combination of categories than the "Work" combination. A real difference between Indians and whites lies in the importance of work in the life of the child. Work carries a high moral value in Southwest Indian cultures. Ten per cent of Midwest responses fell in the "work" area, as compared with 18 per cent for Sioux and 30-50 per cent of the Southwest Indian responses.

"Self-restraint"

On this theme, Indian children are markedly different from white. While there is some variation among Indian groups (they range from 6 per cent for Zuni to 14 per cent for Shiprock), that variation is small when compared to the 26 per cent given by Midwest children. (The Sioux, who resemble the whites on the "Work" theme, resemble the Southwest Indians on the "Self-restraint" theme.)

It would seem that for white children the control of impulse life consitutes a real moral problem. Self-restraint and self-indulgence carry strong moral overtones; and the child is aware of a whole range of behaviors in this area that are condemned or rewarded, approved or disapproved. The white child, more than the Indian child, is concerned over what amusements he may or may not properly engage in; what people he should or should not associate with. Categories 8, 9, and 10, for example ("right people," "etiquette," "rowdy behavior") were mentioned frequently by white children; almost never by Indians. Curiosity, self-control, recklessness, general aggressivity—these carry moral implications for the white child.

It must remain for the anthropologist to say whether or not these Indian cultures in reality place less emphasis upon self-restraint—or, better, the concern over self-restraint—than does our own culture. From these data, it seems evident at least that white children seem more

preoccupied with the moral implications involved, and probably with conflict, in adapting impulsive behavior to the demands of society for self-restraint.

"Personal Virtues"

In this area of experience, there is no marked difference between white and Indian children. It is the Navaho Mountain children who give a large proportion of their responses (27 per cent) to this theme, as compared with all the other tribal groups.[11] (The range for the other groups is from 6 per cent for Sioux to 17 per cent for Shiprock, with 13 per cent for Midwest.)

Thus all the cultures studied place about the same emphasis upon the child's developing certain positive patterns or traits of behavior, such as industry, honesty, courage, modesty, and so on—traits which consistently carry positive moral value.

"Relations to Authority"

On this theme, white children again are markedly different from Southwest Indian children; and, again, the Sioux resemble the whites. While Navaho Mountain children are at the extreme low end of the scale, with only 2 per cent of their responses falling in this area, the other Southwest Indian groups are very similar, ranging from 7 to 10 per cent. Midwest, on the other hand, gives 20 per cent of its responses in this area, and Sioux, 15 per cent.

White children, then, seem much more concerned over relations to authority than do Southwest Indian children. It would seem fair to say that the white child and the Sioux child are preoccupied with problems of obedience and disobedience as regards parents, teachers, and other adults and that these problems have strong moral implications. For the Southwest Indian child, his relations to authority constitute only a secondary theme of morality.

"Regard for Others" and "Service"

These two themes together constitute, for all the tribal groups except Navaho Mountain, from 50 to 70 per cent of all the responses given on the Moral Ideology Test. This is, of course, not surprising. In a

11. The Navaho Mountain figures are high, owing to the influence of category 7, "industry," which is included under this heading. Navaho Mountain boys give a large proportion of their responses, almost 30 per cent, to the single category "industry"; and it is this fact which is reflected here.

sense, the socialization process itself consists of inculcating in the child a regard for other people and a willingness to do one's share in promoting the group welfare. And these two themes are the foundations of a system of morality (this is not to say that all cultures define morality in interpersonal relations in the same way but rather that interpersonal relations form the nub of any set of moral values).

At the same time that all the groups studied (except Navaho Mountain) place primary emphasis on these two themes, the range of response on each of the two is relatively great. Thus, for "Regard for Others," the range is from 15 per cent for Navaho Mountain to 39 per cent for Zia and Sioux; for "Service," from 11 per cent for Navaho Mountain to 37 per cent for Zuni. Midwest children are about midway on "Regard for Others," but at the low end of the scale on "Service."

"Sex"

As would be expected from the nature of the test instrument, there were few responses in this area given by any of the children in the Study.

Nevertheless, Navaho Mountain stands out from the other groups in showing over 5 per cent of responses on this theme. Since marriage and sex relations within a clan are taboo among the Navaho and since the Navaho Mountain child has infrequent contact with clans other than his own, it might be expected that sexuality would constitute a greater problem at Navaho Mountain than in the other societies. Certainly, the Navaho Mountain child is repeatedly warned against transgressing the sex taboo.

"Social Institutions"

When we look at the social institutions toward which the child's moral behavior is primarily oriented, the findings are what we might have expected. While there is wide range between the frequencies of mention of the family theme among the various tribal groups, the family nevertheless takes clear precedence over other social institutions in all the societies being studied.

The school is of some importance only to white children.

The church figures not at all in the lives of Indian children and only to slight degree in the lives of white children.

Behavior oriented toward the "community" plays almost no role for Indian children; somewhat more for whites. (Since these data were gathered in wartime, a number of responses from Midwest children dealt with such matters as buying war stamps and bonds, helping to collect scrap for war industries, and so on. We would, therefore, anticipate fewer responses dealing with "community," were this test to be repeated now.)

The Navaho Mountain children are lowest, as compared to the other groups, in their mention of the family theme; and in this respect they differ quite markedly from the other Southwest Indian groups. This finding requires further explanation. The original category 41, "work at home," contributed heavily to the family theme; it dealt mainly with tasks the child performs in and about the home itself. The responses given frequently by Navaho Mountain children dealt with sheepherding for the boys and with weaving and basketmaking for the girls. These responses were categorized as 5, "job," or 7, "industry"—thus they do not appear in 41, or, consequently, in the family theme. Sheepherding and weaving are, we know, carried on within the family unit at Navaho Mountain and should properly be seen as family-oriented activities. The difference, then, between Navaho Mountain and other Southwest Indian groups is probably an artifact resulting from the method we used in categorizing responses. The same may be true for the Sioux, though to a lesser extent. The same is not, however, true of Midwest. In Midwest, responses dealing with work in and about the home or with work that might have been interpreted in any way as family-oriented occurred relatively infrequently. There is a real cultural difference between white and Indian children in this respect.

"Property" and "Stealing"

It is evident, when we examine the frequencies for each tribal group on both "Property" and "Stealing" that responses having to do with stealing constitute the bulk of the "Property" theme. The differences between groups on "Property" are therefore largely differences in the emphasis placed upon stealing. Here the Midwest children stand apart from the Indian children, with the Indians mentioning this theme from four to seven times as frequently as did the white children.

Judging from these data, we may question the strong emphasis upon property rights in modern white society, as it has so often been described by anthropologists and sociologists. In comparison to the Indian groups here studied, our own culture seems to place only secondary value upon respect for property. This may, of course, be a reflection of the difference between Indians and whites as regards material wealth—in general, these Indian groups are characterized by poverty, and it may be that the Indian child, as a consequence, is more concerned over receiving and protecting property than is the white child.

Moral Behavior in Each Tribal Group

Returning, now, to the seven major themes of moral ideology, we can highlight intertribal comparisons if we approach these data in a somewhat different way.

Table 25 shows the rank order of the seven themes within each tribal group. (Thus, for example, the "Competence" theme ranks first for Navaho Mountain children and sixth for Midwest children.)

For each society, the two highest-ranking themes account for more than 50 per cent of the total number of responses given on the test. Using this criterion (the two highest-ranking themes) to differentiate between the tribes, three general patterns are found.

1. For Zuni, Hopi, Papago, Zia, Sioux, and Shiprock (except Shiprock boys), the bulk of responses occur on the "Regard for Others" and "Service" themes. This pattern suggests that these are cultures in which the locus of morality lies in interpersonal relations and in the group good. The group, rather than the individual, is categorically valued. Goodness and badness for the child lie primarily in how he relates himself to other people; and "that for the sake of which" one is praised or blamed is external to the self.

2. For Navaho Mountain the pattern is different. Here, with the bulk of responses occurring on "Competence" and "Personal Virtues," the locus of moral value seems only secondarily to lie in the child's relations to the group around him. Remembering again that category 5, "job," is included in the "Competence" theme and that category 7, "industry," is included in the "Personal Virtues" theme and remembering that Navaho Mountain children give such a large proportion of their responses in these two categories, we may conclude that it is this emphasis upon work and industriousness that is reflected here.

The social isolation of Navaho Mountain children is also important

TABLE 25

MAJOR THEMES OF MORAL IDEOLOGY: RANK ORDER WITHIN EACH TRIBAL GROUP

Themes	Tribal Group															
	Papago		Hopi		Zuni		Zia		Navaho Mt.		Shiprock		Sioux		Midwest	
	Boys	Girls	Boys	Girls	Boys	Girls	Boys	Girls	Boys	Girls	Boys	Girls	Boys	Girls	Boys	Girls
Competence	4.5	4	5	5	5	5	5	5	7	7	6	4	5	3	2	2
Self-restraint	4.5	3	2.5	2	2	1.5	4	3	3	3.5	5	2.5	3.5	4	7	5.5
Personal Virtues	3	5	4	4	3	3.5	2.5	4	6	6	4	5	2	1.5	3	3
Relations to Authority	2	2	2.5	3	4	3.5	2.5	2	1	1	2	2.5	3.5	5	5	5.5
Regard for Others	6.5	6	7	7	6	6	7	7	5	5	7	6	7	7	6	7
Service	6.5	7	6	6	7	7	6	6	4	3.5	3	7	6	6	4	4
Sex	1	1	1	1	1	1.5	1	1	2	2	1	1	1	1.5	1	1

in this connection, perhaps accounting for this picture of a morality which involves only secondarily the group good—for this is a society characterized by minimal social relations outside the family.

3. For Midwest the pattern is again different. The two highest themes are "Self-restraint" and "Regard for Others" (for girls, "Relations to Authority" is also high). Here the primary value lies neither in the individual nor in the group, but rather in a balance between the two. For the Midwest child, his task may be seen as one of "management"—managing to develop the self at the same time that one respects the rights of other people (in this light, "Regard for Others" in Midwest may become a matter of "how to get along" with others). One might say that in modern white society, as compared to the Indian societies, the greatest moral good is to be "adjusted"—to adjust one's own impulses to the group demands, to maximize gratification while minimizing conflict with others.

Sex Differences

Referring back to Table 24 and looking first at the differences between boys and girls within each of the tribal groups, the following findings emerge:

For Zuni, there are no marked sex differences on any of the major or subsidiary themes. While girls exceed boys in their mention of the "Sex" theme and the "Family" theme, and boys exceed girls on "Competence" and on "Work," still these differences are not large.

For Hopi, there are no striking differences. Boys exceed girls on "Competence"; and girls exceed boys on "Family"; but, as with the Zuni, one is impressed more with the similarities than with the differences between sexes.

For Papago, the situation is similar, except for the "Property" theme, where boys give 23 per cent of their responses on this theme as compared to 11 per cent for girls.

For Zia, girls are more concerned over the "Personal Virtues" theme than are boys and, like the other Indian groups, give more responses in the area of "Family" than do boys.

For Shiprock, sex differences are somewhat greater. Here the boys mention the "Self-restraint" theme much more frequently than do girls,

and the "Service" theme much less frequently. Shiprock girls show the same greater pre-occupation over "Family" as is true of other girls; but, contrary to other Indian groups, it is the Shiprock girls rather than the boys who mention the "Work" theme most frequently.

For Navaho Mountain, there is a striking difference between girls and boys on "Personal Virtues," with boys mentioning this theme twice as frequently as girls; and there is considerable difference between the sexes on "Work," where the boys' responses are predominant.

For the Sioux, the girls are more concerned than the boys over "Authority," less concerned over "Regard for Others," and less concerned over "Property."

In Midwest, the sexes are strikingly similar. While the differences on "Self-restraint" (where boys' responses predominate) and on "Authority" (where girls' responses predominate) are statistically reliable, these differences are not large in size.

Looking at the over-all pattern of sex differences in these data, there is something of a general tendency for boys more than girls to mention "Competence" and "Self-restraint" and for girls more than boys to mention "Authority" and "Sex." There is a consistent sex difference on the "Property" theme, where in all eight societies boys mention this theme more frequently than do girls. (The same is true of "stealing"; but this was to be expected, since "stealing" is subsumed under the "Property" theme.)

The difference between boys and girls is most marked in the area of "Family," where in all eight societies girls mention this theme more frequently than do boys and where in all eight the differences in percentage of mentions between boys and girls are sizable.

In general, then, for the girls in this Study, the moral issues of life tend to be associated with family relations, sexual behavior, and the girl's relations with authority figures. For the boys, moral issues are more often related to life outside the home, to competence, self-restraint, and regard for the property rights of others. These over-all findings are scarcely surprising; yet it is of interest to note how well they fit the commonly accepted notion of the "feminine," as compared with the "masculine," role.

Seen from another point of view, however, one is impressed more by the similarities between the sexes than by the differences. It may be assumed that in real life differences in behavior and attitudes are more marked between boys and girls than is evident from these data. This, in turn, may be seen as supporting our original assumption that the Moral Ideology Test—at least, as it was used in this Study—gives information about the moral ideology of a culture at a generalized level. It taps the official set of moral values common to the culture at large. In future research, should the investigator wish to discriminate between subgroups in a society (such as sex, age, social class, or ethnic groups), it would be well to use less generalized questions than those used here. Thus, to study sex differences, instead of asking "What is something a boy or girl of your age might do that would be a good thing to do . . . etc.," the question might be ". . .something a boy could do . . . etc.," or ". . .something a boy, but not a girl, could do. . . ."

Age Trends

Regarding age trends, we can make no generalizations which would be meaningful in comparing the various cultural groups. The data are too complex to be easily summarized and are therefore presented in appendix form (see Appendix C-3). This is not to say that significant changes with age do not appear within and between tribal groups on the various themes of moral behavior but rather that there are no over-all consistencies. The reader might better study age changes within the particular tribal group which interests him, giving attention to sex differences and to the relations between the various themes as they show increases and decreases with age.

Section 3. THE DATA ON MORAL SURROGATES

The data on the surrogate responses from the Moral Ideology Test are summarized in Table 26. (These data are given in greater detail in Appendix C-4, where, for each Indian tribe, the surrogates have been separated into praisers and blamers and are given for each age and sex group.) The difference between two frequencies in the table must be at least five to eight percentage points to be statistically reliable, where frequencies are of the order of 10-20 per cent. When the frequencies are less than 10 per cent, the difference between two frequencies may be as low as two or three percentage points and still be statistically reliable.

Intertribal Comparisons

Looking at the "Average" columns in Table 26 and considering each category of response as it varies from one tribal group to the other, the following conclusions emerge:

Family

The "family" categories constitute from 40 to 70 per cent of all surrogate responses for the various tribal groups. This is not a surprising result but merely supports the fact that the family constitutes the primary social group and is the foremost agent of society in providing moral training for the child. The Southwest Indians mention family members more often than do the white children (although Zia and Hopi approach the white figures); the Sioux, less often. This suggests that, for Southwest Indian cultures, the locus of moral authority for the child is more exclusively vested in the family than is true for the white child.[12]

Father

When we separate out mentions of father alone, there are wide differences between tribal groups. The Zuni give 24 per cent of all surrogate responses to mentions of the father. At the other extreme, only 1 per cent of Shiprock responses go to father alone.

Mother

The mother is mentioned much more frequently than the father in all groups, thus suggesting that it is the mother more than the father who is seen as the "socializer" or moral teacher of the child. It is only the Navaho children (both Shiprock and Navaho Mountain) who fail to single out the mother to any appreciable extent.

Grandparents

Grandparents alone are seldom mentioned, except by Navaho children. (For Midwest, these responses were not tallied separately.)

12. These data on the family as "surrogate" should be studied in relation to the data on the "family" theme of "behavior," as described in the preceding section. For example, the Navaho Mountain children mentioned the family theme of "behavior" much less often than did the other groups; yet, as "surrogates," the Navaho Mountain children mention family members more frequently than does any other group. That is to say what the Navaho Mountain child does may not be oriented toward the family; yet it is the family which approves or disapproves whatever he does.

TABLE 26[a]

MORAL SURROGATES FOR INDIAN AND MIDWEST CHILDREN (PERCENTAGES)

	Papago			Hopi			Zuni			Zia		
	Boys	Girls	Average	Boys	Girls	Average	Boys	Girls	Average	Boys	Girls	Average
No. of responses	305	320	625	332	495	827	259	232	491	133	94	227
Family (1, 1a, 2, 3, 4, 22)	71	74	73[b]	44	53	49	77	72	75	47	56	51
Father (2)	24	15	19	15	5	10	38	10	24	18	. .	9
Mother (3)	20	40	30	14	29	21	18	43	31	19	51	35
Grandparents (22)	5	4	4	3	1	2	4	3	4	2	. .	1
Elders (5, 6)	2	1	2	8	3	6	3	1	2	12	7	10
Age-mates (7, 8, 9, 10)	5	6	5	11	11	11	2	3	3	4	. .	2
Teacher (11)	3	5	4	7	5	6	6	16	11	5	3	4
Clergy (13)	. .	. .	. .	. .	. .	. .	. .	. .	. .	. .	. .	. .
Everybody (14, 14c)	9	8	8	13	15	14	3	1	2	11	10	11
Government (15)	1	. .	1	1	. .	1	1	. .	. .	. .	. .	. .
Self (16)	1	1	1	1	1	1	1	1	1	1	2	2
Recipient (17)	7	3	5	11	10	11	6	1	4	6	16	11
Deity (18)	1	1	1	. .	. .	. .	. .	. .	. .	2	. .	1

a. Indian children are aged eight to eighteen; Midwest, ten to eighteen.

b. These percentages are given in round numbers, as they were rounded after averaging the age subgroups. This accounts for the seeming inconsistencies in the "Average" columns, inconsistencies, of course, which are always within 1 per cent.

TABLE 26—Continued

	Navaho Mountain			Shiprock			Sioux			Midwest		
	Boys	Girls	Average	Boys	Girls	Average	Boys	Girls	Average	Boys	Girls	Average
No. of responses	235	158	393	311	318	629	307	318	625	5,723	8,617	14,340
Family (1, 1a, 2, 3, 4, 22)	74	82	78	67	77	71	32	47	39	47	43	45
Father (2)	6	8	7	2	1	1	8	6	7	7	3	5
Mother (3)	9	15	12	4	7	5	13	25	19	14	15	15
Grandparents (22)	12	14	13	8	10	9	. .	2	1	. .	. .	. .
Elders (5, 6)	1	. .	1	5	2	4	8	1	5	1	2	1
Age-mates (7, 8, 9, 10)	2	1	2	6	5	5	11	6	9	10	8	9
Teacher (11)	6	7	6	10	6	8	9	14	12	14	18	16
Clergy (13)	. .	. .	. .	. .	. .	. .	. .	. .	. .	1	. .	1
Everybody (14, 14c)	14	8	11	9	7	8	12	14	13	12	16	14
Government (15)	. .	. .	. .	1	. .	. .	3	. .	2	5	3	4
Self (16)	1	1	1	. .	. .	. .	1	. .	. .	3	3	3
Recipient (17)	3	2	3	2	1	1	14	11	13	4	3	4
Deity (18)	. .	. .	. .	. .	. .	. .	4	3	3	1	1	1

"Everybody"

The "everybody" category draws roughly 10 per cent of the surrogate responses from the various tribal groups. (The Zuni are an exception; they use this category only 2 per cent of the time). This suggests, if "everybody" is used to symbolize the society at large, that "society" runs a poor second to "family" as the locus of moral authority for the child—again, scarcely an unexpected finding.

Age-Mates

Age-mates, while mentioned to some extent by Hopi, Sioux, and Midwest children, constitute at most a secondary source of approval and disapproval.

Teacher

The teacher as a moral surrogate seems important only in the lives of white children. It may be inferred from these data that Indian children in general (although this is somewhat less true for Zuni and Sioux), viewing the teacher as alien, remain generally indifferent to her—they do not see her as an important moral force in their lives, either as a praiser or as a blamer.

Recipient

The recipient of the act (the person upon whom the child's act has direct and immediate effect) is mentioned as the surrogate about 10 per cent of the time by Hopi, Zia, and Sioux children; very infrequently by the other groups. Responses in this category imply that the child narrows his attention to the particular person involved in his act and does not generalize to any broader social context. Why this phenomenon should operate for Hopi, Zia, and Sioux children more than for others is not clear.

Moral Surrogates for Each Tribal Group

Looking now at the pattern of surrogate responses within each tribal group, we find the following results.

For Navaho Mountain, four-fifths of the surrogate responses are family members, signifying that for the Navaho Mountain child it is almost exclusively the family who controls his moral conduct. Grandparents alone are mentioned relatively frequently, suggesting that the Navaho grandparent has a closer relationship to his grandchildren than in other cultures and that he wields greater moral authority. These

findings are probably related to the fact, described earlier, that the Navaho Mountain people live in isolated family units rather than in communities. The low mention of age-mates is perhaps another reflection of the situation—the Navaho Mountain child is less in the company of age-mates than is true in the other groups we are studying.

For Shiprock, surrogate responses show the peculiarity that father and mother appear extremely rarely as separately mentioned surrogates. Since this is also true, though to lesser degree, in Navaho Mountain responses, we may conclude that the Navaho child (both Shiprock and Navaho Mountain), as compared to other children, sees the family as a unit—he tends to give the response "family" rather than "mother" or "father" when asked who praises or blames him for his conduct. The "recipient of the act" is mentioned rarely by Shiprock children, as is also true of Navaho Mountain.

For Papago, surrogate responses are high for family members (especially for mentions of father alone and mother alone), with no other category receiving an appreciable proportion of responses. We have here again the picture of a group of children who see the family as the primary, almost exclusive, locus of moral authority.

For Zuni, the pattern is very similar to that for Papago. The only major differences between the two groups are that Zuni children mention the teacher more frequently and "everybody" less frequently. The Zuni mention the father alone more frequently than does any other group, suggesting that the Zuni father is unusually strong as a moral surrogate. The low mention of "everybody" is surprising, since the Zuni have the reputation of being a group heavily controlled by community opinion.

For Hopi, the family categories receive relatively less mention (though still nearly 50 per cent) than in other tribal groups. Age-mates, "recipient," and "everybody" each receive about 10 per cent of the mentions. The impression is of a group where community or tribal moral controls are strong and where the child looks to more than the one source, family, for approval and disapproval.

For Zia, we have a pattern similar to that of the Hopi, in that the family is less exclusively the focus. In Zia, however, the mother alone obtains a higher proportion of responses. It is interesting that not a single Zia girl mentioned the father as a praiser or blamer. The Zia children use the category "elders" more frequently than does any other group, and the category of age-mates less frequently.

The Sioux surrogate responses are closer to the responses of white children than are those of the other Indian groups. The Sioux are the lowest of all in mentioning family members as surrogates, and they use "age-mates," "teacher," "everybody," and "recipient" fairly frequently. This is the pattern, again, of some variety in the sources of moral authority for the child.

The Midwest pattern is, similarly, one of spread in moral surrogates for the child. With the family first in importance, there is, nevertheless, considerable importance attached to the teacher, to "age-mates," and to "everybody."

"Praisers" versus "Blamers"

As has already been indicated, the data on surrogates for Indian groups were tabulated separately for praisers and blamers (for Midwest, this was done only for mentions of father alone and mother alone). This breakdown of the data is not shown in Table 26 but is given in Appendix C-4. The findings are as follows:

On the whole, for all the groups studied (including Midwest), the mother is mentioned more frequently as a praiser than as a blamer, while the father generally is mentioned about equally as both. (Exceptions to this rule are found at Zuni, where this difference does not appear; at Shiprock, where the father is never mentioned as a blamer and the mother receives equal mention on both; and at Navaho Mountain and Hopi, where the father is mentioned more frequently as a praiser.) Other than this, the separation of surrogates into praisers and blamers has produced no over-all generalizations of major importance as regards cross-cultural comparisons.[13]

13. Since these data on praisers versus blamers may be of some significance to the anthropologist who has special interest in one or another of these cultures, we may summarize our results as they appear in Appendix C-4 as follows:

"Family members" are mentioned as praisers more frequently than as blamers by Hopi, Papago, Zia, and Navaho Mountain subjects. For the other tribes they are mentioned equally often in the two roles.

"Age-mates" are mentioned more frequently as praisers by Zuni and Sioux; equally as both by Shiprock and Navaho Mountain; and more frequently as blamers by Hopi, Papago, and Zia.

"Everybody" is mentioned more frequently as praisers by Sioux only; equally as both by Hopi, Zuni, and Shiprock; and more frequently as blamers by Papago, Zia, and Navaho Mountain.

"Recipient" is mentioned more frequently as blamers by Sioux,

Sex Differences

For all the groups studied, differences between boys' and girls' mentions of surrogates lie almost entirely in the "family," father alone," and "mother alone" categories.

Considering, first, those other categories which show any sex differences at all, "elders" are mentioned more frequently by boys at Hopi, Zia, and Sioux (for other groups, this category shows no sex differences).

The "teacher" draws more responses from Zuni girls than from Zuni boys, and from Sioux girls than from Sioux boys; otherwise there is no sex difference among the groups on "teacher."

The "recipient" draws more responses from Zia girls than from Zia boys; more from Zuni boys than from Zuni girls.

Age-mates are more frequently mentioned by Sioux boys than by Sioux girls.

"Everybody" obtains greater mention by Navaho Mountain boys than girls.

These sex differences are peculiar, then, to the individual tribal groups in which they occur.

Returning, however, to the family categories, there are consistent sex differences. Girls, except in Midwest and Zuni, give a higher proportion of their responses to the family than do boys, signifying that for girls in general the locus of moral authority lies more exclusively in the family than it does for boys.

In all societies the mother (as compared to the father) is clearly the principal surrogate figure for girls. Her importance as a surrogate for boys, however, varies somewhat from society to society. Clearly, she seems less important than the father for Papago and Zuni boys; but more important than the father for Sioux and Midwest boys. We might say, then, that the girl in all societies looks to the mother as the source of moral authority but that there are interesting cultural differences as regards boys. In some of the cultures here studied

Navaho Mountain, Zuni, and Hopi; and equally as both by Shiprock, Zia, and Papago.

"Teacher" is mentioned more frequently as praiser by Papago; equally often as both by Zia, Zuni, Sioux, and Shiprock; and more frequently as blamer by Hopi and Navaho Mountain.

(Papago and Zuni), the boy looks to the father; in others (Hopi, Zia, Shiprock, Navaho Mountain), the boy looks equally to father and mother; in others (Sioux and Midwest), the boy looks to the mother.

As regards our own culture, these findings are in line with the phenomenon so often described (and often deplored)—the importance of the mother in the life of her son. This phenomenon among the Sioux may be related to the "loss of role" suffered by the men, as described by MacGregor.[14] For the Hopi, Zia, and Navaho boys, it is interesting that the father does not occupy the clearly predominant role that we might have expected.

Age Trends

Here, as with the data on "behaviors," we have made no attempt to summarize the complexity of the data on age differences, but refer the reader to Appendix C-4. The reader may wish to analyze age trends within one or another tribal group, giving simultaneous attention to differences between boys and girls and to differences between praisers and blamers. Since age trends are not consistent from tribe to tribe, such differences as occur will take on meaning as they can be interpreted in the light of the anthropologist's knowledge of the culture in which they occur.

14. Gordon MacGregor, Warriors without Weapons: A Study of the Pine Ridge Sioux (Chicago: University of Chicago Press, 1945).

CHAPTER V

MORAL JUDGMENT: ATTITUDES TOWARD RULES OF GAMES

The essence of morality is respect for rules. Various societies use various means of teaching their children rules of behavior and attitudes toward such rules. Hence it might be expected that the attitudes of children toward rules would differ from one Indian tribe to another, and surely between the Indian and Midwestern children.

To study children's attitudes toward rules, we turned our attention to the rules of games. Games are important to children—they may be considered the "real business" of children. In the course of playing games the child learns to get along with his age-mates, to regulate his own behavior, and to develop certain moral attitudes toward rules in general.

The pioneer work in the study of moral judgment through children's experience with games was done by Piaget.[1] Based on his studies of Swiss children, he predicted that children of primitive societies would have a different experience with rules of games than children of modern societies. In our study we adapted Piaget's technique and were able to test his hypotheses.

Piaget put questions about rules of games to Swiss children and found the following: Children of six to ten years thought that rules of games could not be changed and had been made by someone in authority (God, father, the government). As the age of ten was approached, an increasing proportion of children thought that rules could be changed, provided that the players all agreed. By observation and participation in the game of marbles, Piaget found that children's behavior corresponded to their beliefs about rules. From seven to about ten, they adhered strictly to the rules as they understood them. At about eleven to twelve, they became interested in rules as such, codified them, discussed them at length, and made changes to fit various situations.

1. Jean Piaget, The Moral Judgment of the Child (New York: Harcourt, Brace & Co., 1932); and "The Moral Development of the Adolescent in Two Types of Society, Primitive and 'Modern,'" lecture given July 24, 1947, at the UNESCO Seminar on Education for International Understanding, UNESCO, Paris (mimeographed).

Piaget then made a distinction between "morality of constraint," or "heteronomous" morality, and "morality of agreement," or "autonomous" morality. In the stage of morality of constraint, children accept rules from outside authority and consider rules as absolute and unchangeable. They progress to a stage of morality of agreement, in which they learn to make rules for themselves by common agreement among those who are involved. A child develops from the level of heteronomous to that of autonomous morality as a result of his social experience with age-mates, who are his equals—in contrast to his parents and other adults, who gave him his first rules. Through the give-and-take of play with age-mates, the child learns that rules are man-made and can be changed by agreement of the players. He generalizes this, more or less thoroughly, to cover other rules, including the rules of moral conduct. Thus he comes to feel personally responsible for morality, because he has participated in the process by which moral rules are made.

In his book Piaget suggests that the attitudes of children toward rules in primitive societies should <u>not</u> show a development parallel to that in a modern society. This suggestion is expanded in the lecture which has been cited. He says:

> In so-called "primitive" societies the economic division of labor is unknown; and as a consequence so also are individual psychological variations, "social classes," and conflicting ideologies. The sole fundamental differentiation known to them, apart from sex, is that of "age-groups":—childhood, adolescence (including initiation), young adults, mature men, and the "Elders" who are the true heads of the tribe. The Elders have authority over all the lower age-groups, but, far from being freer than the young, they are themselves abject slaves to the will of the spirits, to that of their ancestors, and to the traditions linked thereto. Thus the dominant note in such a society is the constraint exercised by earlier generations over their successors, and this "gerontocratic process" explains why the individual is progressively less free as he grows older.
>
> Among primitive peoples childhood is the only age of freedom. . . . In contrast, the serious side of life begins with adolescence. Hitherto the individual has been a child outside the corporate life of the tribe; he must now be absorbed into the ranks of the tribal initiates. The neophyte must therefore acquire a practical, effective and ideological knowledge of the sacred traditions whose guardians are the Elders. Accordingly, for anything from a few months to two years or more, the adolescent must undergo rites of initiation to whose impressive and sometimes cruel nature all ethnographers bear witness. In the presence of Masters masked to heighten the air of mystery, the young man undergoes every kind of physical test, while at the same time—in an atmosphere of emotional tension and submission to the spirits—he absorbs the body of sacred beliefs and practices which will transform him into an adult member of the clan. Thus, founded as it is on mystical authority, the upbringing of the adolescent in primitive societies ruled by tribal custom tends essentially to conformity. On the one hand, intellectual conformity: there is nothing to induce in him the habit of reflection or the critical spirit, for in every field (from true techniques to mystical representations and from magic to the causal explanation of phenomena) his thoughts are ready-made for him and he bows to the collective notions of the tribe handed down from generation to generation. And, on the other hand, moral conformity: sacred duties and ritual prohibition (taboos) leave only the narrowest margin to action not governed by rules.

Piaget contrasts this situation with that in "modern" societies:

> Sociologically, it is in respect of childhood that, with us, the greatest degree of intellectual and moral constraint, exercised by the older upon the younger generations, is observable, while the normal adult gradually frees himself from the bonds of tradition so as to acquire for himself a personal view of the world. In contrast with the state of affairs obtaining in primitive societies, where the individual becomes progressively more enslaved by collective pressure, the specialized individual, characteristic of societies in which economic work is elaborately divided up, thus achieves relative autonomy. In this respect adolescence is a decisive turning-point—that at which the individual rejects, or at least revises his estimate of, everything that has been inculcated in him, and acquires a personal point of view and a personal place in life. Whereas the duty of the primitive "initiated ones" was to submit to an already established truth, the first duty of the modern adolescent is to revolt against all imposed truth and to build up his intellectual and moral ideal as freely as he can.

What may we expect of children growing up in a society which is dominated by the traditional tribal religion and which retains much of the old social structure, but exists only as an island in the surrounding "modern" culture and is accepting more and more of this surrounding culture? Such are the Hopi, Zuni, Zia, and Navaho cultures.

What may we expect of the Papago children, whose parents retain relatively more of the traditional cultures but have adopted Christianity?

What may we expect of the Sioux children, whose primitive culture has nearly vanished?

And what differences may we find between Navaho children who are exposed to the dominant American culture at the busy and accessible community of Shiprock, and Navaho children who are almost isolated from the white man in the distant and out-of-the-way Navaho Mountain area?

Procedures

A series of questions was asked the Indian children concerning rules of games. The interviewer asked the child what games he knew, how they were played, and whether or not he knew what a rule was. Usually the child could name a game and state one of its rules. There followed a series of questions, to which the subject's answers were taken down verbatim in the test booklet:

Q: Do you know a rule in this game? A:
Q: What do you think, who made this rule first? A:
Q: Can boys or girls like you make new rules? A:
Q: Can small children make new rules? A:
Q: Can bigger boys and girls make new rules? A:
Q: Can rules be changed? A:
(if "Yes") Q: How can rules be changed? A:
Q: By whom? A:

In case the child did not know what a rule was but understood how to play some games, the following alternative was used:

A record was made of the conversation in which the child described a game he liked to play. Then he was asked:

Q: Is it right to play another way? (e.g., describe a change in the rules) A:
(if "Not") Q: Why not? A:
Q: Is it right for bigger boys and girls to play another way? A:
(if "Not") Q: Why not? A:
Q: Is it right for anybody to play another way? A:
(if "Yes") Q: Who can play another way? A:

The questions on rules of games came at the end of the interview (see Appendix A).

The shortcomings of our method are fairly evident. First and most serious, we allowed the subject to select his own game, because there was no one game that would be familiar to everyone. Consequently, some subjects chose games like basketball, where the rules are well codified and quite rigid, while others chose hide-and-seek or some local game, in which the rules are quite variable and change of rules is a common experience for boys and girls.

Another shortcoming lies in the fact that we asked the children about games of the white culture, which in most cases they learned at school and which often were unknown to their parents. Whereas the "white" games are traditional in white American culture and presumably are well integrated into the mores, we do not know how well integrated these same

games are into the present-day Indian cultures, nor can we be certain that the games have the same significance for children in the various Indian tribes.

Another difficulty lies in the phrasing of the inquiry. We found a number of responses in which a subject apparently contradicted himself. For example, it was not uncommon for a thirteen-year-old boy to say that smaller children cannot make new rules, children his own age and older boys and girls can make new rules, but rules cannot be changed. This seeming contradiction probably has two reasons behind it. First, the question "Can rules be changed?" may signify a general change applying everywhere, whereas the other question "Can boys and girls like you make new rules?" may signify a local, temporary change. A fifteen-year-old Sioux boy said, in response to the question whether rules can be changed, "Not in a regular game. They have rule books and have to go by them. But when us smaller boys play we shorten the field or something like that." Second, the question "Can rules be changed?" coming after three more specific questions about changes in rules, may act as a challenge to the subject, who thinks that his previous answers have not satisfied the administrator (usually a teacher), and he may change his answer.

The Groups Studied

Children between six and eighteen were tested in the Navaho, Sioux, Papago, Hopi, Zuni, and Zia tribes. These particular questions were not put to Midwest children, but Piaget's results on Swiss children had previously been confirmed, in a general way, by informal questioning of American white children.

With respect to the adequacy of the sampling of children in the various communities, the conclusions of chapter ii may be applied here. The children who answered with least completeness were those aged six to seven, many of whom did not yet know the games that were popular at school and did not think to mention their tribal games, in case they were familiar with such games.

At Shiprock, 70 of the 99 children responded to questions about rules of games. At Navaho Mountain, 53 of the 61 children were asked about rules of games. When the interviewer noted that so few of the subjects knew enough about white games to respond, she began asking about the rules of Navaho games and secured responses from 39 children on these tribal games. This was the only group that gave any responses concerning native games.

With the Sioux, as with the other groups, many of the younger children did not respond to the questions about rules of games. There were 81 responses from the 136 children. To increase the number of responses, 20 responses from children of another Sioux community, Wanblee, were added (Wanblee children were not included in other aspects of the Study).

Among the Papago, 75 out of 129 Topawa children on the roster answered questions on games, and 35 of 119 Hickiwan children; the latter area was not well represented because a number of the younger children had no experience with organized games.

Among the Hopi children the answers were quite complete—97 out of 109 children of Third Mesa and 72 out of 81 at First Mesa. However, there was one difficulty at Third Mesa: although it had not been intended that the interviewer should suggest a game to a child, one interviewer at Third Mesa prompted most of the children, when they had difficulty in describing a game they knew, to speak of the game of cat-and-mouse. This game is played by younger children with only rudimentary rules that are frequently modified by the players as they go along. It is quite different from the games with more rigid rules, such as baseball and basketball, which made up the great bulk of games mentioned. Accordingly, it was decided to omit the answers dealing with cat-and-mouse. This reduced the number of Third Mesa subjects to 58, which is still a good sample of the children over eight years of age.

At Zuni, 89 out of 103 in the sample answered questions concerning rules of games. At Zia, 47 out of 67 in the group answered these questions.

In general, it appears that, with the exception of children below eight or nine, a fairly representative sampling was obtained from the Hopi, Sioux, Zuni, and Zia groups, as well as from the Papago (Topawa) group.

Results

The "white" games which were mentioned by the Indian children were the same games as would be named by white children in American culture. Basketball or baseball was mentioned most frequently by every group. Football was also frequently mentioned, as were jacks and marbles. Other games mentioned more than once were: dodge ball, volleyball, hide-and-seek, run sheep run, London Bridge, New Orleans, ring-around-a-rosy, drop the handkerchief, farmer in the dell, cat-and-mouse, and checkers. These games are listed in Table 27 together with the frequencies of mention by various tribal groups.

TABLE 27

FREQUENCIES OF GAMES MENTIONED BY INDIAN CHILDREN

Game	Tribe																							
	Papago			Hopi						Zuni			Zia			Shiprock			Sioux			Total		
				Third Mesa			First Mesa																	
	M	F	T	M	F	T	M	F	T	M	F	T	M	F	T	M	F	T	M	F	T	M	F	T
Baseball	27	28	55	3	6	9	1	3	4	6	12	18	15	13	28	30	9	39	10	11	21	92	82	174
Basketball	9	7	16	15	1	16	12	2	14	30	11	41	0	0	0	2	4	6	25	11	36	93	36	129
Football	6	0	6	2	0	2	2	0	2	6	0	6	0	0	0	3	0	3	12	0	12	31	0	31
Soccer	0	0	0	0	0	0	5	12	17	0	0	0	0	0	0	0	0	0	0	0	0	5	12	17
Volleyball	0	2	2	0	2	2	0	6	6	0	4	4	0	0	0	0	0	0	0	0	0	0	14	14
Marbles	14	0	14	9	0	9	3	0	3	0	0	0	3	0	3	1	0	1	0	0	0	30	0	30
Cat-and-mouse	2	2	4	25	13	38	0	1	1	0	0	0	0	0	0	0	2	2	0	3	3	27	21	48
Jacks	0	4	4	0	3	3	0	4	4	1	1	2	0	0	0	0	15	15	0	10	10	1	37	38
Hopscotch	0	0	0	0	0	0	0	3	3	0	0	0	0	2	2	0	1	1	0	0	0	0	6	6
Hide-and-seek	0	0	0	0	4	4	0	1	1	0	0	0	0	1	1	0	0	0	2	1	3	2	7	9
Drop the handkerchief	0	3	3	3	0	3	0	0	0	0	0	0	0	0	0	0	0	0	1	5	6	4	8	12
Dodge ball	0	0	0	0	0	0	0	0	0	3	5	8	0	0	0	0	0	0	0	0	0	3	5	8
Checkers	0	0	0	0	1	1	2	3	5	1	1	2	0	0	0	1	1	2	0	2	2	4	8	12
Miscellaneous	1	4	5	1	2	3	1	3	4	1	1	2	5	2	7	0	2	2	6	19	25	15	33	48
Total	59	50	109	58	32	90	26	38	64	48	35	83	23	18	41	37	34	71	56	62	118	307	269	576

The results for the several tribes are summarized in Tables 28 and 29. Table 28 gives the percentages of "Yes" answers or answers saying that rules can be changed, for each sex and age group in each tribe and for each of the four questions that were answered. The higher the percentage of "Yes" answers, the greater is the latitude allowed by the subjects for change of rules. Table 28 also shows the total numbers of children answering each question. Table 29 summarizes the answers to the questions "Who made this rule first?" and "Who can change the rules?"

Table 28 contains responses from more children than does Table 29. The reason for this is that not every child answered every question. This was due mainly to the fact that the child's answer of "No" to the question "Can the rules be changed?" precluded his answering the question "Who can change the rules?" Similarly, his answer that he did not know a rule of a game precluded his answering the question "Who made the rule first?" Also some questions were occasionally omitted by the interviewers.

In Tables 27, 28, and 29, data from the three Sioux communities have been grouped together, and the data from the two Papago communities have been grouped together. The original intention had been to look for differences between communities within the same tribe--communities which had experienced different degrees of assimilation into the white culture. But, as has already been described, the testing in the less acculturated communities tended to select out the children who were in school and who had the most contact with white culture. Hence, whatever differences actually existed between the more and the less acculturated communities were obscured by our method of sampling. It did not seem justifiable, for this reason, to present the data for single communities of Sioux and Papago. Furthermore, the numbers of subjects in some of the communities were too small to allow the investigators to draw conclusions. The two Hopi groups were left separate, since they were numerous enough to be treated separately. The Navaho Mountain group was kept separate from the Shiprock group, because, as has already been described, Navaho Mountain children gave responses dealing with traditional Navaho, rather than "white," games. Results on the Navaho will be discussed later.

Sex Differences

It is difficult to draw conclusions from these data concerning sex differences, because the number of subjects in each group is relatively

TABLE 28

ATTITUDES TOWARD RULES OF GAMES: CAN RULES BE CHANGED?

Yes		Papago M	Papago F	Papago T	Hopi Third Mesa M	Hopi Third Mesa F	Hopi Third Mesa T	Hopi First Mesa M	Hopi First Mesa F	Hopi First Mesa T	Zuni M	Zuni F	Zuni T	Zia M	Zia F	Zia T	Navaho Shiprock M	Navaho Shiprock F	Navaho Shiprock T	Sioux M	Sioux F	Sioux T
Age Group 6-7																						
Can rules be changed by:																						
Younger children?	Per cent	25	0	20	--	--	--	33	--	33	0	50	40	--	--	--	--	67	67	0	--	0
	Total N	4	1	5	--	--	--	3	0	3	1	4	5	0	0	0	0	3	3	1	0	1
Same age?	Per cent	64	86	72	--	--	--	43	33	36	0	17	9	0	25	13	--	75	75	57	0	36
	Total N	11	7	18	--	--	--	7	4	11	5	6	11	4	4	8	0	4	4	7	4	11
Older children?	Per cent	67	88	75	--	--	--	83	100	90	20	0	9	25	25	25	--	100	100	60	75	67
	Total N	12	8	20	--	--	--	6	4	10	5	6	11	4	4	8	0	4	4	5	4	9
Can rules be changed?	Per cent	58	71	63	--	--	--	71	67	70	40	17	28	25	25	25	--	100	100	60	25	45
	Total N	12	7	19	--	--	--	7	3	10	5	6	11	4	4	8	0	3	3	5	4	9
Age Group 8-10																						
Can rules be changed by:																						
Younger children?	Per cent	11	0	7	0	100	50	17	20	18	0	0	0	33	50	42	38	25	33	29	100	38
	Total N	9	5	14	1	1	2	6	5	11	11	7	18	6	6	12	8	4	12	7	1	8
Same age?	Per cent	40	33	37	28	50	33	60	42	50	25	36	30	30	50	38	83	56	71	31	37	34
	Total N	20	15	35	7	2	9	10	12	22	12	11	23	10	6	16	12	9	21	16	19	35
Older children?	Per cent	74	53	65	28	50	33	67	58	62	43	64	52	50	43	47	91	60	77	71	55	62
	Total N	19	15	34	7	2	9	9	12	21	12	11	23	10	7	17	11	10	21	17	20	37
Can rules be changed?	Per cent	50	27	40	43	50	44	56	67	62	43	54	48	50	71	59	78	80	79	60	55	57
	Total N	20	15	35	7	2	9	9	11	21	12	11	23	10	7	17	9	10	19	15	20	35

TABLE 28 — Continued

Yes	Papago M	Papago F	Papago T	Hopi Third Mesa M	Hopi Third Mesa F	Hopi Third Mesa T	Hopi First Mesa M	Hopi First Mesa F	Hopi First Mesa T	Zuni M	Zuni F	Zuni T	Zia M	Zia F	Zia T	Navaho Shiprock M	Navaho Shiprock F	Navaho Shiprock T	Sioux M	Sioux F	Sioux T
Age Group 11-13																					
Can rules be changed by:																					
Younger children? Per cent	0	0	0	0	50	33	40	8	16	0	13	8	33	0	20	0	0	0	18	45	32
Total N	3	4	7	2	4	6	5	14	19	11	15	26	6	4	10	8	3	11	11	11	22
Same age? Per cent	40	21	31	50	56	53	60	67	65	8	53	33	29	75	45	63	50	59	36	41	39
Total N	15	14	29	10	9	19	5	12	17	12	15	27	7	4	11	19	10	29	14	17	31
Older children? Per cent	40	33	37	70	56	63	100	92	94	67	67	67	71	75	73	95	90	93	64	76	71
Total N	15	12	27	10	9	19	5	13	18	12	15	27	7	4	11	19	10	29	14	17	31
Can rules be changed? Per cent	53	15	36	70	44	57	60	77	72	67	38	52	71	75	73	65	80	70	21	50	37
Total N	15	13	28	10	9	19	5	13	18	12	13	25	7	4	11	17	10	27	14	16	30
Age Group 14-18																					
Can rules be changed by:																					
Younger children? Per cent	23	0	11	22	30	27	14	9	11	25	25	25	40	16	27	50	29	33	32	8	20
Total N	13	15	28	9	10	19	7	11	18	20	8	28	5	6	11	2	7	9	25	25	50
Same age? Per cent	50	37	43	69	45	59	50	61	57	45	63	50	100	50	73	50	70	63	32	52	42
Total N	18	19	37	13	11	24	8	13	21	20	8	28	5	6	11	6	10	6	25	25	50
Older children? Per cent	65	68	67	93	69	78	75	77	76	75	75	75	100	84	91	83	80	81	67	72	70
Total N	17	19	36	13	13	26	8	13	21	20	8	28	5	6	11	6	10	16	24	25	49
Can rules be changed? Per cent	65	22	43	86	62	74	50	46	48	35	50	39	80	67	73	50	50	50	54	59	57
Total N	17	18	35	14	13	27	8	13	21	20	8	28	5	6	11	6	10	16	26	27	53

TABLE 29

ATTITUDES TOWARD RULES OF GAMES: WHO MAKES THE RULES? (PERCENTAGES)

	Papago	Hopi Third Mesa	Hopi First Mesa	Zuni	Zia	Navaho Mt.	Navaho Shiprock	Sioux
Who made rule first?								
Players, boys and girls	6	13	10	13	18	5	0	20
Big boys and girls	3	0	10	6	14	20	13	0
Teacher, coach, referee, umpire	55	16	39	57	11	0	29	39
White people	6	31	13	18	29	75	48	2
Inventor of the game	17	31	35	0	4	0	0	34
Miscellaneous	14	9	18	6	25	0	10	5
Total no. responses	36	32	39	62	28	20	31	44
Who can change rules?								
Players, boys and girls	43	61	41	25	47	47	72	54
Big boys and girls	24	2	29	43	11	24	17	15
Teacher, coach, referee, umpire	12	20	15	32	26	12	2	31
White people	5	0	2	0	0	12	6	0
Men, grown-ups	5	11	2	0	11	0	0	0
Miscellaneous	12	6	10	0	5	6	2	0
Total no. responses	42	46	41	28	19	17	47	52

small. There appear to be relatively few systematic sex differences, except perhaps in the case of the Papago, where the boys over ten give consistently more "Yes" responses than do the girls. The Papago girls over ten were definitely more "heteronomous" in their attitudes than were the boys.

Age Trends

Generally speaking, older children are given more latitude than younger ones in changing rules. That is, at all ages, the subjects tend to expect older children to be more free to change rules than younger children.

But this trend is only partially supported when the question is phrased, "Can the rules be changed by children of your own age?" To this question, responses from the Pueblo groups—Hopi, Zuni, and Zia—show that the older age groups allow themselves more latitude than the younger age groups. The Papago and the Sioux fail to show such an age change, the several age groups remaining practically constant with about 35 per cent saying that children of their own age can change the rules. The Shiprock group, which gives more latitude to all ages, also fails to show the age trend found in the Pueblo groups.[2]

There are no strictly comparable data for white children, either from Piaget's Swiss group or from American groups. However, Piaget's findings in his questions about the game of marbles would lead one to expect that, by the age of twelve, practically all his subjects would have said that it was all right to change the rules and that people of their own age could change the rules. Among the Indian groups, only Shiprock approaches this level of freedom or autonomy at the ages of ten to thirteen. The conclusion might therefore be drawn that the other Indian tribes all showed a slower development toward moral autonomy than did Piaget's children.

From the data on Indian children, it appears that attitudes toward rules of "white" games do not change from heteronomous to autonomous

2. The statistical reliability of these statements about age trends were confirmed by a chi-square test. However, the difference between any two age groups is often unreliable, owing to the small numbers in a given tribal age group. In general, in this chapter the trends which are pointed out are reliable, although few of the specific differences which make up these trends are separately reliable.

so early or so consistently as they probably do in modern white societies. In the three Pueblo tribes there appears to be a developmental sequence generally similar to, but slower than, the sequence for white children. In the Papago and Sioux groups, about half the children, even at the ages of fourteen to eighteen, do not believe that they or anybody else can change the rules.

Intertribal Differences

In order to compare the several tribal groups, the data of Table 28 have been treated so as to abstract therefrom an "order of constraint," ranging from groups with relatively low moral constraint (high degree of latitude with reference to change of rules) to groups with relatively high moral constraint (low degree of latitude with reference to change of rules). This was done by ranking the groups in eight different ways. For example, the responses given by the age group five to seven on all four questions were averaged, and the tribes were arranged in order of percentage of "Yes" responses given by this age group. As can be seen from Table 28, Shiprock subjects in this age group gave the greatest proportion of "Yes" responses, and Zuni subjects the smallest proportion. Hence Shiprock is given an order number of 1, and Zuni is given an order number of 7. This was repeated for each age group and resulted in four different rankings of the tribal groups.

Then the answers of all age groups within a tribe given in response to the first question were averaged, and the tribes were ranked on this basis. This was done for each of the four questions, which resulted in four more rankings.

Finally, the eight order numbers for each group were added and a composite order number derived. The order numbers are quite stable and indicate that there is a reliable set of differences between the several tribal groups. These data are shown in Table 30.

Zuni is consistently a group with relatively high moral constraint (low degree of latitude in changing rules). Papago and Sioux are next in order, followed by Zia and the two Hopi groups. The two Hopi groups are close together and might well be combined into a single group. The Navaho Shiprock group is at the low-constraint (high degree of latitude) end of the scale and is, therefore, most like a "modern" group.

This order of constraint for the various Indian groups is not the same as their order of assimilation of white culture. Sioux are probably

TABLE 30

ORDER OF MORAL CONSTRAINT AMONG INDIAN GROUPS[a]

	Tribe						
		Hopi					
	Papago	Third Mesa	First Mesa	Zuni	Zia	Shiprock	Sioux
Average on all four questions by age group:							
6-7	2.5	--	2.5	7	6	1	5
8-10	6	5	2.5	7	4	1	2.5
11-13	7	4	1	6	3	2	5
14-18	7	2	4	5	1	3	6
Average of all age groups:							
Can rules be changed by:							
Younger children?	7	1	5	6	2	4	3
Same age?	4	3	2	7	5	1	6
Older children?	4	5	2	7	6	1	3
Can rules be changed?	6	4	2	7	3	1	5
Total	43.5	24	21	52	30	14	35.5
Composite order no.	6	3	2	7	4	1	5

a. Low order number means low constraint.

more assimilated to white culture than any of the other groups, although Shiprock would probably come second.

Special consideration of each tribal group, taking into consideration its own particular pattern of games and its own pattern of teaching and learning the games, would probably aid in the interpretation of these results. For example, it has been reported by Dr. Florence Hawley Ellis, the anthropologist who studied the Zia, that the Zia boys have made up their own ball-game rules and that they teach these rules to younger children. For this test the Zia children mentioned baseball most of the time, and it is possible that their answers reflect their particular experience with this game, where there is a higher degree of latitude in changing the rules than perhaps is the case with other games. This might account for the fact that in these data Zia occupies a midway position on order of constraint, whereas other types of data show Zia to be a community of relatively high moral constraint.

Native Navaho Games

The Navaho Mountain subjects mentioned three traditional games that are commonly played in that region.[3] In the "moccasin game," one team hides a turquoise in one of a pair of moccasins, and the opposing team tries to guess which moccasin holds the turquoise. "Forty stones," "stick-dice," "three sticks," or "bounding sticks" is a game with three sticks for dice, something like the game of parcheesi as played by white children. While it is considered a woman's game, it is played by both sexes. "Thirteen chips" is played with thirteen chips with designs on only one side. The chips are thrown and, in order to count, must fall between two designated lines and must fall design side up. All three are gambling games, usually played by adults; but children have plenty of opportunity to watch and to play among themselves. The results of the inquiry concerning Navaho games are shown in Table 31.

The Navaho Mountain children were practically unanimous in saying that the rules of the native games cannot be changed. They spoke very freely and definitely on this subject: "the rules never change," "the holy people taught us to play this way," "it would not be right to play

3. For descriptions of Navaho games see Stewart Culin, "Games of the North American Indians," Annual Report of the Bureau of American Ethnology, XXIV (Washington, D.C., 1902-3), pp. 3-809.

TABLE 31

ATTITUDES OF NAVAHO MOUNTAIN CHILDREN TOWARD RULES OF NAVAHO AND OF "WHITE" GAMES

Can rules be changed by:		Age Group			
		Six to Eleven		Twelve to Eighteen	
		Navaho Games	"White" Games	Navaho Games	"White" Games
Younger children?	Yes	1	6	3	8
	No	12	2	22	6
Same age?	Yes	0	5	0	7
	No	13	3	23	7
Older children?	Yes	0	7	0	8
	No	14	2	24	6
Can rules be changed?	Yes	0	7	1	10
	No	14	3	24	3

any other way," "ancient ones taught the right way," " games are very sacred—they are not to be changed," " the animals played that way—the holy people taught them."

These remarks all refer to legends concerning the origins of the games—legends which are well known to the children.[4] The Navaho games were taught to the Dineh (Navaho people) by their ancient supernatural predecessors and are always played the same way. In response to the question, "Who made the rules first?" the answer was usually, "the holy people," though occasionally it was "the animals," often with the explanation that the holy people taught the animals and the animals taught the Navaho.

The only exceptions were made in favor of young children, because they were too young to know better. "Small children aren't like us. They have to change rules to suit their size" (remark made by a girl aged

4. For a report on the mythology connected with Navaho games see Washington Matthews, Navaho Legends ("Memoirs of the American Folk-Lore Society," Vol. V [Boston: Houghton Mifflin Co., 1897]), pp. 83, 240. The versions of the myths that are current in the Navaho Mountain area are reported by Lisbeth Eubank, "Legends of Three Navaho Games," El Palacio (Santa Fe: New Mexico Museum, 1945), LII, No. 7, 138-40.

thirteen). "They [little children] have to play as they can—they are not big enough to play it right, so they change the rules to suit themselves" (remark made by a boy aged eight). The younger children are not considered real players. Their attempts to play at the games do not constitute a real change of rules, and consequently the rules are not thought of as being changed when the younger children play to suit themselves.

Table 31 also contains the answers of some of these same Navaho Mountain children to questions concerning the rules of "white" games. They answered much as the Shiprock Navaho did, giving relatively wide latitude to children in changing rules, and especially to younger children. The contrasting attitudes maintained by a given individual toward the two sets of games are illustrated by the answer of an eighteen-year-old boy who had gone away from Navaho Mountain to an Indian boarding school and who had had a relatively large degree of contact with white culture. He speaks about football and says that the "coaches or head people" get together and change the rules. Concerning Navaho games he says that rules cannot be changed "because the holy people taught us them. It is not right to change them."

The games of the white culture are learned in school from teachers or from older children. The Indian children have the usual experience of white children with respect to the rules of these games. Rules are changed or adapted to local conditions: size of play space, type of equipment, and so forth.

The games of the native culture are not taught to children, in the sense that actual instruction takes place, but are rather observed until prospective players feel sufficiently sure of their skill and grow audacious enough to try. The games are an integral part of the culture of the adult society. The native games are allied with the religious beliefs and the world view of the Navaho. Every game has its legendary origin, told over and over on winter nights around the fire.

There is evidence that the traditional games, in addition to providing amusement and excitement, have an aspect of the supernatural associated with them. Aberle[5] asked a number of Navaho adults in another part of the reservation to tell him about the game of stick-dice. He encountered

5. David F. Aberle, "Mythology of the Navaho Game Stick-Dice," Journal of American Folk-Lore, LV (1942), 144-54.

great resistance on their part to telling rules of the game or to telling myths about its origin. They expressed fear of supernatural punishment for giving away these tribal secrets. What he did find out suggests that successful cheating in the game may give rise to the suspicion that the cheater is a witch. This might help to explain the rigidity of attitudes about obeying the rules, since witchcraft is much feared and abhorred.

Discussion

In the responses of Navaho Mountain youth toward the questions about rules of games we see an illustration of Piaget's theory of the development of a tight, constraining moral view in primitive societies as shown by their responses concerning native games. At the same time, these young people also approach the attitudes of children of a "modern" culture when they are dealing with "modern" games. Perhaps we see in the Navaho Mountain data the side-by-side development of two kinds of morality in the child, one coming from his tribal culture and the other coming from his contact, largely through the school, with white culture.

The tribal morality is a heteronomous morality of constraint, suited to life in a folk society. There is very little reason for changing the rules of life. The old rules, coming from supernatural beings, are the best rules and may not be changed. This morality is the central pillar of life for a member of the Navaho Mountain society.

On the fringe of his life is another kind of morality, the autonomous morality of agreement of the white teacher and the white man's school. Here the rules of life are not sacred. They may be altered by people who know enough or are old enough. If the rules cause trouble enough, people can get together and make new rules.

There is no clash between the two moralities as long as the influence of the white culture is restricted to the periphery of life through school games, style of dress, and so on. But when the white culture encroaches on the core of life and begins, for example, to suggest that there are new rules for getting cured of sickness, rules which work better than the sacred tribal rules, we may expect the individual to show signs of inner conflict.

There may be one set of mores and one kind of morality for the tribal life of the Navaho Mountain individual, and another set of mores and kind of morality for that part of his life which is lived in the white culture.

Conclusions

Nowhere among the Indian groups in this Study do we see the steady growth from moral heteronomy to moral autonomy that we expect in children of a modern society. Among the Hopi, Zuni, and Zia children there is a growth in this direction, but the age group over fourteen are at about the stage where we would expect ten-year-olds to be in a modern society. And there is doubt that these adolescents will progress further toward autonomous attitudes toward rules of games.

Among the Papago, Navaho, and Sioux children there is no appreciable change with age in attitude toward rules of games. The majority of the Papago and Sioux children at all ages show attitudes of heteronomy or moral constraint. The Shiprock children are more autonomous in their attitudes than those of the other tribes at the younger ages but do not increase in autonomy as they grow older.

Thus, in a partial sense, Piaget's hypotheses about children of primitive societies are borne out. But none of these children live in a truly "primitive" society. They are all influenced to some degree by the surrounding modern culture, and they are reporting their attitudes toward rules of games that come from the modern culture.

The only reasonably adequate test of Piaget's hypotheses that we have is in the data on native games from Navaho Mountain children, where Piaget's predictions are verified.

Thus we may perhaps regard the data on attitudes of Indian children toward rules of "white" games as indicating a partial acculturation. They have incompletely adopted the attitudes of the children of the dominant white culture toward rules of games in that culture. At the same time, they seem to be able (if we may generalize from the case of Navaho Mountain) to hold completely heteronomous attitudes toward the rules that are imbedded in their own tribal cultures.

CHAPTER VI

BELIEF IN IMMANENT JUSTICE AND ANIMISM

In every society the child learns that punishment accompanies wrongdoing. Punishment may take the form of spanking, scolding, or a cold and loveless attitude; in any case it is an unpleasant experience which helps the child define a certain act or situation as bad. As the child grows up, his definition of good and bad changes and develops, as does his notion of the relations between punishment and badness. He develops a concept of justice--a concept of how goodness is rewarded and badness is punished.

A child's concept of justice develops partly as a result of certain experiences universal in the life of all children--experiences which accompany growth in size, strength, and intelligence. At the same time, the child's concept of justice depends partly upon the particular culture in which he grows—upon the world view held by the culture and upon its methods of child-training. It is obvious that a society which believes that a spirit world governs the fortunes of men will have a different theory of justice than will a society which does not believe in the existence of supernatural beings. It is also clear that a society in which adult authority is impressed sternly upon children will teach a different theory of justice and punishment than a society in which children have maximum freedom from adult domination.

According to Piaget's theory of moral development, all children grow up in an atmosphere of moral constraint, in which they think of punishment as coming from all-powerful and all-knowing sources. These sources may be parents or other people in authority, or they may be supernatural forces. The child does not at first make the distinction betwee the natural and the supernatural or the living and the nonliving.

In a modern society the child's "moral realism" (the belief that morality is imposed by an unchangeable and unchallengeable external set of moral forces) gradually fades away as he experiences social and moral relations with other children where his own voice counts; as his reasoning power increases; and as he is subjected to the moral theory of adults around him. He learns a theory of co-operative morality--

of justice that works through reasonable human beings; of punishment that depends on wrongdoing being discovered and judged in relation to the intentions of the wrongdoer (except, of course, for the punishment that comes from the individual conscience).

Piaget's moral theory has been described in another context in the preceding chapter. He suggests that the child's moral development will take a different course in a "primitive" society. Such a society will make children more, rather than less, rigid in their moral theory as they grow older and will exercise more, rather than less, moral constraint on them. If this society has a world view which includes a supernatural power that watches over men and rewards and punishes their actions, then belief in immanent justice will probably be as strong in older children as in younger ones, or even stronger. (Belief in immanent justice is the belief that there is a power in the world which punishes people for wrongdoing through its influence over "natural" things and events. The phrase "immanent punishment" is used by some writers instead of "immanent justice."

To sum up, Piaget's theory would lead us to expect that belief in immanent justice will decrease as children grow older in a modern society and will remain unchanged or (perhaps even increase) as children grow older in a primitive society. What may we expect of children's beliefs in these Indian societies, all of which are influenced by modern American culture and all of which have had cultural beliefs in the past which were favorable to a belief in immanent justice?

Procedures

In order to learn something about the development of moral ideas among the Indian children, we told them a story about wrongdoing and punishment and asked them to comment on it. The story was similar to one that was used by Piaget[1] with Swiss children and to variations used by Lerner[2] with white American children and by Dennis[3] with Hopi children. Our form of the story was as follows:

1. Jean Piaget, The Moral Judgment of the Child (New York: Harcourt, Brace & Co., 1932), p. 250.

2. Eugene Lerner, Constraint Areas and the Moral Judgment of Children (Menasha, Wis.: Banta Publishing Co., 1937), chap. vii.

3. Wayne Dennis, "Animism and Related Tendencies in Hopi Children," Journal of Abnormal and Social Psychology, XXXVIII (January, 1943), 21-36.

Story: This is a story about two boys. These two boys, named Jack and Paul, were out walking, and they came to a melon field. Each of them stole a melon and ran off to eat it. But the owner of the field saw them and ran after them. He caught Jack and punished him, but Paul got away. The same afternoon, Paul was chopping some wood, and the ax slipped and cut his foot.

Questions:

A. Why do you think Paul's foot was cut?
B. If Paul did not steal the melon, would he cut his foot?
C. Did the ax know that he stole the melon?[4]

This story appears second in the test booklet. The teachers who gave this test did not report any difficulty with it, except that some of the children could not see any connection between the melon-stealing and the ax slipping and were uncertain as to whether they had caught the point of the story. For those who did not believe in immanent justice, this might pose a problem. Dr. Ellis, the anthropologist who was studying the Zia children, reported the teachers there as feeling that the Zia children were uncertain in their answers. This type of comment was not made to us by any of the people who administered the test, although there were enough contradictory answers on the children's protocols to suggest that at least a few of the children were uncertain about their interpretations of the situation.

Nearly all the children on the selected lists were tested with this story, except for the western Papago at Hickiwan, where only 54 out of 119 were tested (for the reasons given in chap. ii). Thus the conclusions about the adequacy of the sampling which are drawn in chapter ii apply to this part of the Study. The actual numbers who were tested are reported in Table 32.

Scoring the Test

Answers to three questions were scored, as follows:

4. It was thought that stealing melons would have about the same moral significance to children of all the Indian tribes. It would be a fairly common event in the lives of young people, yet one that is definitely disapproved by the adults and one that causes adults a good deal of concern, since melons are highly valued and not very plentiful. In the story used by Dennis, the boys steal fruit from an orchard. This would have been appropriate with the Hopi, but perhaps not for the Papago and Navaho. Dennis, Lerner, and Piaget all had the boys come to a bridge on the way home, a bridge which broke and let the boys fall through. We changed this item because we felt that bridges were not common enough in the experience of the Southwest Indians. On the other hand, chopping wood is a common experience, and the danger that the ax may slip and cut one's foot is a familiar one.

Question A--"Why do you think that Paul's foot was cut?" Many answers were clearly based upon belief in immanent justice, such as "because he stole the melon," "it was his punishment"; others were naturalistic, as "the ax slipped," "he was careless"; and sometimes the answer was "I don't know." The answer was scored as positive for immanent justice only if it was clearly so.

Question B--"If Paul did not steal the melon, would he cut his foot?" If the answer was "No," it was scored as positive for immanent justice. If the answer was "Yes" or "Maybe," it was scored negative for immanent justice. Such answers as "I don't know" were scored as uncertain. To check on the answer to question B, a further question was asked, "Yes, what?" or "No, what?" The purpose of this question was to make sure that the subject had not been confused by the conditional clause stated in the negative form--"If he did not steal the melon, would he cut his foot?" In a few cases, such mistakes were brought to light in this way, and the score on question B was corrected.

Question C--"Did the ax know that Paul stole the melon?" If the question was answered "Yes," it was scored positive for animism. Most answers were "Yes" or "No." There were a few qualified answers, such as "His arm knew," or "He was thinking about what he had done and was careless." These were scored negative for animism. The question of animism will be discussed in the latter part of this chapter.

Reliability of the Test and the Problem of Language

The question of the reliability of the answers to this test was studied in three ways: by using an inquiry at the end of the test interview, by repeating the test in the native language, and by comparing the answers to questions A and B.

The Inquiry

The inquiry was used with a number of Hopi and Navaho subjects. At the close of the test battery, they were asked, "Do you remember the story about the boy who cut his foot? Now suppose that the boy stayed home all day and worked around the house and did not steal any melons. Then, he went out to chop some wood. Would he cut his foot?" This was, in effect, a repetition of question B of the test, and the answers to the inquiry can be compared with the answers to question B.

This inquiry was conducted with fifteen Hopi subjects at Third

Mesa who took the test in their native language. Fourteen of them repeated the answers they had given to question B of the story, and one girl, aged fourteen, changed her answer.

The same inquiry was made of twenty-four Navaho subjects of varying ages at Shiprock, who took the test in English or in Navaho, depending on their familiarity with English. Fifteen of the twenty-four repeated their earlier answers, and nine changed their answers. Seven of the nine changed their answers so as to say that the boy might have cut his foot anyway. Since the Shiprock group showed the least belief in immanent justice of all the groups studied, it is conceivable that a number of children were wavering in their belief and that the repetition of the question may have seemed enough of a challenge, coming from a teacher, to make them change their stand. In any case, there was very little evidence that the subjects were confused by the form of the questions.

Repeating the Test

The test was given first in English and a month or more later in the native language to groups of all ages of Hopi (Third Mesa) and Papago (Topawa). At Third Mesa, out of fourteen test-retests, there were twelve agreements, one disagreement, and one uncertain (neither definite agreement nor disagreement) on question A. At Topawa, out of seventeen test-retests, there were ten agreements, two disagreements, and five uncertain on question A. (The uncertain responses were failures to respond to the question during the testing in the native language.) On question B there was less agreement. At Third Mesa there were eight agreements and six disagreements; at Topawa, nine agreements, six disagreements, and two uncertain. On question C (animism), there was also considerable disagreement. At Third Mesa there were nine agreements, four disagreements, and one uncertain; at Topawa, nine agreements and eight disagreements. At Topawa the tendency was to give more positive responses on immanent justice and animism when the test was given in the native language.

We also conducted an experiment at Third Mesa to test the effect of varying the administrator while using the native language. Two Hopi Indian teachers, using the Hopi language, each tested the same fifteen subjects ranging in age from six to eighteen. One of the Hopi teachers used her own translation of the test, and the other used a translation

made by a linguist in the Indian Service (Dr. Edward Kennard). The tests were given about six months apart. On all three questions the two testers got identical group results. That is, they got the same numbers of positive and negative answers. However, there was some variation among individual children: child X would answer positively to one tester and negatively to the other, while child Y would reverse the process, thus keeping the total numbers the same. (This happened with two children on questions A and B and with four children on question C.)

Comparing Questions A and B

Another way of checking the reliability of the responses on immanent justice consists in comparing the answers to questions A and B. We find that question A draws a fairly high proportion of immanent-justice responses in some groups and a low proportion in others. A significantly higher proportion of immanent-justice responses is obtained on question B at First Mesa, Shiprock, and Zuni (twelve to eighteen years). But a significantly lower proportion of immanent-justice responses is obtained on question B at Kyle, Pine Ridge (twelve to eighteen), and Zia (six to eleven). How can this result be accounted for? One possible reason is that some subjects may have become confused by the form of the question and answered "Yes" when they meant "No." There is little reason to expect this, except possibly at Zia and Topawa among the younger children. The older children at Pine Ridge, Kyle, and Third Mesa gave more immanent-justice responses on question A than on question B, but they are the ones with relatively good command of English.

Another possibility is that some of the subjects felt that they were being challenged by the tester in question B and consequently hesitated to repeat the immanent-justice response they had given to question A. If this actually happened, it would be best to take the higher of the two proportions as the correct one; that is, to use the proportion of immanent-justice responses to question A if that is the higher, and to use the proportion of immanent-justice responses to question B if that is the higher.

We may summarize the consideration of the question of reliability of the test by saying that the Indian children's answers are stable, on the average, although there is a good deal of individual variation--that is, an individual child will sometimes change his answers when the test is repeated.[5] But the individuals change in both directions to about an

5. See chap. ix, p. 204, for a discussion of the possible significance of such variations.

equal extent, so that the results for a group are stable and reliable enough for us to base generalizations on group averages.

Results on Immanent Justice

The results on questions A and B are given in Table 32, for the age groups six through eleven and twelve through eighteen. For groups of the size with which we are dealing, a difference between two groups must be at least 15 per cent to be statistically reliable. Hence it will be seen that, in general, differences among the tribal groups are not reliable, except for Shiprock, which is definitely below the others.

As for age differences, with the exception of Shiprock, the proportion believing in immanent justice is, for ages twelve to eighteen, of the order of 85 per cent. At the younger ages the proportion believing in immanent justice tends to be smaller.

To get a rank order, the tribal groups were arranged in order of the proportion believing in immanent justice, using for each group the response on question A or question B, whichever was higher. A composite rank for each group was obtained by averaging the ranks for the two age levels.

The rank order, with the group showing the least belief in immanent justice first, is as follows: Navaho, Hopi First Mesa, Zia, Papago, Hopi Third Mesa, Zuni, Sioux, Navaho Mountain.[6] (The two Papago and the two Sioux groups are combined because they fall together in the rank order.)

Since the differences between any two groups in Table 32 are seldom reliable, we are not justified in placing a great deal of reliance upon the rank order. Nevertheless, when based upon the two age levels combined for each tribal group, the ranking becomes reliable enough to permit distinctions between the top, middle, and bottom ranks, at least.

This rank order might be called an order of "moral constraint" or "moral rigidity" and may be compared with the rank order obtained from the study of attitudes toward rules of games.[7]

6. In computing the rank order, there might be an advantage in taking the average of the percentages on questions A and B rather than the higher of the two percentages. If this had been done, the rank order would have been changed by an exchange of places between Papago and Sioux.

7. This point is discussed in chap. viii, pp. 193-94.

TABLE 32[a]

BELIEF IN IMMANENT JUSTICE AMONG INDIAN CHILDREN: PERCENTAGES OF RESPONSES INDICATING BELIEF IN IMMANENT JUSTICE

Group	Ages Six to Eleven			Ages Twelve to Eighteen		
	No. Responding	QA	QB	No. Responding	QA	QB
Papago						
Topawa	46	80	50	49	87	83[b]
Hickiwan	31	60	71	23	90[b]	91[b]
Hopi						
Third Mesa	51	69	82	48	90[b]	77
First Mesa	40	45	60	31	66[b]	84[b]
Zuni	41	73	82	51	68	88
Zia	31	67	48	17	76	88[b]
Navaho						
Navaho Mountain	23	91	86	29	97	86
Shiprock	53	14	62	36	24	58
Sioux						
Pine Ridge	23	90	92	15	93	67
Kyle	39	78	61	46	100[b]	89[b]

a. QA - "Why do you think Paul's foot was cut?"
QB - "If Paul did not steal the melon, would he cut his foot?"
b. Statistically reliable increase with age.

Discussion

Since most of the Indian groups show either an increase or no change with age in their belief in immanent justice, it is clear that Piaget's theory of belief in immanent justice in a primitive society is borne out by these data.[8]

8. To clarify the difference between these Indian children and children of a "modern" society: Piaget and his students found, for a group of 167 Swiss children, the following percentages of belief in immanent justice (one-fifth of the answers were uncertain):

Age	6	7-8	9-10	11-12
Per cent	86	73	54	39

All the Indian groups behaved more like what we should expect of a primitive society, then, with an actual increase of belief in immanent justice or at least no decrease with age. Even Shiprock, although at the bottom of the rank order in terms of degree of belief, shows a higher

Dennis[9] secured some evidence on belief in immanent justice from Hopi children aged twelve to seventeen at First and Third Mesas about a year before our tests were given. In his story a bridge broke under two boys who were coming home after stealing fruit. He asked "Now tell me, why did the bridge break?" He next asked "Did the bridge know that the boys had been stealing?" If a subject gave a response to the first question suggesting belief in immanent justice and answered the second question by saying that the bridge knew, he was then asked, "Is that why the bridge broke?" If the answer to this question was "Yes," his responses were scored as positive. If his answers appeared to contradict each other, he was finally asked "Now tell me, what do you really believe? Why did the bridge break?" If he answered this question with a statement suggesting immanent justice, his response was classified as positive. Thus it was possible for a subject to be scored as believing in immanent justice, though he said that the bridge did not know that the boys had been stealing. Dennis secured the following results:[10]

	Age		
	12-13	14-15	16-17
Number in group	44	32	22
Per cent of I.-J. responses	64	47	9

We did not get the decrease of belief in immanent justice between ages twelve and seventeen which Dennis found. Thus our results on the Hopi are somewhat at variance with those of Dennis. Our results on the Hopi are, however, consistent with our results for the other Indian groups, none of which showed any marked decrease of belief in immanent justice within the age range twelve to eighteen.

It is a striking fact that degree of acculturation is not reflected in Table 32. If it were, we should expect to find the Sioux, whose accultu-

degree of belief than Piaget's Swiss children at the older ages and shows no decrease with age.

9. Op. cit.

10. It should be noted that if a child appeared to contradict himself by giving one naturalistic and one immanent-justice answer to the two questions as to why the bridge broke, he was finally asked — "What do you really believe? Why did the bridge break?" In Dennis' 98 sets of responses, there were 25 children who gave contradictory answers to the two questions about why the bridge broke, and their answers were classi-

ration has proceeded furthest, to show the least belief in immanent justice. The only evidence in favor of an acculturation hypothesis is furnished by the two Navaho groups, which are at the two extremes of the rank order. Still, the relatively acculturated Shiprock group does not show a decrease of belief in immanent justice with age, which we would find in a modern culture.

As a further test of the hypothesis that the Indian groups with more contact with white culture would show less belief in immanent justice, we studied the Hopi Third Mesa results by dividing the subjects into three groups with differing degrees of acculturation, as follows:

Group A — residents of Old Oraibi, all of whom are conservative of tribal ways; also the residents of New Oraibi who are conservative in following the Hopi way and also conservative economically in their farming and housekeeping methods.

Group B — dwellers in New Oraibi who are progressive in farming and housekeeping methods. Some of them are conservative of the tribal ways, and some are not.

Group C — residents of New Oraibi who are under christian influence, either active church members or only nominally Christian.

The results on immanent justice and animism for these groups are as follows:

	Group		
	A	B	C
Per cent of immanent-justice responses	76	85	84
Per cent of animistic responses	70	74	64

These three groups are hardly distinguishable. Other groupings of the Third Mesa subjects also failed to show differences related to acculturation.

We are brought to the conclusion that an explanation of these results is impossible if we try to base it simply upon the concept of "primitive" cultures subject to varying degrees of influence from a modern culture. Rather,

fied on the basis of this last question. According to our scoring, however, all these 25 would have been classified as believing in immanent justice under either question A or question B of our story. If we should add these 25 to Dennis' figures, his percentages would still fall below ours for the age group twelve to eighteen.

we must look for total environmental factors within each group of Indians and of whites to explain the results given by that particular group. Shiprock differs from Navaho Mountain, First Mesa from Third Mesa, Kyle from Pine Ridge; and the differences are not simply due to different degrees of contact with white culture.

Dr. Laura Thompson has studied these findings on immanent justice in relation to basic religious orientations of the Sioux, Navaho, Papago, and Hopi societies.[11] She points out that all four societies (and we can probably add Zuni and Zia as somewhat similar to Hopi) have basic attitudes toward supernatural power-sources which she believes may have developed from a common world view that was widespread among hunting tribes. The Dakota Sioux world view of the past century was still quite close to this early version and is summarized by Thompson from Macgregor's account[12] as follows:

> 1. The traditional Dakota world is pervaded by a great, mysterious power which encompasses all the supernatural, though without a clear-cut organization.
> 2. Men, both as individuals and as a group, are dependent on this power and must humble themselves and supplicate it for successful living.
> 3. There are sanctioned mechanisms to accomplish this, both for the individual and for the group.
> 4. Power in this hunting society reveals itself at the individual level mainly by success with animals (i.e., success in hunting) and entails the winning of an animal guardian.
> 5. If man does not fulfil his role in the scheme, he will suffer sickness or other misfortune (i.e., the traditional Dakota world view includes a belief in immanent justice).

Thompson believes that "this over-all orientation concerning the nature of the universe and the role of men and animals in it persists among these Sioux Indians despite loss of their hunting economy, most of their hunting grounds, their ritual, and much of their social structure."

The other three tribes are shown also to believe in a supernatural source of power, but they do not see man as so helpless in dealing with it. Thompson says:

> With the development of a more systematic control of the food supply by means of social organization and farming technologies,

11. Laura Thompson, "Attitudes and Acculturation," American Anthropologist, L, No. 2 (April-June, 1948), 200-215.

12. Gordon Macgregor, Warriors without Weapons: A Study of the Society and Personality Development of the Pine Ridge Sioux (Chicago: University of Chicago Press, 1946).

> man's concept of himself, in relation to nature and especially to animals, apparently changed from that of a helpless supplicant toward disparate superhuman guardians who controlled the power supply, to that of a power entity in a correlative system wherein his distinctively human role, including the development of his will, was indispensable. Nevertheless, he remained the conservator and protector of life in all its forms, and the propitiator of animal guardians, some of whom came to be regarded as peers. Moreover, he still believed that the universe was immanently just and that sickness was due to his failure explicitly to fulfill his role, although that role was extended to include not only observation of the rules at the overt-behavioral level but also "keeping a good heart."

After describing the Navaho, Papago, and Hopi views of the supernatural power source and men's relation to it, she says:

> The foregoing findings and generalizations, I submit, suggest that in the tribes studied, basic orientations regarding the nature of the universe, man's relation to it, and to its nonhuman component, including animals, are major psycho-cultural structures, deep-rooted in the tribal past and persisting through millennia, despite far-reaching changes in the group's ecology, economy, sociology, and ritual expressions. Whatever their historic origin, the evidence leads to the assumption that once such basic attitude patterns become firmly entrenched in the tribal culture (probably in the symbol system) and in the communal personality structure, their inner morphology tends to endure despite changes in content and emphasis.

This account would lead us to expect all the groups we have studied to show a high degree of belief in immanent justice, even though they are partially acculturated. But how does this theory fit the facts of the difference between Navaho Mountain and Shiprock, which are at the two extremes of the Indian groups in their belief in immanent justice? Thompson suggests that this may be due to the fact that the Navaho believe supernatural power to be localized in numerous disparate personal entities, the Holy People, and also in Earth People, in the form of witches and ghosts. Men may compel and propitiate the superhuman entities by following detailed rules and using appropriate ritual formulas. For the traditional Navaho at Navaho Mountain, stealing may bring on misfortune, such as sickness or accident caused by a superhuman power. But as the Navaho become acculturated at Shiprock, so that they engage in irrigated agriculture and attend missions and schools, the emphasis in their thinking may shift from superhuman to human power entities. They may come to view man as relatively more effective in dealing with the universe than do the more traditional people at Navaho Mountain. Consequently, the Shiprock children may show less belief in immanent justice. This would be more probable among acculturated Navaho than among acculturated Sioux or Hopi or Papago people, because the Navaho see the supernatural power as distributed in a mosaic of unrelated and unreliable personal-power entities, none of which is all-powerful; while the other groups all see supernatural power as more coherent and more difficult for men to ignore by bad behavior. In other words, Shiprock children may be more able to deny supernatural or immanent punishment because their traditional world view never endowed superhuman beings with as much coordinated absolute power over human beings as did the world views of the other tribes.

TABLE 33[a]

ANIMISM AMONG INDIAN CHILDREN: PERCENTAGES OF RESPONSES INDICATING BELIEF IN ANIMISM

Group	Ages Six to Eleven		Ages Twelve to Eighteen	
	No. Responding	QC	No. Responding	QC
Papago				
Topawa	46	65	50	44[b]
Hickiwan	30	80	23	65
Hopi				
Third Mesa	52	71	47	66
First Mesa	40	63	30	30[b]
Zuni	41	60	51	52
Zia	32	68	17	82
Navaho				
Navaho Mountain	21	90	26	58[b]
Shiprock	55	53	35	25[b]
Sioux				
Pine Ridge	23	82	13	47[b]
Kyle	37	72	45	62

a. QC - "Did the ax know that he stole the melon?"
b. Statistically reliable decrease with age.

Results on Animism

The results of this test on animism will be discussed separately from those dealing with immanent justice, because they show different age trends, as can be seen in Table 33. Five of the ten tribal groups show statistically reliable decreases in animism with age, two more decrease

measurably, and three (Zuni, Zia, and Hopi Third Mesa) do not change reliably with age.

Lerner[13] studied white American children of two contrasting socio-economic groups. He told a story of a boy who had done wrong and on his way home he came to a bridge which broke and dropped him into a stream of water, where he got wet. He asked his subjects, aged six to eleven, whether the bridge knew that the boy had done wrong and whether the bridge could punish the boy. His results are as follows:

PER CENT OF ANIMISTIC RESPONSES

Socio-economic Status	Age		
	6-7	8-9	10-11
High	62	50	15
Low	82	70	31

Averaging Lerner's percentages for the age group six to eleven, we get 61 per cent of the children of low socio-economic status giving animistic responses, which is about what we find for the three Indian groups which are lowest in animism.

We can also compare our results on animism with those of Dennis and Russell.[14] Dennis interviewed all Hopi school children aged twelve to seventeen at First Mesa and Third Mesa. He used a list of twenty items and asked each subject whether these items were living or dead. From the responses he classified his subjects into four stages, which had been defined by Piaget as follows: Stage I, everything which is useful, unbroken, and in good condition is alive; Stage II, only things which move are alive; Stage III, only things which can move themselves are alive; Stage IV, only plants and animals are alive.

In order to compare our results with those of Dennis, we must assume that attributing consciousness to something (e.g., the ax knew the boy stole) is equivalent to saying that the thing is alive. Fortunately, Dennis tested this assumption with Hopi children by asking them concerning each of the

13. Op. Cit.

14. Dennis, op. cit.; R. W. Russell, "Studies in Animism. IV. An Investigation of Concepts Allied to Animism," Journal of Genetic Psychology, LVII (1940), 83-91; and W. Dennis and R. W. Russell, "Piaget's Questions Applied to Zuni Children," Child Development, XI (1940), 181-87.

twenty items on his list "Does the ______ know where it is?" He found that the Hopi subjects were a little more likely to say that a thing was alive than to say that it was conscious, but there was not much difference between their application of the two concepts to his list of items. Consequently, we may suppose that our results slightly underestimate the amount of animism as it might be determined by asking the question "Is the ax (or other item) alive?"

Dennis found that 47 per cent of his group aged twelve to seventeen were in Stage I of animism, where they would say that an ax is alive, and that there was no reliable age trend within this age range. If we combine our First and Third Mesa subjects into a single group, we find that 52 per cent of those in the twelve to eighteen group were in Stage I. We also note that there was no reliable age trend among our Third Mesa subjects but that the First Mesa group decreased in animism from ages six to eleven to ages twelve to eighteen. Dennis does not report his data separately for the two localities.

Russell,[15] using subjects from a variety of schools and communities, gives the following data on the proportions of white American children in Stage I of animism:

	Age					
	6-7	8-9	10-11	12-13	14-15	16-17
Percentage in Stage I	48	43	40	29	1	0

We can also compare our results on Zuni children with a study made by Dennis and Russell[16] on 24 Zuni children aged eight to sixteen whom they questioned on animism in 1938 and 1940. Seventy-six per cent of these children were in Stage I, which is somewhat higher than we found, but the difference is not statistically reliable for this small group.

Thus we find our results to be in fair agreement with those of Dennis and Russell on Hopi and Zuni children; and our results show the various Indian groups to be more animistic than most white American groups,

15. R. W. Russell, "Studies in Animism. II. The Development of Animism," Journal of Genetic Psychology, LVI (1940), 353-66, and "Studies in Animism. V. Animism in Older Children," ibid., LX (1942), 329-35.

16. Dennis and Russell, op. cit.

though white children of lower socio-economic status aged six to eleven are not different from the least animistic of our Indian groups.

Discussion

Piaget regards young children as universally animistic. He believes that at first they ascribe life to all objects and then, as a result of their experience with the world of man and nature, they gradually develop naturalistic attitudes. He says, concerning the child: "Liberation from the bond that ties him exclusively to his parent and the freeing of his own point of view on self seem thus to be the two principal factors that explain the progressive decline of animism and of artificialism. . . . According as man ceases to be a god in the child's eyes and as nature appears less to gravitate around us and our interest, the child seeks to explain things by means of themselves."[17]

Therefore, it would be only in a society where the adults believed that certain inanimate objects possessed life that the children would tend to retain their early animistic attitudes.

As far as we know, none of the Indian societies we studied is animistic in the sense that adults believe an ax is alive. According to Dennis,[18] adult Hopi who are well acquainted with English include among living objects the sun, moon, stars, wind, clouds, permanent springs of water, permanent rivers, and fire — in other words, objects which endure and move. Other "primitive" people have somewhat similar ideas. It is toward this kind of conception that we would expect children to move in the Hopi society. Yet Dennis found only two children who possessed the adult Hopi concept and two others who had the adult American concept. About half of Dennis' subjects, and of ours, in the age range twelve to eighteen were in the first stage of animism, which considers an object such as an ax as alive. And roughly half or more of the twelve to eighteen group in all the other tribes except the Shiprock Navaho also regarded the ax as alive. Further, the younger children were not nearly 100 per cent animistic, except at Navaho Mountain, Hickiwan, and Pine Ridge. Three Pueblo groups — Third Mesa, Zuni, and Zia — do not show a decrease of animism with age.

17. Jean Piaget, The Child's Conception of the World (New York: Harcourt, Brace & Co., 1929), pp. 385-87.

18. Op. cit.

We might explain the slow decline (or the failure to decline) of animism as due to a general tendency toward animism which is illustrated by the Hopi adult belief and which is contrasted with the prevailing naturalism of the high socio-economic groups in America whom Lerner studied. Thus we would expect Shiprock to show less animism than Navaho Mountain because of Shiprock's relatively high degree of acculturation to American ways.

As for the failure of most of the groups to show 100 per cent animism at the earlier ages, perhaps we should question Piaget's hypothesis. This is done by Huang,[19] who summarizes the evidence on children's animism and shows that it supports a hypothesis of the existence of what we may call a "childish naturalism." According to this hypothesis, some young children at least will naturally give naturalistic explanations of the world. In their early concepts of what is alive and not alive, they will place axes and such objects in the not-alive categories. Then, if the adult society has certain animistic beliefs, the children will learn these as they grow older. It is parallel to the idea which was presented in chapter v that some young children are "not old enough" to understand rules of games, and so they do not treat them as sacred.

Margaret Mead[20] leans toward this hypothesis about animism in one of the groups she studied. She found no evidence among Manus children of spontaneous animistic thought, even though the adult culture uses many animistic concepts. She believes that the Manus children have very practical materialistic attitudes and are not taught the religious concepts of adults until they reach puberty.

These various considerations may have some bearing on animism among the Indian children, but they do not offer a clear, unambiguous explanation of the data we have obtained. For instance, they do not explain the apparent increase of animism in the older children's group at Zia. Probably some specific cultural factors, peculiar to a given tribal group, must be brought in to account for our results.

19. I. Huang, "Children's Conceptions of Physical Causality: A Critical Summary," Journal of Genetic Psychology, LXIII (1943), 71-121.

20. "An Investigation of the Thought of Primitive Children, with Special Reference to Animism," Journal of the Royal Anthropological Institution, LXII (1932), 173-90.

CHAPTER VII

THE FREE DRAWINGS OF INDIAN CHILDREN

Section 1. ANALYSIS OF CONTENT

Making pictures is very nearly a universal method of expression and communication. Among young children there appears to be little or no inhibition in drawing. They usually draw what they want to draw, regardless of technical difficulties. However, in some societies, including modern American society, as children reach their teens, their production becomes inhibited; self-criticism reduces the quantity of production and probably limits the selection of content. Similarly in the Indian societies, by the early teens there appears to be a growing awareness of technique and technical problems in drawing, but productivity is not much reduced.

In collecting the "free drawings" of the children in this Study, it was expected that Indian youth might report more freely about themselves through their drawings than through speech and that a study of their drawings might enable us to see the world through their eyes. Two ways of studying and analyzing the free drawings were utilized.

1. Analysis of the content of the drawings, based on the assumption that the interests uppermost in the children's minds and the experiences most familiar and most meaningful to them would be expressed in the content of their drawings. This type of analysis forms the main body, Section 1, of this chapter.

2. Analysis of the artistic qualities of the drawings--discovering stages of artistic development, comparing the sexes, and comparing the several Indian tribes among themselves and with other societies. This has been done for the Hopi Third Mesa group, in comparison with a Cleveland, Ohio, group of urban American children, and is reported briefly as Section 2 of this chapter.[1]

1. There is a third method: analysis of personality of the children who make the drawings— search for cultural similarities among the children of a given tribe, together with systematic personality differences between children of different tribes. Using the drawings as projections of the children's personalities and subjecting them to analysis according

The content of the free drawings was analyzed according to categories that were expected to throw light upon the emotional and moral development of the children. What experiences were most significant to children at various ages? To what extent did the landscape impress them? To what extent were they concerned with their homes, with human beings, with animals? How much did the objects of the surrounding "modern" civilization come within their field of attention?

Previous work along this line had been reviewed critically by Anastasi and Foley,[2] who dealt with the question of the relative importance of environmental stimuli and maturational processes in the drawings of children. These and other authors felt that too much credence had been placed in the view that the development of children's drawings is a result of innate maturational factors, independent of specific environmental stimulation. They admit that studies of children's drawings made in various cultures indicate that there is something of an orderly progression through stages of technique and representation of various types of content, but they also point to great differences of content among children of the same age but different cultures. The conclusion from these studies is that children's drawings are to some extent "cultural" or the results of environmental stimulation, to some extent "individual," and to some extent "universal," showing stages of development which are common in all human experience.

to principles that have been developed for "projective techniques" was the original intention of the Study. Projective analysis of children's drawings had been made by Schmid-Waehner, by Alschuler and Hattwick, and by other workers. Several exploratory studies of this type were carried through, with interesting results; but this approach was discontinued when it became clear that the Rorschach and Thematic Apperception Test results would adequately meet this research need. These latter tests were given under more carefully controlled conditions than the Free Drawing Test, and it seemed hardly worth while to supplement the results of these tests with a projective analysis of the free drawings. The principal interest in such a project would have been that of establishing the validity of the analysis of the Free Drawing Test against the Rorschach and TAT analyses and against the life-history data on the children. The projective analysis of the free drawings could hardly have added new information on personality to what was already available.

2. Anne Anastasi and John P. Foley, Jr., "An Analysis of Spontaneous Drawings by Children in Different Cultures," Journal of Applied Psychology, XX (1936), 689-726.

Procedure

The directions for the Free Drawing Test are given in Appendix A. They were part of a mimeographed "Guide for Field Workers" that was distributed to all teachers of the children to be tested.

In most cases the drawings were made by the children in their regular classrooms. The practice of drawing during "free" periods was fairly common in Indian schools at the time these drawings were made. According to the teachers, these children enjoy drawing and look upon a period of free drawing as a pleasure. Thus the experience of being asked to draw whatever they pleased was not strange to most of the children.

For children not in school the free drawings were more difficult to obtain. Dr. Dorothea Leighton secured drawings from nonschool Navaho children at Navaho Mountain and Ramah, while Miss Jane Chesky obtained drawings from a few nonschool Papago children in the Hickiwan district. Since tables or other convenient flat places were rarely to be found outside school, nonschool children usually drew on paper laid out on the ground, or on a flat stone, or occasionally on a wagon bed.

In only one of the communities of this Study had the children any skilled instruction in art. The rest of them had much the same experience in school as children in most elementary schools in town and rural districts in America, where there is no special art teacher. Fred Kabotie, an Indian artist, taught at Third Mesa school for the Hopi and administered the Free Drawing Test there. His own interest in painting katcinas and ceremonial dances may well have influenced the choice of content by some of his pupils.

The plan was to procure eight drawings from each child. If the child did not draw a face or human figure in the first five or six drawings, he would be asked to draw or paint one or the other, or both; and he would be asked to make a picture of himself doing something. The request to draw a face or human figure was seldom necessary, and the request to make a picture of himself was apparently seldom made, even though such a figure had not been drawn. This inference is drawn from the fact that very few such pictures were sent in.

In order to limit the content analysis to subjects drawn spontaneously, all pictures were discarded on which it was indicated that a specific direction as to subject matter had been given. (However, it is possible that some of the teachers omitted to note such directions on drawings made by their pupils.)

In any case, somewhat less than eight pictures were obtained and analyzed for a number of the children, as can be seen from Table 34, which shows the number of children whose drawings were analyzed and the number of drawings they made. The six- to seven-year-old group was not represented by an average of 7 to 8 pictures from the Kyle, Navaho Mountain, and Hickiwan groups. All groups except Navaho Mountain averaged 7 to 8 pictures at ages eight to thirteen. Navaho Mountain, Ramah, and Hickiwan, gave fewer pictures per child at the fourteen to eighteen age level.

Adequacy of Sampling

The question should also be raised as to whether the children whose drawings were analyzed were representative of the children in the communities being studied. Reference to the numbers of subjects enrolled in the Study and the numbers of subjects actually in the age group six to eighteen (see Table 1, chap. ii), when considered in relation to Table 34 (see also Table 46, Appendix D-2), suggests the following conclusions:

The group who submitted free drawings were fairly representative of the Study group in Kyle, Pine Ridge, Shiprock, Ramah, Topawa, Third Mesa, and Zuni. The age group least well represented was the fourteen to eighteen group, of which as many as three-fourths were included only at Zuni, Kyle, Shiprock, and Ramah. The age groups best represented were those from eight to ten and eleven to thirteen. No claims can be made for a representative sampling of subjects in the Free Drawing Tests at Navaho Mountain or Hickiwan. The six to ten group was adequately represented at Zia; the six to thirteen group was fairly well represented at First Mesa.

Methods of Analysis

The individual picture, rather than the individual child, was used as the basic unit for analysis. Ten basic categories were devised into

TABLE 34[a]

SAMPLES OF FREE DRAWINGS FROM INDIAN CHILDREN

	No. of Children			No. of Drawings			Average No. of Items per Drawing		
	M	F	Total	M	F	Total	M	F	Total
Papago									
Hickiwan	30	26	56	213	155	368	5.7	6.3	5.9
Topawa	43	44	87	300	305	605	5.0	6.0	5.6
Hopi									
Third Mesa	39	44	83	307	337	644	3.9	4.6	4.2
First Mesa	23	35	58	183	268	451	5.3	4.4	4.8
Zuni	46	45	91	358	365	723	4.6	5.9	5.3
Zia	24	18	42	186	135	321	6.8	6.3	6.6
Navaho									
Shiprock	37	45	82	260	324	584	7.1	8.0	7.5
Ramah	17	17	34	161	132	293	3.5	3.5	3.5
Navaho Mt.	21	11	32	106	34	140	6.1	7.3	6.7
Sioux									
Kyle	29	41	70	210	310	520	5.2	5.7	5.5
Pine Ridge	17	17	34	137	140	277	4.5	4.8	4.6

a. Ages eight to eighteen.

which were grouped all the items appearing in the pictures:

1. Landscape (including plants)
2. Dwellings (including household furnishings and equipment)
3. Human beings
4. Other structures and miscellaneous tools
5. Animals and birds
6. Transportation
7. War and patriotism
8. School appurtenances
9. Ceremonials
10. Crafts

The attempt was made to make the number of categories as small as possible and, at the same time, to keep separate the different types of interests exhibited in the drawings. (Appendix D-1 shows the categories with their component items.)

A few explanatory comments will help to clarify the scoring procedure. For example, in pictures where a group of trees appeared, rather than count the entire number of trees, the group was given one count under the heading of "woods." Several clouds, several hills and rocks, or several fields in the same picture were given only one count for each type of item. However, if two or three prominent trees appeared as the main subject matter of the drawing, two or three tallies were made in this category. By the same token, a sketchy group of dwellings in the distance, where other objects of interest occupied the foreground, was given one count under "village." In other words, the attempt was at all times to make the emphasis in our scoring coincide as nearly as possible with the apparent degree of emphasis placed upon various objects in the drawings.

Occasionally the same item occurs in two different categories. The airplane was listed under transportation and also under war and patriotism. Where from the context of the drawing it was obvious that the airplane was seen only as a vehicle, it was counted under the first category. To take another example, if a flag was pictured waving over an army camp, its patriotic meaning was taken to be important. If it appeared in front of the school building, however, the chances are that it was simply considered another piece of school equipment.

In the category of "ceremonials" are included objects and designs which might have a religious significance. However, a number of the designs and symbols certainly were not intended by the children to have a religious meaning. For instance, the feathered serpent and the conventionalized cloud of rain design of the Southwest pueblos are intended as a pleasing bit of design and are frequently used on jewelry and pottery made for sale to tourists. Hence they do not necessarily signify a religious feeling on the part of the child who draws them.

One other thing deserves mention. For white children, Christmas trees, Christmas gifts, etc., cannot be subsumed under the heading of "school appurtenances." But for the Indian children, school is the only place in which children have experience with these objects.

Besides subjecting the drawings to the scheme of content analysis just described, they were used as a basis for making inferences about acculturation. All items in the drawings were divided into four categories: (1) those which are native to the old culture; (2) those which were introduced from white culture by indirect contact or many years ago; (3) those recently acquired from white culture; and (4) "neutral" landscape items. By finding the percentage of appearance of items in each of these categories, we have an index for the degree of material acculturation which exists in each community. The children are recording, presumably, those things in their environment in which they take special

interest — those things which are important to them. Unconsciously, they tell us whether life as they find it is filled with many things reflecting the influence of white culture. It is understood, of course, that this index will show nothing more than the degree of material acculturation and will reflect nothing directly of acculturation on the social or ideological levels.

For the five Southwest groups, the representations included in the category "early introductions" were those reflecting Spanish influence. Such things as the horse, fruit trees, sheep, and the Catholic church come under this heading. Items introduced after approximately 1850, usually by direct white contact, were put under "late introductions."

For the Sioux, the items placed in "early introductions" were those of early, indirect white influence--such as the horse. The recent period for the Sioux is the reservation period, which began after 1890. The categorization of items was determined in each case by consultation with a person who was an expert on the particular culture involved.

As has been said, the picture was used as the basic unit for analysis. Results were tabulated as follows: (a) total number of items per picture (shown in Table 34); (b) number of items of each category per picture (Table 35); and (c) percentage of items of a given category, based on the total number of items (Table 35). This method of analysis loses sight of the individual but is appropriate for studying differences between groups.

Reliability of the Analysis

Assuming that most of the samples of children are fairly representative of the communities where they live, there remains the problem of the reliability of the analysis: Would another person obtain the same results by using the same scheme of analysis?

Mrs. Inger Olson Klumpner analyzed the Hopi and Papago drawings and compared her results with those of Mrs. Brooke Mordy, who had made the original analysis. The numbers of items noted per picture varied somewhat in the two analyses. There was probably greater than chance difference between the two analysts on this point, for Klumpner noted somewhat more items per picture in twelve of sixteen subgroups.[3]

3. Average number of items per picture were: for Third Mesa, 4.8 for Klumpner, 4.2 for Mordy; for First Mesa, 5.4 and 4.8; for Topawa, 5.9 and 5.6; for Hickiwan, 6.1 and 5.9.

TABLE 35

COMPARISON OF INDIAN GROUPS ON CONTENT OF FREE DRAWINGS (PERCENTAGES)

Group		Land-scape	Animals	Humans	Dwell-ings	Other Structures	Transpor-tation	War and Patriotism	School	Crafts	Cere-monial
Hickiwan	Male	30	4	14	9	16	9	17	1	0	0
	Female	43	2	17	21	10	1	3	4	0	0
	Average	37	3	15	15	13	5	10	2	0	0
Topawa	Male	59	8	6	8	9	3	5	1	0	0
	Female	60	4	7	17	9	1	1	2	0	0
	Average	60	6	6	13	9	2	3	2	0	0
Total Papago	Male	43	6	10	8	13	6	11	1	0	0
	Female	51	3	12	19	10	1	2	3	0	0
	Average	48	4	11	14	11	4	7	2	0	0
Third Mesa	Male	55	10	3	10	8	1	3	1	0	9
	Female	42	2	6	30	12	0	0	1	1	5
	Average	48	6	5	21	10	1	2	1	1	6
First Mesa	Male	40	16	15	9	11	5	1	1	0	2
	Female	30	4	15	26	13	2	0	3	4	2
	Average	35	11	15	17	12	1	1	2	2	2
Total Hopi	Male	46	14	10	10	10	3	2	1	0	5
	Female	35	4	10	29	13	1	0	2	2	4
	Average	41	8	10	19	11	2	1	2	1	4
Zuni	Male	35	18	10	9	14	6	0	2	0	6
	Female	37	5	11	22	15	1	0	3	6	0
	Average	36	11	11	16	15	4	0	2	3	3
Zia	Male	37	38	6	5	8	3	0	0	0	2
	Female	22	8	23	28	13	2	0	0	0	3
	Average	30	22	15	17	11	3	0	0	0	3
Shiprock	Male	36	11	14	9	10	4	12	3	0	0
	Female	40	4	9	28	8	3	1	6	1	0
	Average	38	7	11	19	9	4	6	5	1	0

TABLE 35 — Continued

Group		Land-scape	Animals	Humans	Dwell-ings	Other Structures	Transpor-tation	War and Patriotism	School	Crafts	Cere-monial
Ramah	Male	22	26	17	4	8	8	5	0	8	0
	Female	37	14	16	14	3	3	1	0	13	0
	Average	31	20	16	9	5	6	3	0	11	0
Navaho Mt.	Male	50	14	11	11	10	2	1	0	0	0
	Female	34	8	21	26	6	6	0	0	0	0
	Average	42	11	16	19	8	4	0	0	0	0
Total Navaho	Male	39	15	13	9	10	4	6	1	2	0
	Female	37	8	15	24	6	4	0	3	3	0
	Average	38	11	14	17	8	4	3	2	2	0
Kyle	Male	40	5	7	19	16	5	9	1	0	0
	Female	43	7	8	20	16	2	0	3	0	0
	Average	41	6	7	19	16	4	4	2	0	0
Pine Ridge	Male	32	4	10	15	7	5	20	2	0	0
	Female	46	7	15	19	8	1	2	7	0	0
	Average	39	5	13	17	8	3	11	5	0	0
Total Sioux	Male	37	4	11	17	12	5	14	2	0	0
	Female	44	7	9	19	12	2	1	5	0	0
	Average	40	6	10	18	12	3	7	3	0	0

The number of items per picture is undoubtedly less reliably noted than the categories of the items. The analyst has greater latitude for personal judgment, for example, in deciding whether to count a small group of animals as one item or to tally each one separately, than in deciding to what category they belong.

The extent of agreement between the analysts in assigning items to categories is a more significant question for us. This was studied by comparing the percentage frequencies which the two analysts assigned to the various categories for the several age and sex groups of the Hopi and Papago tribes. Mrs. Klumpner found no differences that are reliable at the 5 per cent level of probability among about fifty comparisons for First Mesa; only one such difference for Topawa; five for Third Mesa; and thirteen for Hickiwan. The fact that most of the larger discrepancies were located in one set of data (those from Hickiwan) suggests that these drawings offered special difficulties to the analysts.

To summarize: it appears that the relative frequencies of items in the various categories are reliably determined at least for most of the tribal groups, when judged by the test of consistency between two analysts working independently. The number of items noted per picture is not so reliably determined and may differ systematically from one analyst to another.

Results

Results will be given first from the "interest" analysis. These are expected to answer the question "What objects and what experiences are uppermost in the minds of these boys and girls, objects and experiences which they are willing and able to portray in their drawings?"

Table 35 reports the percentage frequencies of categories for the two sexes, for the community groups, and for the tribal groups as a whole. Each percentage is calculated by totaling the number of items in a particular category for the particular group of children and dividing that number by the total number of items in the pictures of that group.[4]

4. In testing the statistical significance of differences between the percentages shown in Table 35, it is necessary to know approximately how many items were counted for each group of children. This can be computed by reference to Table 34, which shows the number of children in

Intertribal differences

This collection of free drawings from children of six different societies gives us an opportunity to test the hypothesis that there are common features in the content of children's drawings which appear in different cultures. We were impressed more by the differences between tribal groups than by the similarities.

Of course, the content was the same for all groups if we consider only broad categories, such as animals, human figures, dwellings, and landscape. There was little else that the children could conceivably draw, if they drew real objects in their environment. Also there were certain things that were drawn very seldom by any of the children. They seldom drew interiors of houses, for example, and they almost never drew an arrangement of flowers or fruit or a water pitcher — the sort of thing we would call "still life." Perhaps the most general statement that might be made concerning the content of the drawings was that they reflected a rural life. But rural life was differentiated from one tribe to another, as was the landscape they presented.

The differences among the several tribes are concentrated mainly in three categories: animals, landscape, and ceremonials. The Sioux and Papago children drew fewer animals than did the other groups, while

each group, the number of drawings, and the number of items per drawing. For comparisons of percentages based on 1,000 items, differences of 3-5 per cent have only a 5 per cent probability of occurring by chance, so long as the percentages compared do not fall below 6-10 per cent.

This method of computing statistical reliability is open to some objection, since the unit of sampling is the item and each item is not independent of all other items. The items of a given picture may be related to those of six or seven other pictures that were produced by the same child, the same principles of individual interest operating to produce all the items drawn by a given child. A more conservative estimate of reliability would have been obtained by using the child as the unit of sampling and comparing the numbers of a given category of items per child, or comparing the percentages of children who drew a given category. Finding the average number of a given category, e.g., animals, drawn per child and comparing these averages for the different tribal and age and sex groups would probably be the most defensible procedure, but it would be a tedious process. Comparing the percentages of children who drew a given category would have been useless in cases where 100 per cent of the children drew one or more items in a given category, as they did in several categories.

The present method is a simple one, but the statistical reliabilities of the percentage differences should be interpreted conservatively.

the Zia children are at the high end of the scale, with 22 per cent of their items animals. The Zia boys are responsible for this difference, since 38 per cent of their items are animals, compared with 8 per cent for the Zia girls. The boys are encouraged to draw animals from an early age, according to an anthropologist who has studied Zia childhood:[5]

> From the time a boy can handle a pencil or a brush he is encouraged to draw and to paint. His subjects are usually animals, although cowboys riding or roping are likewise frequent subjects. Even the figures of dancers are represented, but these are never supposed to be shown to white people. Parents and siblings encourage the youngsters with admiration and criticisms. Girls rarely draw pictures except in school, but by the time the children start school the boys already are much more advanced in their ease of handling pencils and colors and even more in their ability to put their accurate observations of animal forms and movements on to paper. The pueblo expects its boys to be able to paint animals upon house walls at Christmas, to encourage fertility, as well as to work later at painting the ceremonial masks, altars, and other ceremonial paraphernalia. Girls are expected to paint nothing but the conventionalized designs used on pottery.

Landscapes are less frequently drawn by Zia and Zuni, and most frequently by Papago. The Papago predominance is due to the very high proportion of landscapes drawn by Topawa children (60 per cent as compared with 37 per cent at Hickiwan). The Topawa landscape is dominated by the sacred mountain, Baboquivari, which might account for the difference between the two Papago communities. In general, the interest and variety of the actual landscapes are not sufficiently different to account for the differences in landscape drawings among the several cultural groups.

Ceremonial objects and symbols are drawn only by the Pueblo children of Hopi, Zuni, and Zia.

Differences between tribes and between communities within a tribe may be attributed to actual differences of interest. It is possible, however, that these differences are partly due to "fashions" in drawing. For instance, 27 per cent of the items in drawings of Hopi children aged fourteen to eighteen at Third Mesa are ceremonial objects and designs, compared with 4 per cent from the same age group at Hopi First Mesa (see Table 46, Appendix D-2). This is perhaps due to the influence of the art teacher at Third Mesa, which has already been referred to. While no art teachers are present in the other communities, it might be that a style had been established, with or without the leadership of teachers,

5. Quoted from a memorandum written by Dr. Florence Hawley Ellis.

which encouraged children to specialize in one or another subject.

Sex Differences

Looking at the eleven communities, there are some consistent sex differences which are undoubtedly due to actual differences of interests. The masculine interests are items indicative of war and patriotism, such as airplanes, big guns, and flags. Animals are drawn mainly by boys (the one exception is the Sioux, where there is no sex difference on this category). Transportation items, while they show less striking sex differences, are also mainly masculine, with airplanes, autos, trucks, and wagons (the exception occurs at Navaho Mountain, where the girls draw more transportation items than do the boys).

The girls in all the tribal groups draw pictures of houses (the "dwellings" category) much more frequently than the boys. Also feminine are drawings of crafts — pottery, weaving, basketry, and other craft designs. Drawings of school appurtenances are given more frequently by girls.

As regards the magnitude of sex differences, Zia shows the greatest amount of difference. At the other extreme we find Kyle (Sioux) and Topawa (Papago), where little sex differentiation occurs. The other eight communities all show a substantial degree of sex differentiation.

Age Differences

These data on the content of free drawings have been analyzed by age groups within each tribal group and are so presented in Appendix D-2. In summary, there are a few age differences which appear to be common to all the groups in the Study. They lie principally in the categories of landscape, human figures, and dwellings. There is a general tendency for the frequency of landscape objects to increase with age; the frequency of human figures to decrease with age; and dwellings to be relatively frequent only among the six- to seven-year-old group.

Acculturation

Do the free drawings of children reflect the degree to which their societies have become acculturated to the dominant American culture? Remembering that we are limiting our remarks to material acculturation, we may compare the frequencies of "native" items and "acculturated" items in the children's drawings.

Before making the actual comparisons, we asked a group of anthropologists who knew American Indian cultures to rank the communities in the order of acculturation. While opinions varied somewhat among those questioned, the various rankings were averaged and arranged as shown in the first column of Table 36. The data on percentage of items showing acculturation, native culture, neutral (landscape), and early introductions from white culture are given in Table 36 for each community as a whole.

The rank order for acculturation as given by the judges agrees in general with the data, but there are some interesting exceptions. Hickiwan is such an exception. On the "acculturation ratio" of acculturated to native items, Hickiwan is second only to Kyle (Sioux). Another exception is Shiprock, which, according to this index, should occupy a place below both Papago groups and at the border line between the relatively acculturated and the relatively unacculturated communities.

Indeed, the division into two rather separate groups, with Shiprock in the middle, is a striking phenomenon of Table 36. This may be related to the fact that the "unacculturated" communities are relatively little Christianized in the formal sense, while all the "acculturated" communities are Christianized. Retention of the traditional religion may be a good single criterion of lack of acculturation.

Sex Differences

As might be expected, the girls tend to draw more native items than the boys, because the houses and items having to do with the home are nearly all of native origin in the Southwest tribes. The ratio of acculturated to native items is higher for boys than for girls in all the communities except Zia and Pine Ridge, as is seen in Table 37. These two exceptions are probably to be understood by the following considerations:

At Zia the boys draw very many animals, including native animals as well as horses (the latter are categorized as early introductions of white culture). Thirty-eight per cent of the boys' items are animals, as against 8 per cent for the girls. This has the effect of forcing down the proportion of acculturated items drawn by the boys, relative to the girls.

At Pine Ridge the boys and girls are about equal in proportions of acculturated items, but the boys drew 24 per cent native items as against 16 per cent for the girls. This may be due to a tendency of the boys to

TABLE 36

COMPARISON OF EXPERT JUDGMENTS ON DEGREE OF ACCULTURATION WITH EVIDENCE FROM FREE DRAWINGS

Order of Acculturation Ranked by Experts	Percentage of Items Showing:				
	Acculturation	Native Culture	Landscape	Early Introduction from White Culture	Ratio: Acculturated to Native Culture
Pine Ridge	41	20	37	3	2.05
Kyle	40	13	44	3	3.08
Shiprock	35	20	37	9	1.75
Topawa	23	13	55	8	1.77
Hickiwan	42	19	32	7	2.21
Zuni	25	30	38	8	0.83
First Mesa	23	38	33	7	0.60
Third Mesa	16	33	48	3	0.49
Zia	20	42	27	11	0.48
Ramah	22	30	34	14	0.73
Navaho Mt.	15	30	43	13	0.50

draw "Indian" scenes in which the male is given a role which he does not have in real life. The absence of satisfactory male roles in present-day Sioux society has been reported on by Macgregor.[6]

Age Differences

As Table 37 shows, there is no consistent pattern of age changes in the proportion of acculturated or of native items, or in the ratios of ac-

6. Gordon Macgregor, Warriors without Weapons: A Study of the Society and Personality Development of the Pine Ridge Sioux (Chicago: University of Chicago Press, 1946).

culturated to native items. Within the contrasting communities of Shiprock and Navaho Mountain, the ratio of acculturated to native items goes down with increasing age at Shiprock and up at Navaho Mountain. For Hickiwan the ratio increases with age; but for Topawa this is not true. Kyle has a decreasing ratio with increasing age; but this is not matched at all by the irregular results from Pine Ridge.

From these data it seems best to conclude that several different factors are affecting the frequencies of the various categories of items as they occur in the different age groups, with degree of acculturation being only one such factor.

TABLE 37

PERCENTAGES OF ITEMS SHOWING ACCULTURATION AND NONACCULTURATION, BY AGE AND SEX

	Acculturated	Early	Native	Landscape	Ratio: Acc./Native
	Hickiwan				
6- 7	46	5	24	25	1.9
8-10	46	8	17	30	2.7
11-13	36	5	18	40	2.0
14-18	37	9	11	43	3.4
Male	49	5	16	30	3.1
Female	35	8	21	36	1.7
Average	42	7	19	32	2.21
	Topawa				
6- 7	24	6	18	53	1.3
8-10	26	8	13	54	2.0
11-13	24	8	12	56	2.0
14-18	20	10	11	60	1.8
Male	22	9	11	58	2.0
Female	25	7	15	53	1.7
Average	23	8	13	55	1.77

TABLE 37- Continued

	Acculturated	Early	Native	Landscape	Ratio: Acc./Native
	Total Papago				
6-7	37	6	21	36	1.8
8-10	36	8	15	41	2.4
11-13	29	7	14	50	2.1
14-18	28	10	11	51	2.6
Male	36	7	14	43	2.6
Female	30	8	18	44	1.7
Average	33	8	16	44	2.06
	Third Mesa				
6-7	20	5	48	27	0.42
8-10	17	3	23	57	0.74
11-13	13	3	31	54	0.42
14-18	18	3	45	33	0.40
Male	13	4	26	56	0.50
Female	18	3	37	41	0.49
Average	16	3	33	48	0.49
	First Mesa				
6-7	26	10	34	30	0.76
8-10	20	6	35	40	0.57
11-13	24	7	42	27	0.57
14-18	25	3	38	32	0.66
Male	18	15	32	36	0.57
Female	27	1	41	30	0.41
Average	23	7	38	33	0.61
	Total Hopi				
6-7	23	8	39	30	0.59
8-10	18	4	29	48	0.62
11-13	16	4	34	45	0.47
14-18	22	3	42	32	0.52
Male	15	8	29	47	0.52
Female	22	2	39	37	0.56
Average	19	5	34	42	0.56

TABLE 37-Continued

	Acculturated	Early	Native	Landscape	Ratio: Acc./Native
			Zuni		
6-7	34	6	41	20	0.83
8-10	27	9	27	37	1.00
11-13	21	5	27	48	0.80
14-18	13	13	34	38	0.38
Male	24	12	26	37	0.92
Female	25	5	32	37	0.78
Average	25	8	30	38	0.83
			Zia		
6-7	20	15	46	19	0.43
8-10	17	11	41	30	0.41
11-13	22	7	41	30	0.54
14-18	18	2	45	35	0.40
Male	12	16	40	32	0.30
Female	30	3	46	21	0.65
Average	20	11	42	27	0.48
			Shiprock		
6-7	51	13	18	18	2.83
8-10	40	5	20	36	2.00
11-13	31	8	21	40	1.48
14-18	15	13	25	47	0.60
Male	36	11	17	36	2.12
Female	33	8	23	36	1.43
Average	35	9	20	37	1.75
			Ramah		
6-7	29	21	36	14	0.81
8-10	22	11	32	35	0.69
11-13	14	12	36	38	0.39
14-18	26	17	25	31	1.04
Male	24	14	27	34	0.90
Female	18	14	34	34	0.53
Average	22	14	30	34	0.73

TABLE 37-Continued

	Acculturated	Early	Native	Landscape	Ratio: Acc./Native
			Navaho Mountain		
6-7	12	18	42	27	0.29
8-10	10	16	23	51	0.43
11-13	17	8	28	47	0.61
14-18	20	8	28	43	0.71
Male	12	11	25	52	0.48
Female	16	15	34	34	0.47
Average	15	13	30	43	0.50
			Total Navaho		
6-7	32	17	30	21	1.07
8-10	24	10	24	43	1.00
11-13	22	8	27	42	0.82
14-18	20	12	26	43	0.77
Male	25	12	22	42	1.13
Female	22	12	31	35	0.71
Average	23	12	27	38	0.85
			Kyle		
6-7	69	8	8	14	8.6
8-10	48	4	10	38	4.8
11-13	38	3	12	48	3.2
14-18	32	2	17	49	1.9
Male	39	7	11	42	3.5
Female	40	1	15	44	2.7
Average	40	3	13	44	3.08
			Pine Ridge		
6-7	51	3	18	29	2.8
8-10	45	0	19	36	2.4
11-13	51	3	12	33	4.2
14-18	24	4	27	45	0.9
Male	40	5	24	31	1.7
Female	42	1	16	42	2.6
Average	41	3	20	37	2.05

TABLE 37 — Continued

	Acculturated	Early	Native	Landscape	Ratio: Acc./Native
	Total Sioux				
6-7	60	5	13	21	4.6
8-10	46	3	13	38	3.5
11-13	43	3	12	43	3.6
14-18	31	2	19	48	1.6
Male	40	6	15	40	2.7
Female	41	1	15	43	2.7
Average	41	3	15	41	2.70

Section 2. ARTISTIC ABILITY AND ARTISTIC DEVELOPMENT

Upon looking over the free drawings of Indian children and comparing them with similar collections of drawings by white American children, the layman is impressed with the comparatively good quality of the Indian children's work. Although there are numerous differences between the pictures produced by different tribal groups (enough so that one can tell almost at a glance which tribe produced a given drawing), the Indian children's drawings all compare favorably with those of white children. The observer quickly forms the conclusion that here is a medium of communication or representation in which Indian children are at no disadvantage with respect to white American children.

To put this impression to the test, we asked a teacher of art to study and evaluate the drawings of one group—Hopi Third Mesa—and to answer two questions:

1. How does the artistic quality of Hopi children's drawings compare with that of white American children?

2. Are the developmental stages of drawing for the Hopi children the same or different from those of white American children?

The study was made by Mr. Edward W. Rannells, a faculty member in the Department of Fine Arts at the University of Kentucky. He had, for comparison with the Hopi children's drawings, a report on the development of children's art based upon a study of drawings made by children aged six to fifteen in the children's classes of the Cleveland

museum of Art.[7]

In the following pages we shall quote liberally from a memorandum written by Mr. Rannells in 1943.

> This report, with the accompanying data, concerns an examination of the drawings of ninety Hopi Indian children, boys and girls, ages 6 to 16, all from the Oraibi [Third Mesa] School. The number of drawings is not large enough for any statistical proof of theories about them to be taken very seriously. I can only say that a systematic checking device has enabled me to approach them with some degree of objectivity, and I think what limited data I have obtained appear to be in harmony with my conclusions about them. I have tried to let the drawings speak for themselves: all my inferences are based on them. I found them revealing enough, and particularly interesting as documents of the Hopi culture.
>
> My problem was to see what could be learned from the drawings of these Hopi Indian children that would have any developmental significance from the standpoint of art. And in order for this to mean anything there would have to be some comparison with the developmental stages already known to be characteristic of children's drawings elsewhere. Known in a general way, that is, and determined with some accuracy, for one urban community at least, by Betty Lark-Horovitz' analysis of drawings made by children in the Cleveland public school.
>
> This Cleveland study is the most throughgoing attempt so far made to determine the successive stages in the development of children's drawings and to establish corresponding age norms. Recognizing the fallacy of adult standards in the construction of previous drawing scales, Mrs. Lark-Horovitz sought to establish an empirical basis for the evaluation of children's drawings by using as standards what is found to be characteristic of their product at each age level. And to find this, she and her assistants examined over 10,000 drawings by some 1,400 Cleveland school children, at least 100 representing each age level, from ages 6 to 15. (The ages for the Hopi children range from 6 to 16.)
>
> The Cleveland drawings were analyzed in a definite sequence of stages in representation from the schematic drawings of the very young child to the realism of those by adolescents, on the theory that from the first "the child intends his representations realistically" and that "the process of development in representational drawings is continuous until adolescence." The tentative age norms reported would seem to substantiate this, and it seems just as true of the drawings by the Hopi children. These also develop along the lines of realism very consistently up to the age of 13 or thereabouts, when the tribal symbols begin to appear and the work tends to become increasingly stylized, moving in the direction of conventional patterns that no longer suggest representations of what we would recognize as a real world.

7. Betty Lark-Horovitz, Edward N. Barnhart, and Esther M. Sills, Graphic Work Sample Diagnosis: An Analytical Method of Estimating Children's Drawing Ability (Cleveland Museum of Art, 1939); Thomas Munro, Betty Lark-Horovitz, and Edward N. Barnhart, "Children's Art Abilities: Studies at the Cleveland Museum of Art," Journal of Experimental Education, XI (1942), 97-155.

When we say "representations" we should remember that, up to the age of puberty, a child draws not things so much as ideas of things; he draws visual concepts of things experienced, things remembered, things in mind, rather than "copies" the visual appearance of things as seen at the moment. This would be "observation drawing" and comes later in adolescence. But the child uses lines to indicate his ideas, to signify what he knows. Saying that a child draws chiefly ideas--the things he has in mind--is not to say that these ideas of his are unreal. Indeed, they can be the clearest images of reality possible, and, in any case, their intention is real. Certainly, the Hopi drawings document the real lives of these children, as I shall point out more fully in a moment.

In order to delimit the characteristics of children's drawings as precisely as possible and thus discover what is typical for each age level, the analytical method devised by Lark-Horovitz involves checking each drawing against a long list of variables. This checking scale has nearly eighty items on it, and that means looking at a drawing a lot of different ways. But it is an object lesson in thoroughness, with the result that the "standards" for each age level in the Cleveland study are more acceptable than anything hitherto available, even though these "standards" are based on a highly selective group of children.

By "selective" I mean that, because Cleveland, as a community, offers its children unusual opportunities in art, and, in addition to this general fact, many of the children in the study would be the talented youngsters attending the Staurday classes at the Cleveland Museum of Art, there is every reason therefore to suppose that the "standards" will be high and, on the upper end of the scale, more sophisticated than usual, owing to the advantages of training in art. Hence to compare the drawings of Cleveland and Hopi children is to compare extremes. And yet we shall find that the normal stages in development occur at corresponding age levels for both groups.

It will be profitable to compare first the Hopi child's naïve treatment of space with the urban child's "perspective." It will serve also to explain why I have been unable to use the Cleveland checking scale just as it is, having eventually to construct an experimental one of my own.

One thing that was required of the children in the Cleveland study was a drawing showing the interior of the classroom at school. This was to gauge the child's knowledge of perspective. Now the Hopi child has no need for perspective of this kind. His space problem involves all outdoors and requires not convergence of lines on single points on an eye-level horizon, but expansion along a sky-line somewhat above this, since there are always mountains in sight. Linear perspective is, after all, a scientific device, not an artistic one. It is the kind of thing which can be demonstrated and proved; hence easily taught, learned, and measured; but it is not fundamental. In fact, the Hopi child's naïve representation of space is, on the whole, more directly functional from the standpoint of art. Knowing nothing of perspective, he sees silhouettes, and he sees these as lying in a succession of transverse planes, all parallel to the plane of the picture itself. Starting from this, he draws his silhouettes in planes set one behind another to locate them in depth, creating thereby an illusion of distance that perspective convergence would only hamper. And these superposed planes, being all transverse planes expressed in terms of silhouettes or shapes, refer back again to the surface

plane of the drawing itself. This is not done very consciously, but it is sound pictorial construction, and all the noticeably good Hopi children's drawings employ it. And it is on this basis that any fair appraisal of space as a factor in the Hopi drawings should be made, in contrast to the studio perspective emphasized in the Cleveland study.

My first inspection of the drawings revealed that the interests of Hopi boys and girls become sharply differentiated at a very early age. In developmental terms this means that they accept their sex roles early. The difference shows up most obviously in the drawings in the choices of subject matter. Since the drawings are "free" drawings, and because I know that a child draws in all seriousness what interests him at the moment, I have tried to let the drawings speak for him. I have not investigated written sources on the Hopi culture. All my inferences are based on the drawings. The checking device has merely helped to clarify what is evident in them.

When the Hopi children first come to school they draw houses — houses that loom up very big and close, crowding the page. Their world doesn't go beyond this. But in a year or two the boys have begun to go out into the hills alone and here, quite abruptly, their drawings change. After the eighth year they seldom draw houses any more; they draw landscapes. The girls keep right on drawing houses, as though they were dependent upon the security of the home. And even when they go some distance away from the houses (I learn all this from the drawings), they go in little groups — several children together. The boys are more independent; they seek the solitude of the hills; they picture themselves as alone or, more often, no human being is represented at all. Instead they draw animals; the horse is a favorite motif. The girls never draw animals. And there are some other differentiated interests which my checking list of "subject details" calls attention to.

Less obvious than subject matter as an index of the differences between Hopi boys and girls is the manner in which the drawings are made, the way they are done. Manner is a personal quality, and pretty elusive, but I think it shows up on the checking scale under "Use of Medium." Among the older children, only the drawings by boys are checked as "bold" or, what is even more significant, "discriminating." I haven't found a way to bring out this difference in manner any too well, and I realize that it is an extravagance to cite any tally on such a small number of cases as "significant." But even if the numbers were larger I believe this generalization would still hold. For, as I observe the drawings, it is clear enough to me that the boys draw with increasing assurance, as though they felt secure in what they are doing, whereas the girls seem to draw with increasing hesitation and uncertainty. The difference becomes more pronounced as they grow older. From all of which my inference is that this reflects the differentiated patterns of the culture that controls and shapes their lives.

These differences between the drawings of boys and girls are real differences, and worth noting, I think, in order to point the contrast with the Cleveland diagnosis where the differences aren't as pronounced and not much is made of them. Only in the area of "transportation" are they statistically apparent. The Cleveland boys are like boys everywhere: they draw trains and boats and autos and planes. The Hopi boys don't know trains and boats: they draw horses.

In any analysis of drawings a separate consideration of such elements as line and color and space is always necessary. Space has already been dealt with, and I shall not elaborate on line and color except to say that, for the Hopi child, the lines are most important. They are important to him not only as means of marking off and closing the areas to be filled in with colors, but he values lines in themselves, often going over them afterwards with a brush so as to give them separate emphasis. Other children wouldn't think of using the brush in this way. As for color, the Hopi child uses it descriptively--blue for the sky, white for the cloud, green for the cactus, brown for the earth--without much interest in its quality. He doesn't experiment with color as a thing in itself, nor is he sensitive to color repetitions. This is true all through the "appearance" stage in drawing. But when he comes to the ceremonial designs certain colors have meaning, he has no choice, they must be right. Then it becomes a problem in technique.

Drawing of the figure is also important to consider separately in the analysis of children's drawings. Frontality, profiles and 3/4 views indicate the developmental stages a child has reached; so also the features and details of dress. But whether or not the figure is invested with a sense of life and movement is more an indication of drawing ability, whatever the stage of development. In the early stages the Hopi children draw figures no differently than anybody else, but as they reach adolescence they draw people with a growing detachment, even a sense of unreality, reverting finally to the katcina which alone seems to have meaning for them. A fully developed realism is never achieved. It is not that they find the figure hard to draw — drawing the katcina is not easy — but that it is here first of all that the culture intervenes to determine what shall be done. Eventually realism disappears altogether in the symbolism of a tribal art.

Mrs. Lark-Horovitz describes five stages of development in children's drawings, as follows:

1. Scribble stage (infants)
2. Schematic stage
    a) Primitive schema (5-6)
    b) Schematic stage (6-9)
3. Mixed schema (9-15)
4. True-to-appearance (12-15)
5. Representation-in-space

Advancement into the final stage is, in her view, conditioned by training.

I have accepted the five stages used in the Cleveland diagnosis, wording them as follows: primitive schema, schematic drawing, transition drawing, appearance drawing, spatial drawing. The results are just the same; the years for each stage are almost the

same. Hopi children go through exactly the same developmental sequence toward realism and spatial representation, notwithstanding the parallel development caused by the increasing pressure of tribal conventions which, in the case of the more gifted ones, is destined to supplant visual realism entirely, producing in maturity a completely stylized art. It is interesting to note that a stylized phase occurs also in the work of urban children, though in a more superficial form which the Cleveland diagnosis recognizes as "decorative arrangement." But for the Hopi children this is not just a phase; it is the essence of a mature Hopi style; it is a serious art.

The true Hopi style requires the severest discipline and control over technical means, including mastery of a brush-drawn line unvarying in width and mechanically exact. The best of the Hopi drawings are barely on the threshold of this. The mastery of the brush-drawn line is difficult and slow. But it is the ideal which all those who would be artists in Hopi-land will strive for, even at the sacrifice of skills developed earlier in the service of realism. The peak of realism — that is to say the emphasis upon it — is reached very early at the ages of 12 to 14, but already at twelve the boys are drawing katcinas and the transition to abstract line is beginning. And for a while the quality of the work suffers. If we were to distinguish a "period of repression" for the Hopi child, it would come during late adolescence when he is trying so hard to master this line to bridge the gap from the illusionism of spatial drawing to the precision of a ritual art.

Condensed into brief statements my conclusions are as follows:

1. The developmental stages for the Hopi children correspond to those of the Cleveland children, the only difference being that they develop a year or two earlier, reaching the "appearance" stage toward 12, and seldom going beyond it, to spatial drawing.

2. The quality of the Hopi drawings is not to be compared to that of the selected Cleveland children, which, by our standards, is superior; but quality does not affect the rate or sequence of development.

3. The drawings reveal a sharp division of interest between the Hopi boys and girls; i.e., an early acceptance of sex roles.

4. The drawings indicate a generally superior ability of boys over girls — at least more assurance; this is reflected in data on "use of medium."

5. The Hopi child represents space by the use of multiple planes, not by convergence of lines or by color gradations usually taught the urban child.

6. Line is more important than color in Hopi drawings, and, with adolescence, the emphasis upon it increases, where the opposite could be true of urban children.

7. A fully developed realism is not achieved in figure drawing; the katcina conventions taking precedence.

8. A final change from realism to formalism is inevitable in Hopi drawings; elsewhere it would be optional. But drawings by

youths older than 16 would be necessary to document this change, because at that age it is still in process.

CHAPTER VIII

SUMMARY OF FINDINGS

While we have used a variety of tests in this Study, we have thus far described our findings and drawn cross-cultural comparisons on the basis of each test separately. In this chapter we shall draw together data from the several tests to see to what extent various measures agree or disagree in what they tell us of moral and emotional development in the different cultures.

Accordingly, we have drawn from the several tests a number of variables that seemed to us significant, and we have ranked the tribal groups on each variable. These data are presented in Tables 38 and 39. While these tables can be studied in a variety of ways in drawing cross-cultural comparisons, we have addressed ourselves only to a few major questions:

1. What is the relationship between data obtained from the Emotional Response Test (ERT) and data obtained from the Moral Ideology Test (MIT)?

2. Is there agreement among various indices of the degree of moral constraint that characterizes each of the eight societies?

3. Can we compare the eight societies on the degree of self-centeredness or other-centeredness when we use several indices together?

We then asked another question:

4. How do the roles of father and mother differ for boys and girls in the eight societies? (For this, we drew certain other variables from the Emotional Response and Moral Ideology Tests.)

We shall discuss each of these questions in turn and then offer a very brief description of each society as that description seemed to emerge from the total array of our data.

Emotional Response and Moral Ideology

What similarities may we expect between the emotional experiences reported on the Emotional Response Test and the moral behaviors re-

TABLE 38

RANKS OF CULTURAL GROUPS ON VARIABLES FROM THE VARIOUS TESTS

Test Variable	Test	Papago	Hopi	Zuni	Zia	Navaho Mt.	Shiprock	Sioux	Midwest
Acculturation	Free Drawing	6	3	4	2	1	5	7	8
Animism	Moral Judgment	5.5	3.5	3.5	7.5	7.5	2	5.5	1
Fear of supernatural	ERT	4	6	5	2	8	7	3	1
Moral constraint	Rules of Games	6	3	7	4	8	2	5	1
Immanent justice	Moral Judgment	4	5	6	3	8	2	7	1
Shame: embarrassment	ERT	5.5	3.5	7	3.5	8	5.5	2	1
Individual achievement	ERT	3	6	3	1	7	3	5	8
Competence	MIT	3.5	5.5	5.5	3.5	8	7	2	1
Personal virtues	MIT	4.5	3	2	4.5	8	7	1	6
Self-restraint	MIT	6.5	3.5	1	3.5	3.5	6.5	3.5	8
Self-gratification	ERT	7	4	2.5	5	1	2.5	6	8
Regard for others	MIT	3.5	7	3.5	7	1	3.5	7	3.5
Service	MIT	6.5	4.5	8	6.5	2	4.5	3	1
Smooth personal relations	ERT	4	6	8	7	2	4	4	1
Aggression by others	ERT	4	3	8	7	2	6	5	1
Aggression toward peers	MIT	1	6	3.5	6	3.5	6	8	2
Relations to authority	MIT	2.5	4.5	4.5	6	1	2.5	7	8
Discipline and authority of others	ERT	5	8	7	6	1.5	1.5	4	3
Property	MIT	6	7.5	4	4	2	4	7.5	1

TABLE 38-Continued

Test Variable	Test	Papago	Hopi	Zuni	Zia	Navaho Mt.	Shiprock	Sioux	Midwest
Property and possessions	ERT	2	5	1	7	6	8	4	3
Stealing	MIT	6	7.5	2.5	4.5	2.5	4.5	7.5	1
Work	ERT	3	6	7	1	8	5	2	4
Work	MIT	5.5	3	7.5	4	7.5	5.5	2	1

TABLE 39

RANKS OF CULTURAL GROUPS ON "SURROGATES" AND "PERSONS INVOLVED"

Test Variable	Test	Papago	Hopi	Zuni	Zia	Navaho Mt.	Shiprock	Sioux	Midwest
Family, pos. emotions	ERT	2	3	1	6.5	8	6.5	4.5	4.5
Family, neg. emotions	ERT	4	4	1.5	4	7	1.5	6	8
Family, total	ERT	2	3	1	5.5	8	4	5.5	7
Family, praisers	MIT	6.5	3	6.5	4	8	5	2	1
Family, blamers	MIT	5	2	8	2	6.5	6.5	2	4
Family, total	MIT	5.5	3	7	4	8	5.5	1	2
Father, pos. emotions	ERT	3	5	6.5	6.5	4	8	2	1
Father, neg. emotions	ERT	2.5	7	4	8	1	2.5	5.5	5.5
Father, total	ERT	2	7	5.5	8	1	5.5	4	3
Father, praiser	MIT	7	6	8	4.5	4.5	3	2	1
Father, blamer	MIT	7	5.5	8	5.5	3	2	4	1
Father, total	MIT	7	5.5	8	5.5	3.5	1	3.5	2

TABLE 39 — Continued

Test Variable	Test	Papago	Hopi	Zuni	Zia	Navaho Mt.	Shiprock	Sioux	Midwest
Mother, pos. emotions	ERT	5.5	1.5	1.5	3	5.5	5.5	8	5.5
Mother, neg. emotions	ERT	4	6	4	4	1.5	1.5	7	8
Mother, total	ERT	6	5	1	3	3	3	8	7
Mother, praiser	MIT	6	4	5	7	2	1	3	8
Mother, blamer	MIT	6	4.5	8	7	2	1	4.5	3
Mother, total	MIT	6.5	5	6.5	8	2	1	4	3
They, somebody, pos. emotions	ERT	3.5	5.5	5.5	3.5	1	8	7	2
They, somebody, neg. emotions	ERT	7	6	4.5	2.5	1	8	4.5	2.5
They, somebody, total	ERT	4.5	7.5	3	2	1	8	7.5	4.5
Everybody, praiser	MIT	2	6.5	1	3.5	3.5	5	6.5	8
Everybody, blamer	MIT	3.5	6.5	1	6.5	8	2	3.5	5
Everybody, total	MIT	2.5	7.5	1	4.5	4.5	2.5	6	7.5

ported on the Moral Ideology Test? For instance, if property and possessions constitutes an important focus of emotional experience for a given group of children, do those children show a corresponding moral concern over care of property? Or, to take another example, if the mother is often mentioned in connection with negative emotions, is she also often mentioned as a blamer?

There was a number of general themes which appeared in the responses to both the Moral Ideology and the Emotional Response Tests. Thus "Individual achievement" on the Emotional Response Test is similar to "Competence" on the Moral Ideology Test, in that both have to do with the development of the self.

In Tables 40 and 41, we have selected such similar pairs of variables and compared them. The variables have been taken from Tables 38 and 39; and comparisons are made by computing rank-order correlations for the eight groups of children on the paired variables.[1]

From an examination of Table 40, it becomes evident that only a few general themes carry both emotional and moral value in all eight societies. (Since there were only eight groups being ranked, a coefficient must be as high as .5 to be reliably different from zero.)

The work theme shows a consistent pattern--in societies where work is often mentioned as a source of emotion, work also carries a high moral value.

Where "Smooth personal relations" is an important source of emotion, "Service to others" (and to lesser extent, "Regard for others") is given a high order of moral value.

And the relation between "Self-gratification" (ERT) and "Self-restraint" (MIT) is consistent. It suggests that the groups who get great enjoyment out of amusements, freedom, and personal pleasures also have a moral concern about these things--they evaluate them as good or bad. Or, to put it in still other terms, where self-gratification is highly valued emotionally, it seems to pose something of a moral problem.

---

1. There is, of course, another way of comparing the ERT and MIT: where, instead of selecting only pairs of similar variables for comparison, we systematically compare each variable with every other variable. This procedure was carried out, and the results are shown in Appendixes E-1 and E-2. These appendixes are most impressive, perhaps, for the relatively few significant relationships shown between the variables.

Most themes do not, however, show this consistency. The general conclusion seems warranted that there is relatively little consistency between variables taken from the two tests. (Of 22 coefficients of correlation shown in Tables 40 and 41, only 5 are above .5.)

The two tests were, of course, designed to measure different phenomena. It seems clear from these comparisons that they did, in fact, do so.

Some of the comparisons which yielded insignificant correlations are worthy of further consideration. For example, there is no reliable relationship between "Discipline and authority of others" on the ERT and "Relation to authority" on the MIT. This may mean that the Hopi, Zuni, and Zia children (who are high on the ERT variable) dislike the rather high degree of authoritarianism that they live under and also have a high moral concern over their relations to authority. The Sioux and Midwest children, on the other hand, show a high moral concern over their relations to authority but are less involved emotionally over such constraint as they live under. Hence the correlation is of negligible size.

The low negative correlation between "Property and possessions" (ERT) and "Property" (MIT) may mean that some groups who get much emotional experience out of possession or deprivation of property and personal possessions (Navaho and Zia) nevertheless do not attach great moral significance to the care or destruction of property.

Thus we see that emotional experience in a certain area of life may or may not be connected with a high moral evaluation of this aspect of life. There are relationships between the two, but the relationships are not simple or direct, nor are they consistent in all the societies we are studying.

The differences between the tests are seen even more clearly when we compare the "Persons involved" of the ERT with the praisers and blamers of the MIT. Table 41 shows, in general, no relationship between the two.

At first thought, we might have expected a great deal of similarity between the people who would praise or blame a child for a good or bad act and those who are most involved emotionally with the child. Yet upon further thought, the results of Table 41 might well have been predicted. The MIT asks about behavior which this child or any child might

TABLE 40

SIMILAR THEMES IN EMOTIONAL RESPONSE AND MORAL IDEOLOGY TESTS: RANK-ORDER CORRELATIONS

ERT	MIT	rho*
Individual achievement	Competence	-.05
Individual achievement	Personal virtues	+.27
Property and possessions	Property	-.09
Property and possessions	Stealing	+.12
Smooth personal relations	Service	+.88
Smooth personal relations	Regard for others	+.55
Work	Work	+.71
Self-gratification	Self-restraint	+.60
Discipline and authority of others	Relations to authority	+.29
Aggression by others	Aggression toward peers	+.47

*rho must be greater than .5 to be reliably different from zero.

TABLE 41

PERSONS MENTIONED IN EMOTIONAL RESPONSE AND MORAL IDEOLOGY TESTS: RANK-ORDER CORRELATIONS

ERT	MIT	rho
Family--positive	Family--praisers	+.08
Family--negative	Family--blamers	-.30
Family (total)	Family (total)	-.16
Father--positive	Father--praiser	+.42
Father--negative	Father--blamer	+.25
Father (total)	Father (total)	+.19
Mother--positive	Mother--praiser	-.17
Mother--negative	Mother--blamer	+.25
Mother (total)	Mother (total)	-.13
They, somebody--positive	Everybody--praisers	+.11
They, somebody--negative	Everybody--blamers	-.58
They, somebody (total)	Everybody (total)	+.19

carry out in the future, while the ERT asks about the past experience of this particular child. On the MIT the emotional relations of the past will presumably have some influence over the moral surrogates named, but probably not a controlling influence. For example, a child who never steals might say that the father would blame a child for stealing. He might give this response, even though he has experienced very little blame from his own father and therefore does not report his father as involved in negative emotions.

Our conclusion must be this: that mention of people in the ERT has a considerably different meaning to a child than does mention of these same people as praisers and blamers on the MIT.

To sum up, the two tests tap different areas of life, different as regards behavior, conduct, and events and different as regards persons to whom the child relates.

Moral Constraint

We have three tests of the degree of external moral constraint operating on the children. As has been described in earlier chapters, we are using the concept "moral constraint" in Piaget's terms. The society high on moral constraint is one where morality is "heteronomous" rather than "autonomous"; where morality is vested in external authority--parents, elders, supernatural beings--and where rules of conduct are relatively inflexible. In such a society the child does not develop a sense of personal responsibility for judging right and wrong and for making moral decisions.

The three measures of moral constraint are these:

1. From the Emotional Response Test, responses on "shame" where embarrassment rather than guilt was the source of shame. This point has been developed in chapter iii, Section 5. Here it may be sufficient to repeat that, where a high proportion of responses on shame are of the embarrassment variety, we have interpreted this to mean that the child is controlled by social pressures rather than by internalized conscience; and that, accordingly, we can use this as a measure of the moral constraint that characterizes a society.

2. From the questions on "Rules of games," where proportions of responses indicating that rules are unchangeable were taken as an index of moral constraint operating on the child (see chap. v).

3. From the questions on "Immanent justice," where strong belief in immanent justice (as shown by high proportions of "Yes" responses to such questions; see chap. vi) is seen as a measure of moral constraint.

When the groups are compared on these three measures (see the fourth, fifth, and sixth rows in Table 38), we find over-all consistency--a consistency that cannot be due to chance. Rank-order correlations for the eight groups (including Midwest) were .83 for Rules of games and Immanent justice; .74 for Rules of games and Shame-embarrassment; and .49 for Immanent justice and Shame-embarrassment. The first two are highly reliable coefficients; the last is barely reliable at the 5 per cent level.

In fact, averaging the ranks of the various tribal groups on Rules of games and Immanent justice, we have almost exactly the same ranks as obtain on Shame-embarrassment for Midwest, Papago, Hopi, Zuni, Zia, and Navaho Mountain, although not for Shiprock and Sioux. Thus we can say that the three different measures of moral constraint agree except for Shiprock and Sioux, two relatively acculturated groups which, as described earlier, show contradictory behavior on a number of variables in the Study.[2]

The Rules of games and Immanent justice tests fully support each other. The two support rankings on Shame-embarrassment for all but two of the Indian groups studied.[3]

Self-centered versus Other-centered

Several times in our discussions of individual tests we have noted a tendency for certain groups to be self-centered and self-directed, in comparison with other groups which seem to place less value upon individuality and to be more concerned with smooth relations with others and with co-operation.

We have selected from Table 38 five variables in which the focus is upon the individual himself and seven other variables in which the focus

2. The Shiprock estimates are based on a very small number of responses (37 in all) to the Shame part of the Emotional Response Test, and thus may be unreliable. The Sioux data, however, are based on fairly large numbers of responses.

3. It should be recalled that Midwest children were not tested on Rules of games or on Immanent justice. They were assigned ranks of 1 (the lowest) on the two measures on the basis of our knowledge from other sources that modern White society, as compared with primitive societies, is extremely low on moral constraint.

is upon the group. The five measures of self-centeredness are: Individual achievement, Self-restraint, Self-gratification, Competence, and Personal virtues.

The seven measures of other-centeredness are: Regard for others, Service, Smooth personal relations, Relations with authority, Discipline and authority of others, Aggression toward peers, and Aggression by others. (The reader may consult earlier chapters for a description of each of these measures; see chap. iii, Sec. 3, and chap. iv, Sec. 2.)

We have averaged the rankings for each tribal group on the five measures of self-centeredness and have then established a rank order based on these averages. We have used the same method on the seven measures of other-centeredness. This results in the following new rank orders:

	Papago	Hopi	Zuni	Zia	Navaho Mt.	Shiprock	Sioux	Midwest
Self	5	4	1	3	7	6	2	8
Other	3	6	7	8	1	4	5	2

When we now compute the rank-order correlation on these two sets of rankings, the coefficient of correlation (rho) is –.82, reflecting a high degree of consistency in the data. (A group which is high on self-centeredness is low on other-centeredness.)[4]

Midwest and the two Navaho groups are the highly self-centered groups; the three Pueblo societies (Hopi, Zuni, Zia) are the highly other-centered.

The Roles of Father and Mother

By looking at the data on Persons involved in the Emotional Response Test and on Surrogates in the Moral Ideology Test, we can compare the roles of father and mother in the lives of boys and girls. The relevant data have been taken from Tables 19 and 20 of chapter iii and from Appendix C-4 and are summarized in Table 42.

Looking first at the data for girls, we find that the mother is mentioned much more frequently than the father in all four roles--as a prais-

4. It should be pointed out that the measures of self-centeredness and other-centeredness, having been drawn from different tests, are independent variables.

er, as a blamer, and as a person involved in both positive and negative emotions. (There are a few exceptions. The Hopi and Zuni girls mention father more frequently than mother as a person involved in positive emotions. This is probably due in these matrilocal societies to the position of the father as a gift-giver. The other exception is Navaho Mountain, where the father and mother are about equal as blamers and where neither is mentioned as a person involved in negative emotions.) In general, then, we see the mother as more significant than the father in the eyes of the girls.

The situation is only partially reversed in the case of boys, where there is less consistency in the four roles for the father and less consistency from tribe to tribe. For the boys, there are the following complexities:

As a person involved in positive emotions, the father is mentioned more frequently than the mother (except for Sioux and Midwest).

As a praiser, the father is mentioned more often than the mother at Zuni; he is about equal to the mother for Hopi, Papago, Navaho Mountain, and Shiprock; but he is mentioned less frequently than the mother in Zia, Sioux, and Midwest.

As a person involved in negative emotions, the father is mentioned more frequently than the mother at Zia; is about equal to the mother for Hopi, Papago, Zuni, and Shiprock; but is mentioned less frequently than the mother for Navaho Mountain, Sioux, and Midwest.

As a blamer, the father is mentioned more often than the mother for Hopi, Papago, Zuni, and Zia, but less often than the mother for Navaho Mountain, Shiprock, Sioux, and Midwest.

Thus we find Midwest and Sioux boys consistently giving more attention to the mother than to the father in all four roles--rewarder, praiser, punisher, and blamer. And at Navaho Mountain and Shiprock there is also a trend in this direction.

What appears to be the case, then, is that the father's role is a less important one in the life of the Midwest and Sioux boys than for boys in the other tribal groups and that in these two societies the mother takes a more important place in the boy's life.

TABLE 42

FATHER AND MOTHER AS "PERSONS INVOLVED" AND AS "SURROGATES"

	Hopi				Papago				Zuni				Zia			
	+Emotions		-Emotions		+Emotions		-Emotions		+Emotions		-Emotions		+Emotions		-Emotions	
	B	G	B	G	B	G	B	G	B	G	B	G	B	G	B	G
Father	35	21	8	6	37	8	4	1	41	20	6	0	40	21	16	3
Mother	5	14	10	10	4	23	4	8	6	12	6	9	0	25	8	9
	Praisers		Blamers		Praisers		Blamers		Praisers		Blamers		Praisers		Blamers	
Father	18	5	11	4	25	13	23	17	36	8	39	11	20	0	16	0
Mother	20	30	8	27	25	50	15	30	20	42	16	45	27	61	11	41

	Navaho Mountain				Shiprock				Sioux				Midwest			
	+Emotions		-Emotions		+Emotions		-Emotions		+Emotions		-Emotions		+Emotions		-Emotions	
	B	G	B	G	B	G	B	G	B	G	B	G	B	G	B	G
Father	40	10	0	0	56	18	5	0	15	5	4	4	10	9	4	3
Mother	3	28	11	0	7	24	2	8	19	25	13	11	15	14	12	17
	Praisers		Blamers		Praisers		Blamers		Praisers		Blamers		Praisers		Blamers	
Father	11	9	2	7	3	1	0	0	9	6	8	5	7	3	7	2
Mother	10	21	8	8	4	8	4	6	17	26	10	24	16	17	13	14

The Eight Societies

Midwest

In comparison to the simpler societies of the Southwest Indians, Midwest is a self-centered society, where the individual's responsibility and the individual's feelings are given priority over his concern about the social group.

There is a low order of external moral constraint; and the Midwest child, who feels guilt rather than shame when he does something wrong or ridiculous, is controlled by internal conscience rather than by external group pressures.

Very high in emotional response to individual achievement and to self-gratification, the Midwest child shows less emotionality as regards smooth personal relations with others, aggression by others, or discipline and authority of others.

His moral concerns lie mainly in the areas of personal virtues, self-restraint, and relations to authority, with correspondingly little moral concern over aggression toward peers, care of property, service to others, or competence in doing what is expected of children.

In general, we have the picture of an emphasis upon individual responsibility and self-concern, with clear distinctions between those areas of experience which are emotionally important and those which are morally important.

In interpersonal relationships the Midwest child is high in his perception of the wider community ("everybody") as praisers and blamers (perhaps another reflection of his moral concern over his position vis-à-vis authority figures). Within the family the Midwest child is closely tied to the mother and perceives the father as playing a less significant role in his emotional and moral life.

Navaho Mountain

This group is another self-centered society, but self-centered in a way very different from Midwest. Navaho Mountain is, first of all, the least acculturated of the Indian groups. It is the only Indian society in the Study which can be said to be relatively little affected by the surrounding white culture and is our best representative of a simple, primitive society. This group ranks at the top in animism and in fear of the supernatural but, more important, is at the top as regards moral constraint. Thus the moral character structure of the Navaho Mountain child is different from that of the Midwest child. It involves relatively little development of conscience but high external moral constraint.

The self-centeredness of Navaho Mountain is shown by its high rank on themes of individual achievement, personal virtues, work, and personal competence and in its low rank on themes involving social relations of various kinds: regard for others, service, smooth personal relations, aggression by others, relations to authority, and so on.

Several of these characteristics can perhaps be accounted for by the fact that Navaho Mountain children live in small family units isolated from others, with the family as the economic unit. The emphasis on individual achievement and competence may derive from the early assumption of a worker's role. Their low ranking on a number of social relationships is probably a reflection of the fact that they have so little experience of social relations outside the family, rather than a reflection of active disrespect for the rights and feelings of others.

The factor of geographical isolation probably accounts for the high degree of emotional relations with family members and the extent to which family members are almost the exclusive source of praise and blame. Children are distant from nonfamily members and have low intensity of feeling about things which, in another society, often cause conflict with others. Thus, for example, while Navaho Mountain children value property rather highly, they do not have much moral concern over stealing and care of property — perhaps because the opportunity for misusing other people's property is generally lacking.

While the Navaho Mountain child resembles the Midwest child on many of the test variables shown in Tables 38 and 39, still the over-all picture is quite different. Both groups may be called individualistic; but the individualism of Navaho Mountain is one focused upon industriousness and work (the early assumption of a worker's role) in a setting characterized by the geographical isolation of families who depend on the child's help in economic production. The individualism of Midwest is one in which work and industry are secondary in importance but where the child learns attitudes of self-enhancement and competitiveness and where he comes to expect as a matter of course a considerable amount of friction in his dealings with the people around him.

Shiprock

The test responses of Shiprock children are especially interesting because they can be compared with those of Navaho Mountain and can thus throw light on the question, How does acculturation to the dominant white culture affect the children's moral and emotional experience? Shiprock, which is much more acculturated than Navaho Mountain, is a curious mixture of change and tradition. While, in general, the two Navaho groups are very similar (as seen in Tables 38 and 39), on certain test variables Shiprock is at the other extreme from Navaho Mountain.

The most marked differences between Shiprock and Navaho Mountain are on degree of moral constraint (as seen from Rules of games), on belief in immanent justice, and on animism. (Shiprock comes closest to Midwest in these respects, while Navaho Mountain is the farthest from Midwest.) These differences would appear to be the result of specific teaching by whites.

Some of the differences between the two Navaho groups may also be explained by the differences in social living conditions. Whereas Navaho Mountain families live in social isolation, Shiprock families live as a community, and Shiprock children are subject to the typical community influences. (This difference in living conditions is perhaps reflected in the use of the "They, somebody" category on the ERT, for example, where Shiprock children mention this category more often than does any other group; Navaho Mountain, least often.)

The Pueblo societies

The Hopi, Zuni, and Zia are the three other-centered societies where the primary values seem to lie in concern over group welfare rather than concern with self-enhancement. At the same time, there are marked differences between the three groups.

The Hopi show high sensitivity over their relations with other people and over property: regard for others, discipline and authority of others, stealing, and care of property. They are low on external moral constraint. They show an average pattern on competence, personal virtues, self-restraint, service to others, and so on. Thus they seem to be average or slightly above average among the Indian groups in their sense of individual responsibility, while they are high in general moral and emotional concern over their social relations in the village. They are high in their perception of "everybody" as praisers and blamers; and clearly they experience more emotion and more moral concern in relation to people outside the family than do the pueblo-dwelling Zuni.

The Zuni children occupy the extreme high or low ranks on a large number of test variables. They are high in moral constraint (as contrasted with Hopi and Zia); high on the importance of work; high on the importance of smooth personal relations and service to others. The Zuni children have relatively weak feelings of personal guilt; and their relations with the family do not seem to produce much intensity of emotion, even though they are under continuous family pressure.

A surprising feature is the Zuni's low mention of the community ("everybody") as a source of praise and blame. In view of their close communal life, we might expect them to be much involved emotionally and much concerned about praise and blame from community members, as is true with the Hopi; and we might also have expected this from statements made by anthropologists that Zuni parents do not punish or threaten their children as much as in most other societies, but depend on nonfamily members to do much of the scolding of children. Instead, we have found just the opposite — that community members are not seen as blamers or praisers to any considerable extent at Zuni, while it is the family which takes higher precedence. (The family seems to have much more influence as a socializing agent with the Zuni than with any other group except Navaho Mountain.) The father at Zuni is highly important as praiser and blamer.

Thus we see the Zuni children as living under strong moral constraint to be good workers and peaceful, co-operative citizens. The moral pressure is exerted mainly by the family, but in such a way that it remains external to the child, who does not develop a strong sense of guilt or internalized conscience.

The Zia children are more sensitive to the group of variables dealing with relations to other people than any other group, though they are close to Zuni in this respect. Also, like Zuni, they are low in the area involving individual competence and achievement. (The Zia are high on animism, but low on fear of the supernatural.)

Papago

In general, the Papago are our "average" group among the Southwest Indian tribes. They have the fewest extreme rankings of any of the

groups. The Papago are high in self-gratification (ERT) and self-restraint (MIT), which suggests that gratification of impulse life is emotionally important and is also invested with important moral connotations. The father takes a relatively important role as praiser and blamer in the life of the Papago child.

Sioux

The Sioux are the most highly acculturated of the Indian groups in the Study. At the same time, as has been mentioned earlier, there is a high degree of culture conflict which is reflected in many of our test results.

The Sioux are high on a cluster of characteristics which may be interpreted as moral concern over hostile impulses: regard for others, aggression toward peers, relations to authority, stealing and care of property, self-gratification. While on two indices of moral constraint (Rules of games and Immanent justice) the Sioux are high, they are, at the same time, high on the guilt-shame ratio, indicating a considerable degree of internalized conscience as the source of moral authority. As regards their emotional and moral relations to other people, the Sioux children are much like the Midwest children.

CHAPTER IX

CONCLUSIONS: SOCIOPSYCHOLOGICAL RESEARCH ON CHILDREN OF DIVERSE CULTURES

The studies reported in this volume were all part of a co-ordinated effort to use sociopsychological techniques in a cross-cultural study of child development. Since the techniques were all originated for use in our own society, it was evident at the outset that there would be problems in transposing these techniques to cultures quite different from our own, and it was by no means certain that the effort would succeed.

Our experience includes both successes and failures and serves to point out the major difficulties in an enterprise of this sort. It also enables us to sketch out a procedure that could be used with maximum efficiency in field work by the anthropologist.

Successes

We have succeeded in getting reliable and substantial data on the basic emotional relationships, the common values and aversions, and the basic moral attitudes of children in several cultural groups. These data have been obtained for the most part on adequate samples of children in the various communities that we studied. Thus we are able to make some general statements about the children of these communities—statements which can be compared to those made by ethnologists on the basis of their own more orthodox ethnological methods.

One thing that has impressed us is the considerable degree of individuality shown by the children of these communities. There are such wide individual differences that we should be wary of taking any very small number of children as representative of a whole community. We do not generalize for a modern American community on the basis of a small sample. Yet investigators are often misled by the supposition that the Indian cultures are "simpler"; and they often generalize from knowledge about only a handful of children. Such a procedure is not justified in the light of what we have discovered about the degree of individual differences among the Indian children.

Difficulties

The difficulties we have found lay (1) in the adapting of sociopsychological instruments for use in cultures for which they were not originally intended; (2) in the interpreting of the results; and (3) in the administration of the tests.

The transposing of the technique seems to have been most successful with the Emotional Response Test, the Moral Ideology Test, and the Free Drawing Test. Judging by the volume of response obtained from the children and by the relative ease with which we were able to devise methods of analyzing the data, these instruments were as successful with the Indian children as they have been with children of the modern American culture.

Somewhat less successful were the techniques we borrowed from Piaget (although the Rules of games and the Immanent justice and Animism instruments did yield somewhat useful data). Other stories and questions that we employed in the battery of tests of moral judgment have not been successful (see pp. 216-21 in Appendix A). Even though they were tried out in various versions with Southwest Indian children before drawing up the form for use in the Test Booklet, nevertheless we obtained results which often seemed inconsistent or even contradictory when we tried to interpret and score these tests as Piaget had done with his Swiss children.

It may be, of course, that these seeming inconsistencies are in themselves useful data. This was the position taken by Eugene Lerner (who had taken the lead in formulating the Piaget-type questions) when we discussed with him the problem of interpreting our data. He said that it is as important to find seeming inconsistencies and contradictions in our data as to find regularities. He suggested that children may be so uncertain about their own moral ideas or so ambivalent about them that they will give inconsistent answers within a period of a few minutes. For instance, a child may be uncertain about belief in immanent justice, and consequently may give inconsistent answers. Such an inconsistency may not mean lack of comprehension of the test.

It might even be possible to get a measure of the inconsistency of response of a given child and to interpret this as a measure of his uncertainty over moral ideas. Such uncertainty could be due to transition from one stage to another in his culture or to conflict between the native and the white American cultures.

Similarly, it might be possible to record inconsistencies between communities within a tribe or within the responses of a given community group, such as very probably appear on the Emotional Response Test and the Moral Ideology Test. This inconsistency might be due to a kind of tribal ambivalence, or to compensation due to conflict in the tribal culture.

Analysis of this kind might have proved worth while, but we did not attempt it. Professor Lerner's untimely death prevented him from following up his suggestions.

Thus we must record most of the Piaget-type tests as unsuccessful, though perhaps these tests would have been useful had we employed a more subtle form of analysis.

The second type of difficulty lay in interpreting our results in relation to the concepts of acculturation, conscience-formation, animism, and immanent justice. Here we had partial success but also a good deal of difficulty, as we have shown in the preceding chapters.

There is the third difficulty of administering tests of this sort to children of an alien culture. Kluckhohn and Rosenzweig considered this factor in evaluating the use of these tests with Navaho children. They took account of the use of the Navaho language by the tester as compared with an interpreter, and the degree of familiarity between the tester and the child. They conclude that "psychiatrists and psychologists should not anticipate that primitive children can be tested adequately on the basis of casual rapport established in a few hours or a day. At least as regards quantity (of response), the familiarity between tester and child is crucial."[1]

The degree of rapport between tester and child in our Study varied from the high rapport that exists between a familiar and favorite teacher and the pupils whom she may have known intimately since they first came to school, to the strangeness that exists between a child and a strange white adult who speaks through an interpreter. Most of the children were

1. Clyde Kluckhohn and Janine Chappat Rosenzweig, "Two Navaho Children over a Five-Year Period," American Journal of Orthopsychiatry, XIX (April, 1949), 266-78.

tested by teachers with whom they were familiar but who were white people of another culture.

The Uses of Sociopsychological Techniques

In view of these difficulties, it is fair to ask whether the sociopsychological techniques offer any advantage at all as compared with the use of the regular field procedures of social anthropology. Will they repay the anthropologist for his effort if he undertakes to add them to his repertoire?

The argument in favor of their use by the anthropologist is that they represent a systematic way of questioning an adequate sample of a society. Since the anthropologist makes a major use of questioning in any case, this is simply a convenient and efficient way of doing it.

The use of such procedures as a supplement to and a check on the usual ethnological data was explored by Dr. Hilda Davis,[2] who studied the ethnological data on the Hopi, Navaho, and Papago, and then made inferences concerning the children's emotional responses and moral ideology—inferences which she compared with the data from the Emotional Response and Moral Ideology Tests. Most of her inferences were verified by the test data, but not all of them. This left open the question of whether the discrepancy was due to faulty inferences, faulty ethnology, or faults in the tests.

A subcommittee of the Committee on Social Behavior of the Social Science Research Council has recently published a Field Manual for the Cross Cultural Study of Child Rearing, which pays some attention to the matter of using psychological techniques in an anthropological study.[3] On the whole, they recommend a systematic procedure of observation and questioning by the anthropologist, supplemented by some psychological tests of the projective type. But they emphasize the need for obtaining quantitative measurements or judgments of cultural traits; and they give special attention to the problem of sampling and the size of the social unit of observation.

2. Hilda A. Davis, "A Study of the Moral Ideology and Emotionalized Attitudes of Children in Three Tribes of Southwestern American Indians" (unpublished Ph.D. dissertation, University of Chicago Library, 1953).

3. John W. M. Whiting et al., Field Manual for the Cross Cultural Study of Child Rearing: Preliminary Draft (New York: Social Science Research Council, 1953).

Procedures of the type used in our Study would generally be in accord with their recommendations, although there still remains the problem of how we categorized our data. In categorizing what is said by children on a test, it is difficult to avoid ethnocentrism. (Something of the same problem exists, of course, in categorizing what the anthropologist observes.) For instance, the categories which we employed in analyzing the Fear responses of the Emotional Response Test may not be so useful in analyzing the responses of Navaho and Hopi children as they are with Midwest children. Although we tried to use categories derived directly from the children's responses, there was some ambiguity as soon as we applied the same set of categories to any two tribes. And although, by conferring with anthropologists about these societies, we attempted to make the categories have the same psychological meanings for the various groups, it is nevertheless quite possible that our discussions of the problem of conscience and shame and of the problem of immanent justice and animism (and probably, though to lesser extent, our discussions of emotional response and moral ideology) are weakened by our use of categories which come from our own culture and may not be applied accurately to the other cultures. This problem has been discussed by Kluckhohn,[4] but he does not attempt to offer an easy solution.

Probably the anthropologist is the safest person to use such sociopsychological techniques as we have employed, because he would be sensitive to the problems of categorization of data.

What Is a Minimum Program of Social-psychological Testing?

If we were asked to recommend a minimum program of sociopsychological testing which might be undertaken by an anthropologist who was interested in the children of a given society, we would propose the following:

1. The Emotional Response and the Moral Ideology Tests. These secure responses from children easily, the responses are reliable when treated as group data, and the responses can be analyzed meaningfully.

2. A story-test or other questioning procedure of the Piaget type. (Examples are the Rules of games questions and the test of belief in Immanent justice.) These may be used to get at the degree of moral constraint under which the individual has lived. Since the responses are sometimes difficult to interpret, it would be well to try out this procedure on the group being studied and to adapt it to the specific situation.

3. A Thematic Apperception Test or a modification of it. We have not discussed the giving of a projective test of personality, but in the Indian Education Study we actually gave a Rorschach Test and a Thematic Apperception Test to large numbers of children, with good results. We believe that the TAT is more useful than the Rorschach in cross-cultural studies. In our Study the TAT was given in the usual manner, but we used pictures of people dressed in a kind of generalized Indian costume.[5]

Alternatively, the test may be of the Sentence Interpretation type devised by Lowell and McClelland and used successfully with Zuni, Hopi, and Navaho youths aged twelve to twenty.[6]

4. On the basis of our experience we would not recommend the following procedures for inclusion in a minimum program: (a) The several Piaget-type stories which we used as part of the Moral judgment battery see pp. 216-21, Appendix A). These do not seem to warrant inclusion without a considerable amount of preliminary work to adapt them to the particular culture being studied. (b) The Free Drawing Test. This seems to us to be more useful to someone who is interested in the problem of the development of drawing ability than to one who is interested in the moral and emotional development of children. For the latter purpose the Free Drawing Test is not an efficient procedure.

Number of Children To Be Tested

In order to arrive at results which are stable and from which it is safe to generalize, it would be well to test wherever possible at least 100 children aged eight to eighteen. The committee preparing the Field Manual for the Cross Cultural Study of Child Rearing has dealt with the question of sampling in a useful way, by defining a Primary Social Unit (PSU) as a small group of families that live close together, have frequent

4. Clyde Kluckhohn, "Universal Categories of Culture," in A. L. Kroeber (ed.), Anthropology Today (Chicago: University of Chicago Press, 1953), pp. 507-23.

5. William E. Henry, The Thematic Apperception Technique in the Study of Culture-Personality Relations ("Genetic Psychology Monographs," Vol. XXXV, No. 1 [1947]).

6. David C. McClelland, J. W. Atkinson, R. A. Clark, and E. L. Lowell, The Achievement Motive (New York: Appleton-Century-Crofts, 1953).

mutual interaction, and conceive of themselves as some sort of unit. Ideally, they say, this group would approximate thirty families. Such a group might have sixty or more children. All the families of a PSU should be studied, and all the children. (Our Navaho Mountain group probably approaches the PSU as defined by the committee. While too small for the most careful and accurate comparisons with other groups, yet this community, due to its cultural homogeneity, was a relatively easy and satisfactory one to study.)

Conclusions

For the anthropologist who wishes to equip himself with some systematic interviewing or questioning devices in the study of children we recommend these methods, with certain cautions that we have already stated. For the psychologist who wishes to co-operate with the anthropologist in studying children of diverse cultures we offer these methods and findings as a basis for further research, believing that the direction in which we have started will lead to interesting and useful results.

June, 1942

APPENDIX A

(Field Workers Manual and Example of a Child's Responses)

RESEARCH ON INDIAN EDUCATION

Guide for Field Workers (Revised)

PART I

The Office of Indian Affairs and the University of Chicago have initiated a joint research project which aims to study and compare the development of Indian personality in a number of Indian tribes. We hope that the results of this study, planned to extend over a period of two years, will help us to understand the Indians better, especially the Indian children, and to see what influence the white government and culture are having on them.

We are making an attempt to study the whole child as he grows and develops in his total environment. We want to get an accurate picture of him as he is, not only in school, but also on the playground, in his home, in church, at his daily chores, at fiestas, and in every other life situation he experiences. We believe that only by gaining a broad view of the individual as he functions in all his inter-personal relationships can we truly understand the attitudes and values which motivate his behavior in any one situation.

In your close daily contacts with Indian children, you have a rare opportunity to observe many children at work and play, to talk to them and to discover much about them that would take an outsider months to learn. These observations and interviews can be of great value to us in our attempt to get at the child's personality, his emotional as well as his intellectual life, his changing pattern of attitudes and values. You are also in a position to gain the confidence of the child's parents and relatives and to discover by observation and interview many significant details about his home environment and life history.

We are therefore depending on teachers, nurses, and other Indian Service personnel in close touch with the Indians to gather and record for us certain important facts concerning the life history, the home and community backgrounds of the children selected for study and to admin-

ister certain simple tests which require close rapport with the children.

During the three weeks of the Santa Fe Seminar, you have learned by discussion, observation, and actual practice the simple techniques you need in this work. You have not been required to master tests with difficult, elaborate techniques. A few such tests will be given the children by trained experts who will visit your schools to administer them. A health examination will also be given each selected child by our field doctors.

You will not be expected to score or evaluate the results of your testing program. This will be done by specialists.

Selection of Children To Be Studied

One person from each community has been made responsible for preparing a list of children according to a pre-arranged method of selection and for sending this list, before July 1, to Dr. Laura Thompson, Sells Agency, Sells, Arizona.

These persons are:

Mr. Pratt (Polacca and Oraibi)
Mrs. Eubank (Navaho Mountain)
Dr. Leighton (Ramah)
Miss Jordan (Shiprock)
Miss Leverett (Zia)
Mrs. Gonzales (Zuni)
Dr. Macgregor (Pine Ridge)
Dr. Thompson (Hickiwan and Topawa)

Dr. Thompson will assign a project number to each child on these lists. Once these numbers have been assigned there will be no changes in the list. If for any reason data cannot be obtained on any child this should be stated, but no child shall be dropped or added to the list, and no names shall be substituted.

As nearly as possible we wish to study equal numbers of boys and girls, equally distributed in the following four age groups: 6-8 incl.; 9-11; 12-14; 15-18. In determining a child's age for purposes of this study we shall consider his age to be that of his birthday during the calendar year 1942.

In selecting subjects for study in a given community we want to get a representative sample of the age group 6 to 18. There are two general cases to be considered:

1. When all the children in the community are to be studied (e.g., Hickiwan, Topawa, Polacca, Oraibi, Zia, Navaho Mountain);
2. When a sample is to be taken (e.g., Ramah, Shiprock, Zuni, Kyle, Pine Ridge).

1. In the case where all the children are to be studied the person in each community responsible for preparing the list shall simply make out a list from the school census giving the names of all boys and girls who reach the ages of 6 to 18 inclusive, during the calendar year 1942. This list should contain the name, census number, location, school now attended or occupation of each one of the subjects.

2. When a sample is to be selected, a plan has been made explicitly for each community. In general this plan is as follows: The person responsible will obtain a list of all the boys and girls 6 to 18 whose families live in the community. From this list a sample will be selected at random, except that when one child is selected all of his brothers and sisters in the age group 6 to 18 will automatically be included.

Responsibility of each field worker: The children selected from each school will be divided between the field workers from that school and each field worker will be responsible for seeing that the data described in this Guide are collected and filed for the children assigned to him or her.

Method of recording and filing field data: A field envelope for each child will be kept by the field worker responsible for that child. All the data concerning the child will be filed in this folder. Duplicates will be kept by the field worker and originals will be sent to Chicago for evaluation. On these envelopes there will be a form for recording the name of the child, age, school, community, and the name of the field worker, together with a check list of data to be obtained on each child. As each interview or test result is filed, the field worker will check it on the envelope. The Reservation Supervisor will be responsible for mailing the original copies of the field data every two weeks to Dr. Laura Thompson, Committee on Human Development, University of Chicago, for analysis and evaluation.

A personality card will be filled out in duplicate for each child. The field worker will be responsible for recording the data on the personality card.

A school record form will be filled out in duplicate for each child. The field worker will be responsible for this.

A health record form will be filled out in duplicate for each child by the field doctor.

Interviews concerning sociological background and life history data will be recorded in duplicate according to the instructions in Part III of this Guide.

Psychological tests will be recorded in duplicate on test record forms according to instructions in Part II of this Guide.

Period of field work: The field workers have been detailed to begin work on each reservation after the seminar, according to a prearranged plan. With the exception of the period during which they take annual leave, they will continue to work on the project full time during the summer and part time during most of the next school year. All results are to be submitted to the University of Chicago by January 15, 1943.

PART II

Psychological Tests To Be Given to Each Child Studied

The following informal tests, adapted for use with Indian boys and girls, are designed to throw light on moral and emotional development, and to serve as a guide toward the understanding of children's attitudes and values. These technical notes should be studied carefully by the field worker while he is learning to administer the tests.

Variations with age of child. The stories and questions are designed to be used with boys and girls from the age of 6 to 18. Since the stories and questions must be phrased in child-like language to suit the younger children, there is danger that older boys and girls may think them silly and refuse to take them seriously. To avoid this, it may be well to tell the older boys and girls that the stories and questions were written for small children, but that we want to know how grown-ups respond to them so as to see how mature the younger children are.

Variations with sex of child. Most of the stories and questions can be used in the same form for boys and girls. However, in stories A I and A III, and questions A IV and A VI F, it is important for a child to identify himself with one of his own sex and consequently there is a version for boys and a version for girls.

Variations to suit local conditions. There should be very few variations made on account of local conditions. But occasionally a variation will be necessary. Local place names will have to be supplied in several stories. In each case when a local variation is made, the variations should be approved by Dr. Thompson as Coordinator of the project, and then should be followed carefully.

Check on "Yes" and "No" responses. There is evidence that many Indian children use "yes" and "no" uncertainly when responding to rather complex questions. In some tribes the child may automatically answer "yes" to show that he understands the question, then think a while, and finally give his answer to the question, which may be "no" or "yes." It is important to check on this point with every child tested. This may be done by repeating the child's answer and adding "what?" e.g., "Yes, what?" or "No, what?" This should result in the child's making a further statement which will show what he really meant. For example, in story A I, if the child says "yes," the tester says "Yes, what?" and the child will then say "it was right," if he really intended to say "yes" in the first place. The tester should speak in a neutral tone in asking "yes, what?" so as to avoid seeming to challenge the child's answer. If, after this process has been repeated a few times, it is clear that the child is using "yes" and "no" accurately, it need not be continued.

Omissions. The tester should not omit any stories or questions. If, however, an omission occurs, explain the reason fully on the record form.

Additions. Additions to the stories and questions should be made very seldom. But it may be necessary to make certain additions in order to obtain a response from the child. Such additions should be recorded carefully. Sometimes a slight paraphrase is necessary if a child seems to have difficulty in understanding. Such paraphrases should be recorded on the record form.

Verbatim recording. The child's responses should be recorded verbatim, including incorrect grammar. Also the tester's comments, when they depart from the text, should be recorded verbatim.

Record form. A record form has been devised for use with this battery of tests. This form should be filled out as the test proceeds.

Practice by tester. The tester should memorize the stories and questions and practice them on children not in the study group until he feels sure that his technique is well established.

A. Tests of Moral Judgment and Moral Perspective.

The following stories and questions are to be told to each child in the study, in the order given.[1]

I

Purpose of story: To find out whether a child thinks it is fair to give special favors to the better-behaved of two children.

Story (a): (for boys) This is a story about two brothers. One of the boys, whose name was John, was very lazy and would not help his father and mother. The brother, whose name was Dick, was a good boy and always helped his father and mother. So the parents gave Dick a nice red shirt. But they did not give John anything, and he had to wear his old blue shirt to town.

Questions: A. Was it right what the father and mother did?
B. Why?

Story (b): (for girls) This is a story about two sisters. One of the girls, whose name was Mary, was very lazy and would not help her mother and father. The sister, whose name was Ann, was a good girl and always helped her father and mother. So the parents gave Ann a nice red ribbon for her hair. But they did not give Mary anything.

Question: Was it right what the father and mother did?

Answer: No.

Q. No, what?

Ans. One would get so hurt at heart.

Q. Why?

Ans. She may want to die because she may feel she is not wanted by her parents.

II

Purpose: To find out whether a child thinks that wrongdoing is inevitably followed by punishment even though the wrongdoer may not be discovered.

Story: This is a story about two boys. These two boys, named Jack and Paul, were out walking and they came to a melon field. Each of them stole a melon and ran off to eat it. But the owner of the field saw them and ran after them. He caught Jack and punished him, but Paul got away. The same afternoon,

1. The answers given by an 11-year-old Hopi girl are included for purposes of illustration.

Paul was chopping some wood, and the ax slipped and cut his foot.

Q. Why do you think Paul's foot was cut?

Ans. He did wrong.

Q. If Paul did not steal the melon, would he cut his foot?

Ans. No.

Q. No, what?

Ans. He did something wrong by stealing.

Q. Did the ax know that he stole the melon?

Ans. Yes and no. The ax might know that he did wrong because the spider grandmother perhaps told the ax, so the ax punished the boy.

Q. Does this happen only in stories or does it really happen?

Ans. It really happens in life, too.

III

Purpose: To find out how well a child can take account of people's intentions, when the consequences of their actions are bad.

Story: This is a story about two boys (girls). One of the boys (girls), whose name was Pete (Betty), was carrying five bowls for his (her) mother. He (she) fell over a piece of wood and broke all the bowls. The other boy (girl), whose name was Jim (Ruth), took one bowl to play with, when his (her) mother had told him (her) not to. He (she) fell down and broke the bowl.

Q. Was one boy (girl) worse (more bad) than the other?

Ans. Yes.

Q. Which boy (girl) was worse?

Ans. Ruth.

Q. Why?

Ans. She listened to her mother's advice, but she was too careless.

IV

Purpose: To find out how the child is influenced in his notions of right and wrong, fact and fiction, by the opinions of others of his own age, of older people, and of white people.

Question A: A boy (girl) and five others of his (her) own class are quarreling.

Q. Who is right?

Ans. Both wrong.

Q. Why?

Ans. It is not right to quarrel.

Question B: A small boy (girl) and a big boy (girl) are quarreling.

Q. Who is right?

Ans. Both wrong.

Q. Why?

Ans. They are doing wrong by quarreling.

Question C: A young man and an old man are quarreling.

Q. Who is right?

Ans. Both wrong.

Q. Why?

Ans. Because it is wrong to quarrel.

Question D: An Indian boy (girl) and a white boy (girl) are quarreling.

Q. Who is right?

Ans. Both wrong.

Q. Why?

Ans. They should not quarrel.

V

Purpose: To find out whether a child can take various points of view on a moral issue.

Story: This is a story about a boy called Frank. He was lazy, and so his mother told him to bring water without help from the other boys. But his friend, Sam, helped him anyway.

Q. What do you think—was it right for Sam to help Frank?

Ans. No.

Q. What does Frank think—was it right for Sam to help him?

Ans. Yes. Because Frank was too lazy and was glad to get help.

Q. What does Sam think—was it right for him to help Frank?

Ans. Yes. Frank was his friend.

Q. What does Frank's mother think—was it right for Sam to help Frank?

Ans. No.

Q. What does Sam's mother think—was it right for Sam to help Frank?

Ans. No.

VI

Purpose: To find out how the child feels about his own family, community, school, tribe, race, as against those who are outside of these groups.

Question A: If your father and another man are quarreling, who is right?

Ans. Both wrong.

Q. Why?

Ans. They should not quarrel.

Question B: Does your mother love you more than other mothers love their children?

Ans. My mother.

Q. Why?

Ans. Because I am her child.

Question C: Someone told me that the children from (nearby school) sing better than the children from our school. Who do you think sing better?

Ans. (Local school) Hopi High School.

Q. Why?

Ans. They come to school more and study more.

Question D: Someone told me that the people of our village (name it) are bigger liars than the people from (nearby community). Who

do you think are bigger liars?

Ans. People from our village Kyakotsmovi. People from nearby community Oraibi. Both.

Q. Why?

Ans. They both tell lies.

Question E: Which Indians dance better, the (local tribe) Indians or the (neighboring tribe) Indians?

Ans. (Local tribe) Hopi.

Q. Why?

Ans. They dance all the time.

Question F: Who do you think work harder, the white boy (girls) in (neighboring white center) or the Indian boys (girls)?

Ans. White boys (girls). Indian boys (girls). Both.

Q. Why?

Ans. They both work alike, depends on what they know and can do.

VII

Purpose: To find out how the child evaluates various types of punishment.

Story: This is a story of a big boy named Joe who is 16 years old. Joe steals a saddle from another Hopi.

Q. What do you think should happen to Joe?

Ans. He should be punished.

Q. Now I am going to say three things and I want you to tell me one of these things that should happen to Joe:
1) His grandfather should talk to him.
2) The policeman should put him in jail.
3) He should work and pay for the saddle.
(Circle punishment chosen by child)

(no. 3 was chosen)

Q. Which thing is the worst thing that can happen to him?

Ans. If everybody knows he is working to pay back the man for saddle. They would talk about him and he would be so ashamed all the time.

Q. Which thing is the next worst thing that can happen to him?

Ans. To be put in jail.

Q. Which next?

Ans. When grandfather scolds him.

VIII

Purpose: To find out what a child thinks will happen as a consequence of unobserved wrongdoing.

Story: Now, suppose that Joe steals a saddle and sells it in town and spends the money. Nobody finds out about this. Nobody knows that he stole the saddle.

Q. Will Joe be punished?

Ans. Yes.

Q. (If yes) how will he be punished?

Ans. He will worry till he dies.

Q. I am going to say four things and I want you to tell me one of these things that will happen to him:
1) He will get sick. (Why?)
2) He will remember what he has done and feel badly about it.
3) His family will find out and his father will talk to him.
4) Nothing will happen to him.
(Circle possibility chosen by child)

(Chose no. 3, first; no. 1, second. Answered "why?" of no. 1, "He will worry and be so shamed till he dies.")

B. The Emotional Response Test

The purpose of this test is to get a record of a child's experiences which are associated with certain emotions. The tester, after making sure that there will not be interruptions and that the child feels secure, asks the following questions in the following order, and notes the responses.

I

Happiness. Sometimes people are very happy.

Q. Have you ever been very happy?

Ans. Yes.

Q. Can you remember when you were very happy?—Tell me about it.

Ans. When parents give me something.

Q. Can you remember another time when you were very happy?—Tell me about it.

Ans. When my grandmother gave me a blanket.

Q. Can you remember another time when you were very happy?—Tell me about it.

Ans. When the katcinas give me nice things like dolls and pretty piki.

II

Sadness. Sometimes people are very sad.

Q. Have you ever been very sad?

Ans. Yes.

Q. Can you remember when you were very sad?—Tell me about it.

Ans. When I make mistakes in anything.

Q. Can you remember another time when you were very sad?—Tell me about it.

Ans. When I lose some of my things.

Q. Can you remember another time when you were very sad?—Tell me about it.

Ans. When some one dies in our home or in the village.

III

Fear. Sometimes people are very much afraid.

Q. Have you ever been afraid?

Ans. Yes.

Q. Can you remember when you were very much afraid?—Tell me about it.

Ans. When I am out in the dark, especially away from home. I am afraid that the ghost might catch me or the Masawu (dead person) might come to me.

Q. Can you remember another time when you were very much afraid?—Tell me about it.

Ans. When I hear an owl hooting from the horse corral. He might bring evil or even take me away to eat me.

Q. Can you remember another time when you were very much afraid?—Tell me about it.

Ans. One day when grandparents went to field, Betty and I were going to see them. On our way we were passing the old church. From the old church something that looked terrible looked at us, and motioned to us to come to her.

"How terrible! And what did she look like?"

She had big red head and long, thin red arms and had an old Hopi blanket dress. She was looking at us from the window. Betty and I just stood for a long time, could not move. Then we tried to run home with our heads down, but something just lifts our head up. Neither could we run. We were almost sick. Now I am afraid all the time.

"That's too bad. I am sure nothing will hurt you anymore."

IV

Anger. Sometimes people are very angry.

Q. Have you ever been very angry?

Ans. Yes.

Q. Can you remember when you were very angry?—Tell me about it.

Ans. When my playmates steal my things.

Q. Can you remember another time when you were very angry?—Tell me about it.

Ans. When they make me do things that I do not like to do.

Q. Can you remember another time when you were very angry?—Tell me about it.

Ans. I don't remember.

V

Shame. Sometimes people are very much ashamed.

Q. Have you ever been very much ashamed?

Ans. Yes.

Q. Can you remember when you were very much ashamed?—Tell me about it.

Ans. When I make mistakes before other people.

Q. Can you remember another time when you were very much ashamed?—Tell me about it.

Ans. When I am in the programs.

Q. Can you remember another time when you were very much ashamed?—Tell me about it.

Ans. I don't remember.

VI

Best and Worst Thing.

Q. Now I want you to think what is the best thing that could happen to you. Tell me, what is the best thing that could happen to you?

Ans. I wish I could have a new dress.

Q. Now I want you to think what is the worst (most bad) thing that could happen to you. Tell me, what is the worst (most bad) thing that could happen to you?

Ans. That some boy might take advantage of me at night, so I never go away from home at night.

Notes on Procedure: Try to get three responses for each type of emotion, but do not press the child hard if he doesn't give a response. In this case, note and describe his behavior.

Find out what the best Indian word is for each emotion, and use it together with the English word with young children.

For older children (12 or over) who can write fairly fluently, this test may be given as a group test with the children writing down their responses. If you try this as a group test, write a description of your procedure and send it along with your reports. Be sure that the name and number of the child is on his paper.

Be sure to use a matter-of-fact tone with older children, so that they will not think that they are being treated like babies.

C. A Test of Moral Ideology

The purpose of this test is to find out the public, official, moral ideas of a group. The individual's response is not taken to indicate just how he would act in a given situation, but how he thinks people in general would want him to act.

Procedure: Say to the child: I want to find out what boys and girls of your age think are good things to do and bad things to do.

Q. What could a boy (girl) of your age do that would be a good thing to do, so that someone would praise him (her) or be pleased?

Ans. To keep the house clean and orderly.

Q. Who would praise him (her) or be pleased?

Ans. Parents.

Q. What is another thing, a very good thing, that a boy (girl) . . . etc.?

Ans. Grind corn.

Q. Who would praise him (her) or be pleased?

Ans. Parents.

Q. What is still another thing, a very, very good thing, that a boy (girl) . . . etc.?

Ans. Grind corn for grandparents, and sometimes make piki, too.

Q. Who would praise him (her) or be pleased?

Ans. Parents and everybody.

Note — Continue this procedure until you have as many as seven or eight responses, if possible, but stop with three responses if the child has difficulty.

Then, say to the child:

Q. What could a boy (girl) of your age do that would be a bad thing to do, so that someone would blame him (her), or think badly of him (her)?

Ans. To steal from others.

Q. Who will blame him (her) or think badly of him (her)?

Ans. All the people.

Q. What is a very bad thing that a boy (girl) of your age could do, so . . . etc.?

Ans. Tease and fight with other children.

Q. Who will blame him (her) or think badly of him (her)?

Ans. Everybody.

Q. What is still another thing, a very, very bad thing, that a boy (girl) . . . etc.?

Ans. Destroy other people's things and at home, too.

Q. Who will blame him (her) or think badly of him (her)?

Ans. Everybody and parents.

Note—Continue this procedure until you have as many as seven or eight responses, if possible, but stop with three responses if the child shows signs of disturbance.

Notes on Procedure: Be careful never to ask the child directly what he could do that would be good or bad. Always ask what a boy or girl of his age could do. Do not ask leading questions, such as "Can you help your mother?" or "Does your father ever punish you?"

For older children, who can write fairly fluently (12 or above), this test may be given as a group test with the children writing down their responses. If you try this as a group test, write a description of your procedure and send it along with your reports. In this case, show the children how to follow a form which shows clearly what the good or bad action is, who will praise or blame. One line might be used for each with each new response numbered, or four parallel columns might be used. Be sure that the child's name and number appear on his paper.

D. Rules of Games

Purpose: To find out a child's beliefs about the sources of rules and the possibilities of changing them.

Introduction: Commence a conversation about games and find out what games the child likes to play. Select one (baseball, hide and seek, marbles, jacks, etc.) from among those mentioned.

Record of introductory conversation:

"May, do you still like to play Cat and Mouse?"

"Yes."

"Why can't a mouse catch a cat in that game?"

"Because it is not right way to play it."

"Would it be all right to play that game in some other way?"

"No."

"Why?"

"Because it would not be right."

Q. Do you know a rule in this game?

Ans. Yes.

Q. What do you think, who made this rule first?

Ans. White man that made that game.

Q. Can boys or girls like you make new rules?

Ans. Yes.

Q. Can small children make new rules?

Ans. Yes.

Q. Can bigger boys and girls make new rules?

Ans. Yes.

Q. Can rules be changed?

Ans. Yes.

Q. (If yes) how can rules be changed?

Ans. When it is no good.

Q. (If yes) by whom?

Ans. Everybody that do not like it.

Alternative: If the child does not know what a rule is, ask him to tell you about the game. He will probably mention a rule (three strikes, batting order, etc.). Then ask the following questions about this rule, without calling it a rule.

B. 1. Is it right to play another way? (Give specific example of a variation of the rule).

2. (If not), why not?

C. 1. Is it right for bigger boys and girls to play another way?

2. (If not), why not?

D. 1. Is it right for anybody to play this game another way?

2. (If so), who?

E. The Free Drawing Test

Purpose: To secure from each child in school eight free drawings, or paintings, and one drawing of a man made under controlled conditions. The free drawings are to be obtained in such a way that the child is free to choose size of paper, colors to be used, forms and content, and medium.

Material:

1. At least two sizes of paper, approximately 8 x 11 and 13 x 19 inches. (Three sizes, 8 x 11, 11 x 16, 16 x 22, would be preferable.)
2. Hard and soft pencils.
3. If possible, a set of paints for each individual: bright yellow, brown, bright red, dark red, bright blue, dark blue, black, white.
4. At least one thick, full, and one very thin, fine hairbrush.
5. A 10-cent palette from Woolworth with depressions or holes for mixing colors.
6. A receptacle for water for cleaning brushes.

As far as possible, these materials should be provided. In any case, the field worker should give a description of the materials actually provided.

Attitude of the Field Worker

The field worker's attitude should be stimulating only insofar as he has to bring the individual to action. In cases where the children approach the material with shyness, or without any idea what to begin with, he could stimulate them by making a few strokes or spots, but in that case he should use at least two or three colors, he should not represent any object, and he should remove what he drew or painted as soon and as unnoticeably as possible. It is much better if he can make the people draw or paint without doing it himself, and without provoking the situation of his being asked to draw. A friendly neutrality will be the best attitude. He should not influence in any way, either by stimulating or interfering in the selection of subject, material, or form. If he is asked, "What shall I do?" or "How shall I make this?" his answer should always be, "As you like."

Data To Be Noted on the Back of Each Drawing

1. Name.
2. Age (if possible, or at least approximate).
3. Sex of the person.
4. Chronological order of the drawings. Write sequence number of each picture systematically in same (left or right) top corner; in some cases where the child perhaps does not paint or draw realistically this will indicate from which side the child painted his picture.
5. Time taken for the drawing.
6. Coincidental factors, such as spilling, stimulation within the group, or by outside person, or accidental experience which might influence the choice of a theme, or color, etc.
7. Imitating another person's drawing.
8. Position of both individual and material (whether the person is lying on the floor, sitting at table, etc.).
   A level surface is to be preferred to a slanting one.
9. Write the names of objects on the back of the pictures and note their locations, where the objects are not clearly recognizable.
10. Note objects which obviously do not occur in the child's environment, but which he has seen in books or movies or elsewhere, or heard about.
11. Note reason if picture was left unfinished.
12. Make a note on the back of every picture in which the child was asked to do a specific thing. For example, if the child is asked to draw a human figure, note this. But note specifically what was requested. If the sex of the figure was left to the child's choice, make this clear.

Procedure of Test

1. For individual testing the ideal setup is to obtain a sequence of eight free drawings in chronological order (if made in the same session, note 1, 2, 3, etc.).
2. Testing the limits, in regard to form and color. This means if

the individual uses in his free drawings only pencil and never color (or vice versa) ask him to make a picture with the other medium. If he then only uses lines and never spots (or vice versa) ask him to make a picture with the opposite technique.

3. Testing the limits, in regard to content: If the individual does not draw or paint a face or a human figure, or both, ask him to draw or paint each respectively, or both.
4. Ask him to make a picture of himself doing something.
5. For group testing in a small community where individuals and groups of individuals are in contact with each other, the testing of the limits should be postponed until everybody has given a few free drawings.
6. When the series is completed for any one child, clip the drawings together, folding the larger sheets, if necessary, and turn them in to the reservation supervisor who will send them to the Coordinator's Office, University of Chicago.

APPENDIX B-1

EMOTIONAL RESPONSE TEST: HAPPINESS CATEGORIES

I. Amusements, parties, games[1]

1.[2] Playing, playing games, with pets, toys
2. Playing competitive sports—basketball, football
3. Winning games or sports—the team or school
4. Personal achievement in games or sports
5. Watching sports
6. Riding horses, roping calves
7. Singing, hiking, going for a walk, hunting, fishing, swimming, riding bicycle
8. Going to rodeo, circus, movie, fair
9. Going to or having parties, picnics, dances (not tribal)
10. Having a good time, something going on, riding in a car.

Sample responses:
"To ride a horse." (Zuni male, age 10)
"The little dog played with me." (Zuni M10)
"When I got to shoot a gun." (Navaho Mt. M12)
"Singing makes me happy." (Shiprock M8)
"When I went to a party at school." (Papago F16)

II. Holidays, birthdays, ceremonials, fiestas

11. Celebrating native feasts, fiestas, tribal dances without religious significance
12. Tribal ceremonials
13. Participating in tribal ceremonials
14. Celebrating 4th of July, Christmas, or other white-culture holidays
15. Birthdays (own)
16. Weddings

Sample responses:
"When my father took me to the Indian Ceremonial last August." (Zuni M16)
"I was happy at Shalako because I was helping the women that were baking bread." (Zuni F16)
"Last week when we had a carnival at school." (Zia F14)
"When my family had a Sing for me—about two months ago." (Navaho Mt. F17)
"Going to Navaho Fair." (Shiprock M11)

1. Category combination. The combinations which account for the bulk of the responses are shown in Table 4 of the text. Thus, of 22 combinations of Happiness responses, 10 occurred so infrequently as to make statistical treatment meaningless.

2. The original categories which make up the category combination. Certain categories are to be found in more than one combination.

"Christmas makes everyone very happy." (Shiprock F14)
"The first formal dance I went to." (Midwest F14)
"On my birthday." (Hopi F15)
"When the katcinas came to the village and when I see them my heart jumps and jumps." (Hopi M7)
"I rode on the merry-go-round on Fourth of July." (Hopi F11)
"When we had a fiesta right at our house." (Papago F16)

III. Tribal ceremonials, fiestas

11. Celebrating native feasts, fiestas, tribal dances without religious significance
12. Tribal ceremonials
13. Participating in tribal ceremonials

IV. Receiving food, gifts, money

17. Getting food, being given something to eat, goodies, candy, treats
18. Receiving materials, services
19. Receiving money as gift
20. Getting a pet
22. Having food, having something to eat
23. Owning property—horse, clothes, toys
24. Having a pet
25. Having nice things, clothes, etc., new clothes
26. Finding lost property
27. Having money; getting a check; finding, winning money, getting paid

Sample responses:
"When I got a guitar." (Papago M14)
"When I got my dog." (Midwest F15)
"When I got pants like my elder brother—with pockets." (Navaho Mt. M13)
"When my father bought me my first hat. It was a big one, like his." (Navaho Mt. M13)
"When my sheep and horses are many and fat." (Zuni M17)
"Tuesday my father took me to help sell the sheep and he gave me 25 cents." (Zuni M12)
"When the katcinas gave me bow and arrows." (Hopi M9)
"When I have enough to eat." (Navaho Mt. M12)
"When my grandmother bought me shoes. I wanted them so badly; I was tired of moccasins." (Navaho Mt. M12)
"When I got a bike." (Midwest M13)
"I was happy because I got a new skirt and blouse." (Midwest F12)

V. Giving materials and services

21. Giving materials, services, money

VI. Work, earning money

28. Earning money; getting or having a job
29. First job
30. Doing work at home or in the fields—herd sheep, grind corn; working with others, helping with family tasks.
31. Creative work, weave rugs
32. Doing work well; pride in work, getting a raise in pay, learning to do some work
33. Not being lazy

Sample responses:
"When I picked cotton." (Papago F12)
"When I weave rugs in summer time." (Shiprock F17)
"When I cook and make coffee." (Shiprock F6)
"When I made money to get comb for my hair." (Navaho Mt. F15)
"When we go down into the canyon to plant." (Navaho Mt. F10)
"I was happy when I sold my lambs last fall and got money." (Zuni M17)
"When I stay home with my mother working at bead work and baking bread." (Zuni F15)
"When my garden is doing well." (Zuni F14)
"I worked and got money." (Zia M12)
"When I got a job." (Midwest M12)

VII. Travel, going to town, vacation trips

34. Going some place—store, town; going somewhere with the family, short trips
35. Going on journeys, planned or long trips, vacation trips

Sample responses:
"When I went to Albuquerque in a car." (Zia M11)
"When I go to San Isidro in the wagon with my father and he bought me candy." (Zia F8)
"To go to church or to a picture show." (Shiprock F13)
"Last year we went to the cotton fields and every Saturday we went to town to the picture show." (Papago F13)
"When I went on a trip." (Midwest M13)
"A trip to the Army War show." (Midwest M13)
"When we went to California." (Midwest F12)

VIII. Going to school, doing well in school

36. Going to school
38. School subjects — doing arithmetic, reading, homework
39. Passing, graduating, doing well in school, good grades

IX. No school, vacation

37. Not having to go to school—vacation

X. Family solidarity

40. Being with the immediate family—all being at home together
41. Improvement of family situation, finances, etc.
42. Return of absent members of the family
43. Safety of members of family
44. Family gatherings, visits to and from members of family
45. New baby, birth of sib; addition to immediate or extended family
46. Playing with the baby
47. Getting letters, hearing from relatives
48. Family excursion for purposes of work—sheep camp, gathering pinon nuts

Sample responses:
"When I took care of my little sister all by myself for a day when my mother was away." (Navaho Mt. F13)
"When my grandfather told me stories of the long ago." (Navaho Mt. M9)
"When I became an uncle." (Midwest M15)
"When my father comes home to us in the evenings." (Hopi F8)
"When I'm in my house." (Shiprock F8)
"When my younger brother was born. He was so sweet." (Navaho Mt. F 13)
"Play with baby at home." (Zuni F12)

XI. Good relations with peers

49. Making new friends
50. Being with friends
51. Hearing from friends
52. Safety of friends
53. Acceptance into group by peers—getting to do what the others are doing
54. Going to another child's house, having friend visit own home, dates
55. First date
56. Sexual intimacy, kissing a girl, boy
57. Falling in love, being engaged, going steady, having a girl or boy friend

XII. Good relations with peers of opposite sex

55. First date
56. Sexual intimacy, kissing a girl, boy
57. Falling in love, being engaged, going steady, having a girl or boy friend

XIII. Individual achievement, gaining recognition

4. Personal achievement in games or sports
28. Earning money; getting or having a job
29. First job
31. Creative work, weave rugs
32. Doing work well; pride in work, getting a raise in pay, learning to do some work

39. Passing, graduating, doing well in school, good grades
58. Achieving an ambition, meeting an important person
59. Public recognition of achievement
59a. Personal achievement through talent or hard work (anything not included in more specific categories)

Sample responses:
"When I first went out alone to herd the sheep." (Navaho Mt. M11)
"When I learned my first chant perfectly." (Navaho Mt. M17 — son of a medicine man)
"When I do things good." (Shiprock M8)
"When I made the school basket-ball team." (Midwest M14)
"My first successful ski jump." (Midwest M13)
"When I raised my algebra grade." (Midwest M14)
"When I got my honor pin at school." (Papago F18)
"When I was elected president of our class." (Midwest F12)

XIV. Be good

60. Be good, do good, be nice to each other, be nice to somebody

XV. Others be nice to you

61. Others being nice to you, goodness of others—"When children be good"

XVI. Good fortune of others

62. Happiness in good fortune of others

XVII. Humor and jokes

63. Accidents of, errors by, jokes on others
64. Jokes on self
65. Humorous stories, situations

XVIII. Church

66. Going to church, communion, getting religion

XIX. Health

67. Being or getting well

XX. Moving

68. Moving to a new place
69. Moving back to an old place

XXI. Being grown up

70. Being grown up, allowed to do things independently

XXII. Miscellaneous

71. Miscellaneous

APPENDIX B-2

EMOTIONAL RESPONSE TEST: "BEST THING" CATEGORIES

I. Personal achievement[1]

1.[2] Getting an education; learning and achievement in school
2. Specific vocation; doing work very well
3. Special achievement at play (not school or work); development of a talent
4. High ambition
5. Achieve my ambitions
6. Have many friends; be popular

Sample responses:
"To be a football star." (Midwest M12)
"To become a good singer." (Papago F10)
"To be a good Hopi farmer." (Hopi M13)
"To be a great bronc rider." (Sioux M16)
"Be an airplane pilot." (Sioux M16)
"Learn to tap dance." (Sioux F14)
"To be a nurse or go in medical work." (Sioux F14)
"To learn and study well." (Hopi M18)
"Get good enough to play first clarinet." (Midwest M14)
"To win a prize or some high honor." (Midwest F14)
"To be a good medicine man." (Navaho Mt. M17)
"To win a scholarship." (Midwest F14)
"To become president of the Senior Class." (Midwest F14)
"To get many prizes at school." (Zuni F14)
"When basketball season comes, maybe I be on the team." (Zuni M12)
"Learn to sew really well." (Navaho Mt. F13)

II. Personal pleasure and comfort, excitement, be healthy

8.[3] Prestige or money without working for it
10. Getting or having a pet
11. Food treats
12. Going someplace (town; another state, etc.)
13. Train ride; auto ride, wagon ride
14. Attending social event or gathering; something going on; a fair
15. Riding a horse (or chasing, roping, etc.)

1. Category combination. The combinations which account for the bulk of the responses are shown in Table 5 of the text.

2. The original categories which make up the category combination. Certain categories may be found in more than one combination.

3. See combination XV for categories 7 and 9.

16. General happiness
16a. Playing, having a good time
17. Good health; freedom from accident or injury, long life
18. Move back to a nicer place
19. To be free; socially or physically independent

Sample responses:
"To go visiting." (Zia M14)
"That I could stay by the salt weed where it is warm." (Navaho Mt. F15)
"If I could go and see a big town." (Navaho Mt. F17)
"To ride the train." (Shiprock F12)
"Go to California for a visit." (Sioux M15)
"To ride horses." (Sioux M9)
"If they had a fair here." (Sioux M11)
"Go to a dance or bingo or something." (Sioux F8)
"Have a party." (Sioux F11)
"Get a permanent." (Sioux F17)
"To get fat; I'm tired of being skinny all the time." (Papago F18)
"Have all the iced tea I want to drink." (Papago M9)
"I could be happy." (Midwest F13)

III. Meeting social expectations (school, job); growing up (no stress on achievement)

20. Going to school; school activities (learning, achievement in school, etc. not mentioned)
21. Job; employment. (Specific job or training not mentioned)
22. Work activities; industry; helping at home
23. Growing up

Sample responses:
"To grow up and be a farmer." (Papago M11)
"To get through school and go back to Oraibi and farm." (Hopi M16)
"Get an education and learn to do the right thing." (Papago F14)
"Do the right things: not to have any accidents." (Hopi M16)
"To go to herd sheep." (Hopi M9)
"Finish high school." (Sioux M16)
"If I could go to the Army next year." (Zia M17)
"A good steady job." (Navaho Mt. M18)
"To grow up and be a popular person." (Midwest F13)

IV. Family or group solidarity

24. Witnessing or staging ceremonial (native)
25. Return of absent members of family; family solidarity
26. School or family or social group to make outstanding achievement
27. New addition to family

Sample responses:
"Shalako comes." (Zuni M10)
"That I be going back home from school; I get anxious to see my family again." (Navaho Mt. M8)

"To get another brother." (Shiprock F10)
"My mother and father would go back together." (Midwest F13)
"My mother came home from the hospital." (Midwest F13)
"It will rain." (Hopi F11) (Tested in July, at beginning of season when rains come)

V. Good social relations

28. Having visitors
29. Return of friend
30. Getting a date
31. Getting married; fall in love; have a family

Sample responses:
"When people come to see me." (Hopi M10)
"My friends come to Zuni and we play all day and I am so glad." (Zuni F9)
"To get married." (Navaho Mt. F13)
"To keep my temper." (Sioux M9)
"When my girl throws her arms around me and kisses me." (Midwest M13)

VI. Excitement and adventure

12. Going somewhere (town; another state, etc.)
13. Train ride; auto ride, wagon ride
14. Attending social event or gathering; something going on; a fair
15. Riding a horse (or chasing, roping, etc.)
16a. Playing, having a good time

VII. General goodness of character or disposition

32. General goodness of character or disposition; to do right things; to keep good

VIII. Out of school

33. To get out of school for a long time; close the school

IX. Win the war

34. Winning the war; war to end

X. Death

35. To die; to die a happy death; to die and go to Heaven

XI. Restraint from wrongdoing

36. Restraint from doing wrong or committing a crime

XII. Reticence to talk about best thing

37. Reticence to talk about best thing

Sample responses:
"Nothing."
"It's not polite to talk about in the future."

XIII. Be punished

38. Be punished, whipped, etc.; get hurt

XIV. Miscellaneous

39. Miscellaneous

XV. Receiving clothes, property

7. Possession of money, wealth, clothes, property, etc.
9. Receiving presents; getting something new; getting toy or some other thing especially desired

Sample responses:
"Get new clothes and go to a Squaw Dance." (Navaho Mt. F15)
"Have lots of sheep, I guess; but it is not right to think that way." (Navaho Mt. F12)
"Have lots of silver bracelets." (Navaho Mt. F10)
"To have a gun of my very own." (Navaho Mt. M12)
"For Santa Claus to bring me lots of candy." (Zuni M10)
"To get a radio." (Zia F11)
"To get a horse just for me." (Zia M8)
"To get new clothes for Shalako." (Zuni F13)
"My cows to have lots of calves." (Sioux M15)
"Find money that belongs to nobody." (Sioux M14)
"If my mother send me some money that I didn't know she had and was going to send." (Sioux F18)
"My mother give me a ring." (Hopi F14)
"To have a little piano." (Hopi F11)
"The katcinas to bring me some pretty yellow and red piki." (Hopi M6)
"Father give me a horse." (Papago M9)
"If my mother gets me a doll." (Papago F9)
"To get a million dollars." (Midwest M12)
"Have a new bicycle." (Midwest F13)

APPENDIX B-3

EMOTIONAL RESPONSE TEST: SADNESS CATEGORIES

I. Death of someone[1]

1.[2] Death of someone

Sample responses:
"When our baby died." (Zuni M9)
"When my sister and brother died." (Shiprock F12)
"When the medicine man died." (Hopi M13)
"When my brother died." (Midwest M12)
"When my grandmother died." (Midwest M13)

II. Death of a pet

2. Death or loss of a pet

III. Illness or injury of others

3. Sickness, accidents, physical pain, injury

Sample responses:
"The baby got sick." (Zia F10)
"Miguel got burn bad." (Zia M11)

IV. Being punished

4. Punishment, being reprimanded
5. Punishment "when you haven't done anything"

V. Work

6. Having to help, work

VI. Personal failure, inability

7. Inability, doing things wrong, failing in school
8. Doing work poorly, bad work, poor school work
9. Not doing work, being lazy
10. Defeat or anticipation of failure in sports
11. Unemployment, loss of job

VII. Not enough school

1. Category combination. The combinations which account for the bulk of the responses are shown in Table 6 of the text.

2. The original categories which make up the category combination. Certain categories may be found in more than one combination.

12. Inability to attend school; "when there is no school"

VIII. Dislike of school

13. Having to go to school
14. Caught cutting school

IX. Disappointment due to others

15. Disappointment due to others

X. Disappointment due to circumstances

16. Disappointment due to circumstances, failure to get something wanted very much
17. Giving up a pleasant experience
18. Disappointment in relations with peers

Sample responses:
"When I didn't get a date for the dance." (Midwest F14)
"When I can't go hunting." (Midwest M14)
"I was sad because when I combed my hair it didn't turn out good." (Midwest F12)

XI. Loss of property

19. Loss or damage of property—break toys
20. Loss or damage of property due to theft
21. Having one's property given away in accordance with tribal customs

Sample responses:
"When I lost 10 cents." (Zia F8)
"When I lost my ring." (Zia F10)
"When I lose a sheep." (Navaho Mt. F17)
"To lose something which cost a lot." (Shiprock F16)
"When I lost a dollar." (Midwest F14)
"The Navahos stole my father's cow." (Hopi F11)
"When our horses tramped on our melons in the field and spoiled all our melons." (Hopi M8)
"When the front wheel on my bicycle broke." (Midwest M13)

XII. Absence or loss of friends and family

22. Lonesomeness, being alone, being in a lonesome place
23. Being left at home by family
24. Absence of members of family, friends going away, not hearing from friends
25. Family broken—no mother or father
26. Others taking friends away—"stealing friends"

Sample responses:
"When George and Augustine went away to be soldiers." (Zia M10)
"When my brother and sister went away to school." (Zia F7)

"When I don't get letters from my folks for a long time." (Shiprock F16)
"When the boys from here went to the Army." (Hopi M15)
"I was sad when the people were going away to pick cotton." (Papago F17)
"When all my friends left town." (Midwest M13)

XIII. Being bad

27. Being bad, cheating (by self)
29. Stealing (by self)
30. Stealing and being caught
34. Being aggressive; be mean, get angry, fight

Sample responses:
"When I steal something." (Papago M13)
"When we do not obey our father." (Papago M14)
"I get sad when I do something wrong." (Zuni M15)
"After I make my little sister cry." (Shiprock F11)

XIV. Badness of others

28. Badness on part of members of tribe or family who bring discredit to whole tribe or family
31. Stealing in general
32. Aggressiveness and unkindness (verbal or physical; others "mad at" one, mean to, push, hit one)
33. Aggressiveness of others to others, fighting in general, quarreling
35. The war

Sample responses:
"A seventh grade boy scolded me." (Zuni M12)
"When the girls all got mad at me." (Papago F15)
"When somebody scolds us." (Papago M14)
"A big boy slapped my brother and I felt sad." (Zia M14)
"When my uncle scold me for being lazy." (Navaho Mt. M12)
"When my sister takes my toys." (Shiprock F8)

XV. Having to grow up

36. Having to grow up; "when Mother cut my long curls"

XVI. Seeing a sad movie, play, etc.

38. Seeing a sad movie, play, etc.

XVII. Bad weather

39. Bad weather, portents of bad weather

XVIII. Misfortune of others

40. Misfortune of others

XIX. Miscellaneous

41. Miscellaneous

XX. Sickness or injury of self

3. Sickness, accidents, physical pain, injury, when self is the person involved

Sample responses:
"When my tooth hurt." (Zia M8)
"I had the measles." (Zia F7)
"I was sick and could not come to school." (Zuni M9)
"When I was in the hospital." (Hopi M10)
"When the horse kicked me." (Papago M10)
"Because I ate too much chili." (Zuni M8)
"When I had my appendix cut." (Midwest F13)

APPENDIX B-4

EMOTIONAL RESPONSE TEST: FEAR CATEGORIES

I. Supernatural beings[1]

1.[2] Katcinas, Yeibichai, Adashlay, Masawu, and other specific supernaturals
2. Witches; witch power
3. Supernatural spirits of the dead — tchindi
4. Devil
5. The dead (ghosts, skeletons, graveyards, mummy)
6. Animals associated with the dead — owl, mouse, coyote, eagle (defined for each tribe)
7. Animals associated with witches — wolf, bear
8. Animals of the night (associated with the supernatural)

Sample responses:
"Last night I was afraid of the devil." (Hopi F10)
"Afraid of ghosts; they come in the night." (Papago F10)
"Owls." (Papago F15)
"Coyotes." (Papago F13)
"When the katcinas whip me in the kiva; last year I initiated." (Hopi F11)
"I am afraid of witches; they will take me away." (Hopi M11)
"When I was little I was afraid of the owl, I'm not afraid any more. My mother told me about it to make me behave." (Hopi M16)
"The Adashlay came to my house; I was afraid of him; he almost make me cry." (Zuni F16)
"I heard something walking around last night: I looked out and something white passed by my door." (Shiprock F13)
"This summer when a man got killed; we were afraid to go out at night — afraid he might get us." (Zia F18)
"I am afraid of witchcraft. All the Navahos are, you know, all the time." (Navaho Mt. M18)
"I am afraid of snakes-I saw one too close-it may be the spirit of enemy people." (Navaho Mt. M8)
"I do not like to herd sheep in the canyons where the ancient ones lived (cliff dwellers). I am afraid of their tchindis." (Navaho Mt. M9)
"I'm afraid of a Navaho wolf." (Shiprock F6)

1. Category combination. The combinations which account for the bulk of the responses are shown in Table 7 of the text.

2. The original categories which make up the category combination. Certain categories may be found in more than one combination.

"Yeibichai whip children." (Shiprock F7)

II. Subjective danger, night, mysterious incidents

9. The night, darkness, going home in the dark
10. Mysterious incidents and noises — not necessarily at night
11. The unnatural and unexplainable
12. Warnings and forerunners of death and misfortune
13. Being alone; going somewhere alone

Sample responses:
"Afraid to go out in the dark." (Papago F18)
"Once I was going for water and I heard a funny cry somewhere and it made me afraid." (Hopi F6)
"When the dogs bark in the night." (Hopi F12)
"When I sleep alone in the house and nobody's home." (Hopi F15)
"Bad dreams make me afraid sometimes." (Hopi F16)
"When I go to corral in the night." (Zia M8)
"The night I thought there was somebody in the house." (Midwest F14)
"When I walked past the ballpark one night alone after seeing a very spooky show." (Midwest F14)
"When I get lost in Chicago." (Midwest M12)

III. Danger from animals (excludes animals associated with supernatural)

14. Animals, specific situations not given.
15. Danger from animals, actual instances

Sample responses:
"I was afraid when a mad cow ran after us." (Papago F12)
"I almost stepped on a scorpion and I got afraid of him." (Papago F17)
"When I was thrown off a good-sized calf and he kicked and cut my arm." (Papago M12)
"I am afraid of wild animals." (Zuni M10)
"I was afraid when the old cow got after me." (Zuni M16)
"I'm afraid of bulls; some of them are mean." (Shiprock F16)
"Afraid of a mean dog." (Midwest M14)
"When I saw snakes and spiders." (Midwest M18)
"We had an eagle and we were washing his head and he jumped at me and caught me with his claws." (Hopi M15)
"Big sheep run after me." (Zia F7)
"I roped a calf and its mother got mean." (Sioux M13)
"When a big Hereford bull came after me." (Midwest M13)

IV. Danger from natural elements, accidents

16. The elements (storms, thunder, lightning, wind, rain)
17. Physical danger (other than from animals and the elements); accidents
18. Hospitals, doctors, illness, dentist, death of self

Sample responses:
"When I had my tonsils out." (Midwest M10)
"Afraid of a fire in our fields: somebody was smoking." (Papago F17)
"Afraid of the storm." (Papago F18)
"When its thundering." (Hopi F12)
"One time we were riding in a big truck and ran off the road." (Papago F13)
"Once when an electrical storm came up." (Midwest M14)
"Afraid of drowning when I first went swimming in a dam." (Zia M16)
"When I was up high from the earth and looked down." (Midwest F13)

V. Misfortune of others

19. Danger, accident, misfortune, illness, possible death of others; "when something happens to somebody."

VI. Danger or injury to pet

20. Danger or injury to pet

VII. Personal delinquency, misdemeanors

21. Stealing
22. Destruction or damage to property
23. School misdemeanor; failure to conform to school regulations
24. General misdemeanor

Sample responses:
"When I was stealing, my family might find out and spank me." (Midwest M11)
"When I eat pinon nuts in here (school) I afraid you might take them." (Hopi M8)
"When my friends and I get caught busting bottles on the railroad tracks." (Midwest M13)
"When I was caught skipping school." (Midwest M13)
"When I broke a window." (Midwest M12)

VIII. Being punished

25. Discipline; punishment (by parents, by teachers)

Sample responses:
"When I stole something and the man sent someone to punish me." (Zuni M17)
"When my mother is going to spank me." (Papago M8)

"I was going to get a whipping." (Midwest F12)

IX. Aggression by others

26. Aggression, verbal or physical (not in connection with the supernatural). Aggressor may be indefinitely stated, peer of the same or opposite sex, older child, adult, "drunk man," "white man," etc.
27. Potential aggression
28. Fighting (actual aggression by another not stated); "afraid when I fight"
29. Quarreling or fighting on the part of others ("When the man fights with father")

Sample responses:
"I am afraid big boys will hurt me: they twist my arm." (Hopi M10)
"When the big boys fight me." (Zuni M13)
"When a man scold me and chase me." (Zia M12)
"I'm afraid of drunk men." (Shiprock F9)
"Drunken men." (Midwest F15)
"I afraid of Japs. They might drop bombs." (Hopi F12)
"I'm afraid of policemen." (Shiprock M14)

X. Loss of property

30. Loss of property

XI. Being scared by someone unintentionally

31. Being scared by someone unintentionally or in play; startled by a sudden noise, motion, etc.

XII. New and strange situations

32. Strange places and surroundings
33. Having to appear before an audience
34. New situation involving peers - first kiss

XIII. Scary radio program, story, movie

35. Scary radio program, story, movie

XIV. War

36. War

XV. White man's mechanical conveyances

37. White man's mechanical conveyances and contraptions - airplane, train, cars, etc.

XVI. Bad dreams

38. Bad dreams

XVII. Miscellaneous

39. Miscellaneous

XVIII. Examinations

39a. Examinations

XIX. Personal inadequacy

24a. Mistake, clumsiness, error
39a. Examinations
40. Personal inadequacy or uncertainty; fear of failure

APPENDIX B-5

EMOTIONAL RESPONSE TEST: ANGER CATEGORIES

I. Loss of property[1]

1.[2] Loss or destruction of property; damage to property
3. Having property stolen (by peers, siblings, others)
4. Having property taken away ("Robert took my pencil one time")
5. Having property borrowed, used, disposed of without owner's permission

Sample responses:
"One time a boy stole some of my marbles." (Sioux M11)
"My stepfather took my rope." (Sioux M12)
"I lost my bean-shooter. I asked my mother where it was. She said she burned it in the stove." (Sioux M12)
"When they gave my pony away." (Sioux M16)
"One time we play paper dolls. Papa took our dolls to light the fire." (Sioux F14)
"When the Navahos killed our horse." (Hopi M14)
"When a girl stole my money. She was Apache." (Hopi F17)
"When the girls stole my hair oil." (Hopi F14)
"When someone take my eraser." (Zia F9)
"When my mother gave away my best dress without my consent." (Midwest F14)

II. Loss or injury to pet

2. Loss of or injury to pet

III. Restriction on attainment of desires

6. Restriction on attainment of desires

Sample responses:
"When my mother doesn't give me some money." (Sioux M13)
"They didn't let me go swimming." (Sioux F11)
"When my father didn't take us to Hotevilla." (Hopi F15)
"I wanted a new shirt for the fiesta and was angry when I did not get it." (Papago M10)
"When my parents don't let me go some place." (Shiprock F17)

1. Category combination. The combinations which account for the bulk of the responses are shown in Table 8 of the text.

2. The original categories which make up the category combination. Certain categories may be found in more than one combination.

IV. Failure to achieve a goal

7. Failure to achieve a goal (with no mention of restriction by others)

V. Inconsiderateness of others

4. Having property taken away
5. Having property borrowed, used, disposed of without owner's permission
8. Discrimination against the subject ("My brother got a bicycle and I didn't")
9. Someone takes liberties with the subject ("Boys got fresh with me")
17. Inconsiderateness, non-cooperation or selfishness of others

Sample responses:
"The big boys ran off and left me behind." (Zuni M13)
"If I fall down and hurt myself and someone laughs at me." (Sioux F13)
"When they cheat in games." (Sioux M14)
"When the boys hid my bat." (Hopi M13)
"When other people make my house dirty." (Shiprock F12)
"When somebody calls me by the wrong name." (Shiprock F16)
"I am angry at my brother when he rides the horse and I walk." (Shiprock F12)
"When my sister gets into my private things." (Midwest F14)
"When somebody copies my school work." (Midwest F14)

VI. Being disciplined

10. Exertion of authority by others; discipline; punishment (by "someone"; parents; grandparents; older sibling, etc.)
11. Having to perform an unwelcome task; having to work against one's wishes; having to work too hard

Sample responses:
"When they make me do things I do not like to do." (Hopi F11)
"I was very angry when my father spanked me." (Papago F11)
"Last summer my father slapped me because I didn't work for him." (Zia M12)
"I am late to school and teacher tell me to stay in at recess." (Zia M8)
"When my father spank me I am mad." (Zia M9)
"When my mother tells me to go get water." (Zuni M10)
"My grandmother push me out of the house." (Zuni F8)
"When a big man scold me." (Zia M10)

VII. Aggression by others

12. Aggression (verbal or physical) toward subject
13. Being teased
14. Gossip, slander, false accusation
16. Anger on the part of others toward subject
19. Aggression by others directed toward others ("White people kidnapping children")

Sample responses:
"When the Japs bombed Honolulu." (Zuni M17)
"The boys chased me home from school." (Zia M8)
"When other children say things to me." (Zia M10)
"When a Paiute calls me names: I hit him." (Navaho Mt. M13)
"When someone wants to fight." (Zuni M16)
"Nita hit me with the broom." (Zuni F8)
"I have too many sisters and they make me mad, for they tease me." (Navaho Mt. M18)
"Because one girl was talking about me and making up stories about me." (Navaho Mt. M16)
"If my sister hides my dress from me." (Shiprock F10)
"When somebody teases me." (Midwest M14)

VIII. Fighting

15. Fighting (in a mutual sense; aggression by another not mentioned)

Sample responses:
"When somebody fights me." (Sioux F13)
"When I fight with the boys." (Zia M8)
"Tony fight me." (Zuni M8)

IX. Misdeeds, inadequacies of others

18. Misdeeds, inadequacies of others (not directed at subject)

Sample responses:
"When my little brother don't go get the water, I get angry." (Hopi F14)
"When the boys on the team don't play right." (Zuni M14)
"When someone fights with my friend." (Zuni M16)
"I was angry at my sister when she got into a fight." (Zuni M16)
"When a big guy picks on a little one." (Midwest M15)

X. Perversity, errors of animals

20. Perversity, errors of animals

Sample responses:
"We had a little tepee. We put some plates and meat in it. A dog went in there and ate the

meat up." (Sioux F10)
"I was mad at the cows 'cause they got in the cornfield." (Sioux M14)
"I was mad at my horse; he wouldn't run." (Sioux M14)
"A dog tore my pants." (Sioux M12)
"One time I was running after a horse and I couldn't catch him." (Papago F13)
"When my horse kicked me." (Zuni M16)

XI. Perversity of inanimate objects or circumstances

21. Perversity of inanimate objects or circumstances ("When the water go too fast when I was irrigating")

XII. Personal inadequacy

22. Personal inadequacy; mistakes, clumsiness

XIII. Losing a sports event

23. Losing a sports event

XIV. Miscellaneous

24. Miscellaneous

APPENDIX B-6

EMOTIONAL RESPONSE TEST: SHAME CATEGORIES

I. Making a poor appearance, making mistakes[1]

1.[2] Neglect of person, being dirty, unkempt, etc.
2. Lacking proper clothing; old, poor, ragged clothes, not having good clothes, not having necessities
3. Falling, getting dirty, clothing ripped, spilling things
4. Making mistakes and social errors in public; saying wrong thing, poor table manners, not having money when buying something, etc.

Sample responses:
"The wind blow my dress up." (Zuni F7)
"When my stockings have holes." (Zuni F13)
"Because the sheep camp boys put me on the donkey." (Zuni M9)
"I am ashamed of walking like a duck." (Zuni M14)
"I get my clothes dirty." (Zia M8)
"When the doctors examine us and look at my toes." (Navaho Mt. M9)
"If I wear squaw clothes." (Shiprock F12)
"When I was little and failed to show off and mother spanked me in front of guests." (Midwest F14)
"When I was dancing at the fiesta and fell down." (Papago M10)
"When I eat and the food from my fork sometimes falls off." (Papago F15)
"I'm ashamed of that old house we live in. I'm ashamed when anybody comes." (Sioux F18)
"Shoe come off in a track meet." (Sioux M10)

II. Embarrassment in presence of others

5. Embarrassment in presence of others; having to perform before an audience, visitors in home, coming to school the first time, etc.

Sample responses:
"To visit the neighbors." (Zuni F7)
"When the neighbors come to visit my house." (Zuni F7)
"When we are in Gallup and go in the store I am ashamed." (Zuni F8)

1. Category combination. The combinations which account for the bulk of the responses are shown in Table 9 of the text.

2. The original categories which make up the category combination. Certain categories may be found in more than one combination.

"Many girls are in the schoolroom." (Zuni M7)
"When the girls look at me hard." (Zuni M14)
"To sing by myself." (Zuni M17)
"I am ashamed to be in the play tonight." (Zia F15)
"If I take the sheep to water at the Lodge and there are too many white people around." (Navaho Mt. M14)
"When teacher makes me read in front of class." (Navaho Mt. F13)
"When I am in a program." (Hopi F11)
"Because lots of people looked at me." (Papago F12)

III. Poverty, and neglect in home

6. Having old, poor possessions, no money
7. Having old, poor home
8. Having dirty, ill-kept home

IV. Loss or damage to property

9. Having property or money stolen
10. Unintentionally damaging property, losing money or property

V. Personal failure and inadequacy

11. Doing work poorly, lacking skill in work
12. Doing school work poorly, cutting school, lacking skill in school tasks
14. Not knowing what one is expected to know
15. Lacking skill in sports and social techniques: games, dancing, etc.
16. Failure to achieve something desired
17. Anticipation of failure in work or play
18. Carelessness, neglect of obligation by subject, inconsiderateness by subject
19. Childish or immature behavior of subject

Sample responses:
"When I didn't know my lessons." (Zia M16)
"I let the goats eat the needles of the pinon tree: then the needles stick in their stomachs and they die." (Navaho Mt. F10)
"If your mother have a new red bowl, and if you break it, you'll be ashamed." (Navaho Mt. F16)
"When I say it wrong in school, it make me ashamed." (Hopi M10)
"When I don't spell my words right." (Hopi M14)
"I was ashamed of my writing when I come to school." (Sioux F18)
"When I missed a basket in a basketball game." (Midwest M13)
"I took a hammer and broke some spokes on my bike." (Midwest M13)
"When I didn't know how to act at a party." (Midwest F13)
"When I broke my sister's new electric clock." (Midwest F13)

VI. Bad behavior with opposite sex

20. Sexual transgressions
21. Being seen with wrong companions; being seen with a certain boy
22. Being caught in sexual transgressions; being seen kissing a girl

VII. Bad behavior and aggression (may or may not be known to others)

13. Laziness; not working or helping family
23. Stealing
24. Stealing and being caught
25. Lying and cheating
26. Getting drunk
27. Disobedience, disrespect, breaking rules
28. General bad behavior; being bad, using bad words, etc.
29. Being caught in bad behavior
30. Aggressiveness (verbal or physical) of individual toward others
31. Anger, fighting, on part of subject
32. Bad thoughts, evil wishes

Sample responses:
"Sometimes I don't work for my mother." (Zuni F10)
"I was ashamed to talk to Sister Mary Victoria because she tell us to sweep and we don't sweep." (Zuni F14)
"I stole something and someone catch me." (Zia M11)
"I hit the girl; her mother make me ashamed." (Zia F9)
"When I smoke." (Midwest M14)
"When I didn't sweep good." (Shiprock F11)
"When teacher caught me cheating." (Midwest M14)
"When I hit little boys." (Hopi M9)
"When we took the old man's melons; he got after us." (Hopi M13)
"When I got drunk I felt very much ashamed." (Papago F14)
"When I do wrong." (Papago F10)
"I was smoking and my mother saw me." (Sioux F15)
"My mother told me to come after groceries; I spent the money for candy, and cigarettes. That made me ashamed." (Sioux M10)
"One day I was angry at my mother so I took a stick and come to the door but she took it away from me and chased me away. That made me ashamed, so I went behind the house and sat for a long time." (Sioux M8)

VIII. Rowdiness of companions

33. Rowdiness of companions; loud, conspicuous behavior

IX. Bad behavior of others toward others

34. Bad behavior of others toward others; unkindness, selfishness, fighting, etc.

X. Being disciplined

35. Being punished, scolded
36. Being punished or scolded in front of others

Sample responses:
"When a teacher whipped me." (Navaho Mt. M14)
"When I'm sent to bed for doing something bad." (Midwest M12)
"When I get a scolding." (Midwest M12)

XI. Aggression by others

37. Being made fun of, laughed at
38. Being "looked at," having "something" said to you (sexual significance)
39. Aggressiveness (verbal or physical), unkindness of others toward subject
40. Someone takes liberties with subject's person; hair cut off, etc.

Sample responses:
"A little girl fight me and I cried and was ashamed." (Zuni F6)
"When somebody called me a bad name." (Zuni M12)
"I was ashamed that a girl said something to me." (Midwest F12)

XII. Embarrassment of groups to which subject belongs

41. Embarrassing things happen to members of family, or to friends
42. School losing at sports

XIII. Miscellaneous

43. Miscellaneous

APPENDIX B-7

EMOTIONAL RESPONSE TEST: "WORST THING" CATEGORIES

I. Death of self[1]

1.[2] Death of self

Sample responses:
"To die." (Midwest M12)
"To die young." (Midwest M13)
"To be drowned." (Midwest M12)

II. Death of relative or friend

2. Death of relative or friend

Sample responses:
"My grandma to die." (Midwest M12)
"My parents and brothers and sisters to die." (Midwest F12)

III. Accident or illness of self

4. Sickness, accident, injury to self

Sample responses:
"To fall down from the top of the house." (Zuni F15)
"A snake bite me." (Zia M10)
"When a dog bit me." (Zia M12)
"To be struck by lightning." (Navaho Mt. F10)
"To have my legs cut off." (Hopi M14)
"To get sick." (Hopi F13)
"Get hit by a car or train." (Midwest M13)
"To be drowned." (Midwest M12)

IV. Accident or illness of others

4. Sickness, accident, injury to others

V. Frightening experience

3. Be bewitched
5. Hospital, dentist, doctors
6. Frightening experience with supernatural
7. Frightening experience with an animal

---

1. Category combination. The combinations which account for the bulk of the responses are shown in Table 10 of the text.

2. The original categories which make up the category combination. Certain categories may be found in more than one combination.

8. To have bad luck (general or specific instances)

Sample responses:
"Find witches pollen in my food." (Navaho Mt. F13)
"Have a Navaho witch to spit a curse at me." (Navaho Mt. M12)
"The owl to get me." (Hopi M9)
"Something might come to me in the dark like Massawu." (Hopi M9)
"See a tchindi." (Navaho Mt. F10)

VI. Being punished

9. Discipline; punishment
13. Jail

Sample responses:
"To be put in jail." (Zuni M9)
"My family to scold me if I do something bad." (Zuni M14)
"If I stole something and got put in jail." (Zia M17)
"To be expelled from school." (Midwest M14)

VII. Aggression by others

10. Aggressiveness of others (verbal or physical)

Sample responses:
"Two Navahoes fight me and my father in Gallup and break my arm." (Zuni M12)
"The worst thing would be to have everyone quarreling." (Papago F13)

VIII. Bad behavior and aggression

11. General bad behavior (on part of individual himself)
12. Stealing (by individual himself)
14. Damage to other's property (intentional)
15. Sexual transgression
16. Anger, fighting (on part of individual)
16a. Killing somebody
17. Unkindness to others; aggressiveness toward others (other than quarreling and fighting mentioned in 10)

Sample responses:
"To kill somebody." (Zia M11)
"To lie with a boy of my own clan." (Navaho Mt. F13)
"To drink whiskey." (Shiprock F17)
"Become a gangster." (Shiprock M14)

IX. Personal inadequacy or failure

18. Doing things wrong or badly; bad work; breaking something
19. Laziness, shirking work
20. Inability to achieve an important goal
21. To be a failure
22. Loss of a job

Sample responses:
"Being a failure in life." (Midwest M14)
"To be ashamed of my life, ways of living and have my friends look and think of me as an outcast of the world." (Midwest F14)
"To fail in school." (Midwest M13)

X. Misfortune, discomfort

23. Enforced absence from school
24. Going to school
25. Poverty
26. Loss of money or property, or damage to property
27. Loss of a pet
28. Disappointment
29. Having to work too hard or too much

Sample responses:
"To be poor and no food to eat." (Zia M11)
"To have something go wrong with the sewing machine. My father cannot get machine needles now. The storekeeper is stingy for it." (Shiprock F13)
"You could get poorer and not have much to eat or wear." (Midwest F12)

XI. Loss of family or friend

30. Separation from family, not to have a father and mother, to get lost
31. Lose friends; move away
31a. Quarreling with friends or family

XII. Lose the war

32. To lose the war

XIII. World to end

33. World to end

XIV. To go to hell

34. To go to hell

XV. To marry or marry badly

35. To marry or marry badly

XVI. Reticence to talk about it

36. Reticence to talk about it

XVII. Miscellaneous

37. Miscellaneous

APPENDIX B-8

EMOTIONAL RESPONSE TEST:

CATEGORIES OF "PERSONS INVOLVED"

1. Family (relatives)
2. Father
3. Mother
4. Parents; folks
5. Step-father
6. Step-mother
7. Aunt
8. Uncle
9. Grandmother
10. Grandfather
11. Sibling, same sex
12. Sibling, opposite sex
13. Younger sibling, same sex
14. Younger sibling, opposite sex
15. Older sibling, same sex
16. Older sibling, opposite sex
17. Sibling-in-law
18. Cousin
19. Other relatives
20. Peers, same sex (age-mates)
21. Peers, opposite sex (age-mates)
22. Peers in general, boys and girls; playmates
23. Older children
24. Younger children
25. Friends
26. Boy or girl friend
27. Self
28. White children
29. School teacher or principal (white); school in general
30. Indian teacher
31. Adults (Indian)
32. Members of one's own group or tribe (mentioned specifically as such)
33. Indians from other tribes, communities, schools
34. Strange man or men or women
35. Drunk men or tramps
36. Negroes
37. Medicine man
38. Employer
39. Local Indians in authority; (governor)
40. Local whites in authority; police
41. Other white adults
42. Person or persons indefinitely stated (someone, somebody, "they," everyone, others)
43. National enemy (Japs, Germans)
44. Animal

45. Church or Sunday school personnel, church in general
46. "Supernatural" beings, (Katcinas, Yeibichai, Adashlay, etc.)
47. Miscellaneous

APPENDIX B-9

EMOTIONAL RESPONSE TEST: CATEGORY COMBINATIONS WHICH COMPRISE VALUE-THEMES AND AVERSIONS

Theme	
Individual achievement	Happiness XIII; Sadness VI; Fear XIX; Anger IV, XII; Shame V; Best Thing I; Worst Thing IX.
Property and possessions	Happiness IV; Sadness XI; Fear X; Anger I; Shame IV; Best Thing XV.
Self-gratification	Happiness I, II, VII, IX; Sadness VIII, IX, X; Anger III, V; Shame I, Best Thing II minus VI.
Family-centeredness	Happiness X; Best Thing 25, 27; Worst Thing 30.
Smooth personal relations	Happiness XI; Sadness IV, 18, 26, 32, 33, 34; Fear IX; Anger V, VI, VII, VIII; Shame XI; Best Thing V; Worst Thing VI, VII, VIII.
Work	Happiness VI; Best Thing 2, 21, 22.
Ceremonials, fiestas	Happiness III; Best Thing 24.
Aggression by others	Sadness XIV; Fear IX; Anger VII; Shame XI; Worst Thing VII.
Discipline and authority of others	Sadness IV, V; Fear VIII; Anger VI; Shame X; Worst Thing VI.
Death of others	Sadness I; Worst Thing II.
Illness and danger of others	Sadness III; Fear V; Worst Thing IV.
Illness, accidents to self	Sadness XX; Worst Thing III.
Fear of supernatural	Fear I.

Objective danger	Fear III, IV.
Death of self	Worst Thing I.

APPENDIX B-10

AGE TRENDS IN EMOTIONAL RESPONSES

There is a number of factors which would be expected to cause children of different ages to report different experiences on the emotional response test. The younger children have fewer emotional experiences to select from, and the quality of emotion is regarded as naïve by older people. Young children are happy when they receive simple gifts of toys, food, and clothing and when they take a trip or see something interesting. They are sad over illness of themselves and others; they are fearful for subjective reasons; their anger tends to relate to purely personal frustrations.

As children grow older, the sphere of their emotional experience widens, and the quality of emotion becomes more complex. The welfare and feelings of other people influence their own feelings. They become more interested in their own future and in the welfare of their own group.

These age differences probably vary from one culture to another; some will be nearly universal, while others will be limited to one or a few societies.

The data from our test have been analyzed by age into three age groups: 8-10, 11-13, and 14-18, inclusive. The age divisions were made mainly for the purpose of securing nearly equal numbers of subjects in each age group, especially for the smaller Indian groups.

Since the number of responses from a particular age group on a particular emotion is too small to allow for reliable statistical procedures, some combinations must be made if we wish to study age trends and differences between age groups. To accomplish this purpose, as well as to be able to generalize about values, we have combined these responses according to value and aversion themes, with results shown in Table 43. In this table it is useful to compare percentage frequencies only for groups which average 100 or more in size, where a difference of about 10 percentage points is reliable at about the 5 per cent level; or for groups of 500 or more responses, where a difference of about 5 points is reliable at the 5 per cent level.

The Southwest Indian tribes have been combined to give a single average percentage frequency for each age group for each value or aversion, a frequency which can be compared with Midwest data. There are disadvantages to combining the Indian responses in this way, as is obvious from inspection of Table 43. There are also some statistical crudities in this process. But it is a practicable way to make general statements about age differences, and accordingly we have used the method, being rather conservative in our estimates of the statistical reliability of our conclusions.[1]

When these criteria of reliability of differences are employed, it is possible to group the Midwest and Southwest Indian boys and girls into categories, as has been done in the "Chart of Age Differences." For some values and aversions there are no reliable age changes. For others there are fairly steady increases or decreases of frequency of response with age. For still others there is no change from 8 to 13, but a change after 13: and for others the 11-13 and 14-18 groups are similar, but both are different from age 8-10. In a few categories there is a minimum or maximum frequency for the age group 11-13. All these facts can be seen by studying Table 43 in conjunction with the chart.

Discussion of Age Differences

While there are many interesting age changes within and between tribal groups, we shall limit our remarks to comparisons between Midwest and the average for Southwest Indian children. A general summary statement has already been made (see chap. iii, p. 57); but here we shall take up each value-theme and aversion theme in turn.

Individual Achievement

The individual achievement value increases with age. While the increases are unreliable in three groups out of four (Midwest male and female, Southwest Indian male and female) from ages 8-10 to ages 10-13, all four groups show reliable increases from ages 8-10 to ages 14-18.

1. A simple and usable table for determining the amount of difference between two percentages which is necessary if the difference is to be reliable at the 5 per cent level is given by Cuthbert Daniel, "Statistical Significant Differences in Observed Percents," Journal of Applied Psychology, XXIV (1940), 826-30.

TABLE 43: EMOTIONAL RESPONSE TEST: AGE TRENDS FOR VALUES AND AVERSIONS (PERCENTAGE TABLES)

Tribal Group	Male				Female				Male				Female			
	B[a]	C	D	Av. N	B	C	D	Av. N	B	C	D	Av. N	B	C	D	Av. N
	Individual Achievement								Property and Possessions							
Papago	4.7	2.0	5.5	181	1.2	2.2	4.5	180	11	15	11	165	15	12	5	166
Hopi	1.6	3.1	9.5	191	3.8	2.0	4.8	273	21	20	13	174	13	15	7	227
Zuni	2.0	1.5	5.8	239	1.7	3.0	6.3	211	7	8	7	227	7	9	7	198
Zia	0.6	0.	1.4	111	0.	0.	3.5	80	27	22	13	104	26	31	10	74
Navaho Mt.	2.8	2.3	6.2	116	0.	9.1	7.0	81	15	19	19	108	24	24	10	75
Shiprock	3.5	1.7	8.1	119	0.	3.0	3.0	130	28	31	29	112	30	23	14	123
Sioux	1.3	3.2	5.1	239	1.6	4.7	6.0	243	14.1	21	14	220	16	10	6	224
Midwest	7.4	8.7	17.1	666	6.3	7.1	14.1	1078	16	19	10	623	10	15	8	1002
SW. Indians	2.5	1.6	6.1	957	1.1	3.2	4.9	955	18	19	15	890	19	19	9	863
	Self-gratification								Smooth Personal Relations							
Papago	35	32	20	132	30	39	22	131	12	15	18	181	19	13	18	180
Hopi	27	21	20	144	20	19	30	199	14	17	15	191	18	19	16	273
Zuni	28	23	21	180	30	13	16	162	22	21	15	239	20	20	22	211
Zia	28	15	26	81	15	22	39	57	20	20	12	111	21	23	19	80
Navaho Mt.	19	15	15	79	7	7	13	53	9	4	12	116	2	14	7	81
Shiprock	24	21	20	83	19	24	23	93	26	13	5	119	14	14	20	130
Sioux	32	24	22	177	25	30	21	185	14	11	14	239	21	18	14	243
Midwest	33	30	27	525	38	30	30	824	10	12	14	666	13	13	16	1078
SW. Indians	27	21	20	699	20	21	24	695	17	15	13	957	16	17	17	955
	Family-Centeredness								Work							
Papago	1.2	0.	5.0	79	4.1	1.5	7.1	80	4.3	8.9	11.5	62	1.6	3.5	2.5	69
Hopi	1.2	2.7	0.	83	8.8	1.6	6.4	104	5.8	10.2	11.1	70	4.8	6.3	4.7	81
Zuni	3.1	3.1	2.9	78	2.7	4.9	11.9	74	5.8	2.0	11.9	62	11.3	4.6	10.7	59
Zia	4.7	6.1	8.0	41	6.1	3.9	18.2	31	1.8	7.7	5.0	33	0.	0.	3.7	25
Navaho Mt.	8.6	0.	2.3	43	20.0	11.1	10.0	36	0.	19.0	5.7	35	0.	4.3	19.5	27
Shiprock	4.4	1.5	0.	44	11.5	5.4	6.5	51	2.5	3.5	10.0	39	6.1	6.4	8.1	44

a. Age group: B = 8-10 years; C = 11-13 years; D = 14-18 years. Midwest: B = 10-11 years; C = 12-13 years; D = 14-17 years. Av. N = Average number of responses for each age group.

TABLE 43 - Continued

Tribal Group	Male B	Male C	Male D	Male Av. N	Female B	Female C	Female D	Female Av. N	Male B	Male C	Male D	Male Av. N	Female B	Female C	Female D	Female Av. N
	Family-Centeredness								Work							
Sioux	2.2	4.8	4.1	92	7.2	13.0	15.2	95	2.8	3.9	8.2	73	1.5	3.2	4.0	77
Midwest	4.5	2.8	3.6	245	13.7	17.1	7.0	381	6.2	1.8	11.4	202	4.0	0.5	4.6	305
SW. Indians	3.9	2.2	3.0	368	8.9	4.7	10.0	376	3.4	8.6	9.2	301	6.0	4.2	8.2	305
	Ceremonials, Fiestas								Aggression by Others							
Papago	7.2	10.7	9.8	62	1.6	12.3	10.1	66	8	14	9	119	13	12	18	115
Hopi	2.9	5.9	16.7	70	3.2	13.7	12.8	81	13	11	11	124	9	13	13	192
Zuni	5.8	7.8	11.9	62	15.1	10.8	17.8	59	15	17	13	177	21	15	19	153
Zia	1.9	0.	5.0	33	3.6	5.0	7.4	25	14	20	9	78	23	27	4	55
Navaho Mt.	3.6	2.4	14.3	35	0.	0.	4.9	27	10	2	10	81	3	9	2	54
Shiprock	0.	1.7	5.0	39	2.0	0.	8.1	44	24	15	5	80	15	14	18	86
Sioux	0.	0.	1.0	73	0.	1.6	1.0	77	12	10	10	166	17	18	13	166
Midwest	0.	0.	0.	202	0.	0.	0.	305	7	10	8	463	9	7	8	773
SW. Indians	3.6	4.8	10.5	301	3.9	7.0	10.2	302	14	13	10	659	14	15	12	655
	Discipline and Authority of Others								Illness and Danger of Others							
Papago	9.8	2.1	7.9	119	8.7	3.9	6.1	115	5.1	1.6	6.5	78	3.0	5.5	3.9	75
Hopi	5.2	11.4	7.2	124	12.5	10.7	5.9	192	9.0	3.5	10.8	70	1.3	9.6	11.9	121
Zuni	9.0	7.5	7.9	177	3.2	8.0	12.0	153	9.8	14.1	7.4	88	10.6	4.7	11.8	83
Zia	9.6	3.1	3.7	78	9.8	2.2	13.6	55	4.1	5.1	2.9	49	12.5	0.	7.5	37
Navaho Mt.	3.8	3.5	9.1	81	0.	2.3	2.3	54	1.9	3.3	0.	53	0.	0.	6.8	39
Shiprock	4.1	0.	7.1	80	5.3	1.1	3.2	86	0.	0.	7.4	54	0.	0.	4.8	61
Sioux	3.2	0.9	9.3	166	4.9	4.0	5.6	166	3.1	4.7	1.5	99	3.8	2.6	9.6	101
Midwest	3.6	3.0	5.4	463	4.8	4.4	2.4	773	3.4	4.5	5.7	257	6.5	13.1	8.4	441
SW. Indians	6.9	4.6	7.2	659	6.6	4.7	7.2	655	5.0	4.6	5.8	392	4.6	3.3	7.8	416
	Illness and Accidents to Self								Death of Others							
Papago	32	15	15	45	9	16	24	40	11	10	12	45	6	22	22	40
Hopi	31	21	14	44	16	15	11	71	15	3	16	44	16	19	24	71
Zuni	33	15	11	54	6	15	2	46	11	18	17	54	23	18	11	46
Zia	37	24	40	26	29	29	14	20	11	5	5	26	10	6	19	20
Navaho Mt.	8	0	17	25	30	0	4	17	4	10	11	25	0	7	12	17
Shiprock	8	3	7	24	4	8	17	31	8	6	0	24	8	14	16	31
Sioux	26	12	17	55	13	5	12	64	8	12	27	55	11	18	23	64

TABLE 43 - Continued

Tribal Group	Male B	Male C	Male D	Male Av. N	Female B	Female C	Female D	Female Av. N	Male B	Male C	Male D	Male Av. N	Female B	Female C	Female D	Female Av. N
	Illness and Accidents to Self								Death of Others							
Midwest	15	9	5	149	3	4	4	263	10	18	21	149	13	22	24	263
SW. Indians	25	13	17	218	16	14	10	225	10	9	10	218	11	14	17	225
	Fear of Supernatural								Objective Danger							
Papago	15	8	0	33	24	4	8	52	61	71	53	33	56	57	44	52
Hopi	22	46	17	26	24	21	23	50	28	13	13	26	19	23	25	50
Zuni	12	13	13	44	13	9	10	36	59	58	24	44	45	52	23	36
Zia	14	17	0	23	5	7	5	21	47	56	57	23	63	71	37	21
Navaho Mt.	41	50	39	28	40	33	46	22	33	27	25	28	40	28	18	22
Shiprock	29	34	8	29	45	29	19	30	32	38	46	29	19	32	45	30
Sioux	11	16	13	44	4	3	6	43	47	62	32	44	54	58	46	43
Midwest	1	0	2	108	1	0	2	179	67	50	52	108	61	39	38	179
SW. Indians	22	26	13	183	25	17	19	211	43	44	36	183	40	44	32	211
	Death of Self															
Papago	14	0	11	16	17	18	0	14								
Hopi	13	6	35	17	6	4	26	23								
Zuni	8	8	0	15	0	0	18	13								
Zia	10	0	20	7	0	17	17	6								
Navaho Mt.	0	11	0	8	0	0	0	6								
Shiprock	0	18	0	7	0	11	0	7								
Sioux	14	17	17	19	31	0	17	18								
Midwest	26	10	11	42	6	2	1	76								
SW. Indians	8	7	11	70	4	8	10	69								

CHART OF AGE DIFFERENCES

	Value or Aversion	Midwest M	Midwest F	Southwest Indian M	Southwest Indian F
No reliable age differences	Family-Centeredness	X		X	
	Self-gratification				X
	Work				X
	Smooth Personal Relations				X
	Aggression of Others	X	X	X	X
	Discipline and Authority of Others	X		X	X
	Illness and Danger of Others	X		X	
	Death of Others			X	
	Death of Self			X	
	Illness, Accidents to Self		X		
General increase with age	Ceremonials, Fiestas				X
	Smooth Personal Relations	X			
Increase after age 13	Individual Achievement	X	X	X	X
	Smooth Personal Relations		X		
	Ceremonials, Fiestas			X	
	Illness, Danger of Others				X
Increase after age 10	Work			X	
	Death of Others	X	X		X
General decrease with age	Self-gratification	X			
	Smooth Personal Relations			X	
	Illness, Accidents to Self	X			X
Decrease after age 13	Family-Centeredness		X		
	Property and Possessions	X		X	X
	Fear of Supernatural			X	
	Objective Danger			X	X
	Discipline and Authority of Others		X		
Decrease after age 10	Self-gratification		X	X	
	Fear of Supernatural				X
	Objective Danger	X	X		
	Illness, Accidents to Self			X	
	Death of Self	X	X		
Maximum at age 11-13	Property and Possessions		X		
	Illness, Danger of Others		X		
Minimum at age 11-13	Family-Centeredness				X
	Work	X	X		

Property and Possessions

The value-theme property and possessions tends to decrease with age, especially after age 13. (The relative amount of emotion involved in receiving, possessing, and losing property reaches something of a peak in Midwest children at about 11-13.) With the Indian children, as well as the Midwest children, perhaps the emotional sphere widens after age 13 to include many new emotional experiences that reduce the relative importance of property and possessions. The growth in importance of individual achievement at this age is perhaps one example of expansion of emotional experience.

Self-gratification

The hedonistic or self-gratification theme shows a general tendency to decrease with age, except for Southwest Indian girls, where there is a slight increase with age. The other three groups have a maximum of such responses at ages 8-10, which may indicate a maximum at this age of self-centeredness and of naïve pleasure in having possessions.

Smooth Personal Relations

The value of smooth personal relations shows inconsistent trends with age. For Midwest males there is an increase with age; but this is countered by a decrease with age among Indian males. There is no change with age for Indian girls, and an increase with age after 13 for Midwest girls. These results may be explained perhaps by saying that Midwest children are allowed a good deal of freedom to quarrel and be angry while young, but they gradually grow into more co-operative people in adolescence. On the other hand, the Indian children are strongly indoctrinated with co-operativeness and with the feeling that quarreling is bad; and they may lose some of this attitude as they grow older, or at least the relative importance of this training may be lessened as their sphere of emotional experience widens.

Family-Centeredness

The value of family-centeredness does not change with age for Midwest or Indian boys. It rises slightly from ages 8-10 to ages 11-13 for Midwest girls and then drops sharply, perhaps indicating the relative emancipation from family of the Midwest adolescent girl.

For the Indian girls there is a drop from ages 8-10 to ages 11-13, and then a rise to ages 14-18. Possibly this should be interpreted as resulting from a phase of family dependence of younger girls, followed by a period of relative freedom and lack of home responsibility at ages 11-13, after which the family values descend once more upon the adolescent Indian girl, who is now about to start her own family.

Work

The work theme shows interesting differences among the groups. For both Midwest and Southwest Indian boys there is a maximum at ages 14-18, but Midwest boys show a low point at ages 11-13, while Indian boys at this age almost reach the 14-18 peak. Thus it appears that the value of work increases steadily with age for the Indian boys, reaching its high plateau by age 11 or thereabouts, while Midwest boys are singularly free of positive feelings about work at ages 11-13 and then become very much involved with work as they become adolescents.

Midwest girls show much the same pattern of work values as do Midwest boys. Indian girls, however, have a drop at ages 11-13, which is somewhat similar to the Midwest pattern and quite different from the Indian boys' pattern. Possibly here, too, we have evidence of a relatively carefree and irresponsible period for Indian girls in the age range 11-13.

Ceremonials, Fiestas

There is a regular increase in this value with age for Indian boys and girls.

Aggression by Others

There is no change with age in this aversion for any of the four groups. It remains slightly higher at all ages among the Indians than among the whites.

Discipline and Authority of Others

The discipline and authority theme follows a course similar to that of aggression, with no age changes except for Midwest girls, who show something of a decrease after age 13.

Illness and Dangers of Others

For boys of both groups there is no change with age. Midwest girls show a decided maximum at ages 11-13, while Indian girls reach the peak at ages 14-18. The two groups of girls have in common a tendency to be more concerned about the welfare of other people after the self-centered period below age 10.

Illness and Accidents to Self

Concern about illness and accidents to the self have their peak in ages 8-10 in all but the Midwest females, who show no age change.

Death of Others

Concern over death of others rises after age 10 in all except the Southwest Indian boys, who show no age change.

Fear of Supernatural

Fear of the supernatural decreases sharply after age 13 for Indian boys, and after age 10 for Indian girls. Some of this decrease is perhaps due to the fact that the children learn that some of the supernatural causes of fear (such as the owl at Hopi) are not so fearful as they had supposed. The Indian boys, however, reach their peak in fear of supernatural about ages 11-13. The difference between them and the girls may be due to the fact that at this age the boys are more venturesome after dark than the girls, and so run into more fear-arousing situations than do the girls.

Objective Danger

The aversion of objective forms of danger decreases with age in all groups. Among the Midwest boys and girls it falls off sharply after age 10, but this does not occur until age 13 for the Indian boys and girls.

Death of Self

Because there were not enough responses to Worst Thing to permit making comparisons, we can only suggest the probability that the age trends are opposite in the Midwest and Indian groups. There is a downward tendency with age for the Midwest boys and girls. Perhaps as Midwest children grow older, they imagine other more realistic misfortunes than death. For the Indian children there is an unreliable trend upward with age on this theme—certainly no decrease with age.

APPENDIX C-1

MORAL IDEOLOGY TEST: "BEHAVIOR" CATEGORIES

1. Amusements

   "Going to movies," "swimming," "going to school dances," "fishing," "bicycling," "sports," "dating," "go out and have a good clean time."

2. Bad amusements

   "Listening to mystery stories," "playing cards," "going to shows too much."

3. Hobby

   "Have some hobby," "have a hobby you like," "work at some hobby."

4. Achievement in school

   "Getting higher grades," "being an industrious student," "take an interest in your studies," "do school work," "get passing grades."

5. Job and employment

   "Earn your spending money," "find yourself a job," "work after school," "getting a job for the summer," "take care of children."

6. Self-improvement; ambition; talent

   "Educational movies," "educational clubs," "making good any opportunities," "be ambitious," "use good English," "go to college," "speak correctly," "have a lovely voice," "read good literature," "study to learn," "play an instrument well."

6a.[1] Good in sports (with Midwest data, these responses are included in category 6.)

7. Industry; laziness; generalized work

   "Doing your work well," "doing a good job at something," "working carefully," "wasting time," "loaf."

7a. Obedience to employer; loyalty to employer

---

1. These categories were used with Indian data but not with Midwest data. In some cases, refinement of the earlier category was suggested by the anthropologist who had a special interest in one or another Indian culture. In other cases, a new category was added to accommodate responses which had not occurred on the protocols of the white children.

8. "Right people"; "right places"; keeping a "good reputation"

   "Go around with good, clean group of kids," "date women with bad reputation," "go to places where drinks are served," "go to night clubs," "go to taverns," "hang around pool halls," "go around with a fast crowd."

9. Etiquette

   "Eating hoggishly," "being ill-mannered," "learning to use Emily Post," "act the same at a party as you would at home," "act like a lady or a gentleman," "always say 'please'," "don't say 'gimme' when you ask for something," "don't grab for everything," "be noisy," "not have manners," "use impolite or rough language."

10. Rowdy behavior (excludes school behavior)

    "Run around," "be rowdy in drug stores," "being wild," "act like a zombie out of town," "carouse around," "walk the streets."

11. Maturity; acting grown up; recognizing own immaturity

    "Act your age," "be sensible," "not silly like we were when we were kids," "judging for yourself," "listening to experiences," "advising others when you don't know much yourself," "believing an older person," "not taking advice of older people."

12. Running away

    "Work in another city," "leave home."

13. Verbal aggression; arguing; bossing; bullying; quarreling (with peers or younger children)

    "Making trouble," "always starting something," "always criticizing," "telling others where to get off," "being critical of others," "try to discourage people in everything," "calling somebody names."

14. Fighting

    "Picking fights," "fighting all the time," "stop a fight."

15. Sportsmanship

    "Be a good sport," "be a good loser," "be able to take hard knocks," "profit from criticism," "show good spirit on the team," "playing fair," "not fighting fair," "cheating in games."

16. Honesty; cheating; lying; truthfulness

    "Copy," "cheat, especially on a test," "be honest," "be trustworthy," "be fair in school," "deceive your parents," "tell the truth," "be sneaky."

16a. Take blame

"Don't blame somebody else when it's your own fault."

17. Initiative and leadership; self-reliance

"Being Boy Scout leader."

18. Dependability and responsibility; persistence

"Follow instructions," "do things when I'm told to do them," "don't give up without trying," "be a little more dependable," "never give up," "having books etc., ready to go," "don't shirk."

19. Punctuality; procrastination

"Do things on time," "go to school on time," "be on time for appointments," "let things go till the last minute."

20. (This category was later combined with others.)

21. Courage; cowardice

22. Stealing

"Taking souvenirs," "taking things from somebody without their knowing it."

23. "General" good and "general" bad behavior (when specific examples are not given)

"Getting into trouble," "being bad," "being unclean," "being decent all around," "get into mischief," "setting an example for younger kids," "having bad habits," "have high moral standards," "clean social habits," "don't think up ways of doing bad things," "mind signs and obey them," "behave," "build up my character," "get people into trouble."

24. Smoking and chewing tobacco

25. Drinking

26. Swearing; "bad" language

27. Gambling; punch boards

28. Thrift; use of money; borrow money

29. Neatness (excludes school); personal appearance

"Clean up a mess you make at home," "careless in dress," "get too dirty," "clean up before dinner," "don't mess up the house," "brush hair."

30. Health

"Get plenty of sleep," "eat and drink the right kinds of food," "keep up your health," "getting exercise," "play sports to build up your body."

31. Keeping regular hours

"Stay home more at night," "be in early after dances," (for younger children) "come right home after school."

32. Recklessness and carelessness of person (excludes clothing, property)

"Drive carefully," "play with matches," "obey traffic rules."

33. Care of property (excludes school)

"Think they're smart and ruin somebody's home," "wreck the car," "walk across the neighbor's grass," "breaking windows," "clean up after a picnic," "picking flowers."

33a. [1]Care of one's own property (with Midwest data, these responses are included in category 33)

33b. [1]Aggression against property; petty crimes against property (with Midwest data, these responses are included in category 33)

34. Thoughtfulness of others; courtesy; kindness; tolerance

"Remember people with cards on their birthday," "being thoughtless," "being mean," "be kind," "have no regard for the other fellow," "be polite and courteous," "be rude," "being able to see the better part of a person," "hate," "speak well of people with bad 'reps'," "don't make fun of people," "play with someone who doesn't have many friends," "do things not grudgingly."

35. Pleasant disposition

"Controlling temper," "be good-natured," "always be griping," "have a nice personality," "a bad disposition," "grouchy," "be patient," "don't always say 'I don't want to'," "be nice," "be able to take a joke."

36. Friendliness

"Be friendly," "having good friends," "get along with people," "be a real pal to everybody," "be sociable," "like people," "don't say 'I don't like him'," "say hello to the people you know," "good social contact with everyone," "don't chum with just one person."

37. Cooperation; generosity; selfishness

"Whenever asked to do something, do it," "not cooperating with children in clubs, plays, etc." "greed," "share with others," "be stingy," "being stubborn," "wanting your own way all the time," "share hardships," "do your share of work," "take turns."

38. Service to other people (excludes family)

"Be helpful in school," "helping others when they get behind," "rake the neighbor's lawn," "join clubs like the Boy Scouts to help different kinds of people," "save a life," "protecting a little boy," "charity," "join Red Cross."

39. Regard for family; confidence; affection; family solidarity

"Get job if family needs money," "good home life," "not telling my parents my troubles," "go to see your grandmother now and then," "help brother."

39a. [1]Fighting with sibs (with Midwest data, these responses are included in category 39)

"Fight with your brother."

40. Obedience and respect to parents and elders (excludes employer and teachers)

"Respect to elders," "refusing to follow parents' instructions," "going out when I'm not supposed to," "be mean to parents," "come in later than your parents tell you."

40a. [1]Aggression toward parent (with Midwest data, these responses are included in category 40)

"Sass your parents," "kick," "hit," "scold," "talk back to your parents."

41. Work at home

"Help more at home," "doing dishes," "run errands," "do odd jobs without complaining."

42. Conformity to school's expectations and school rules

"Don't skip school," "finish high school," "talk in school," "toss paper on the floor in school," "create a disturbance in school," "behave in school," "don't annoy others," (in school), "close locker door," "close the door," (in school).

42a. Care of school property

"Tear books," "carve desks."

42b. Neatness in school

"Keep school ground clean," "pick paper off floor."

43. Respect for and cooperation with teachers; obedience to teachers (where teacher is specifically mentioned—otherwise 40)

44. Extracurricular activities; school loyalty

"Enter strongly into school activities," "go out for all the games and cheer the team."

45. Religious observance

"Go to church," "attend Sunday school," "prepare Sunday school lessons," "loyalty to the church," "shouldn't work on Sunday," "say your prayers," "fool around and not pay attention while in church."

46. Taking part in church activities

"Help serve at church suppers," "sing in the choir," "go to a Bible camp."

46a. [1]Tribal religious ceremonies

47. Reverence; sincere religious conviction

"Trust in God," "be religious," "obey ten commandments," "say your prayers."

48. General social participation

"Be a Boy Scout," "join Y.M.C.A.," "take part in everything," "join clubs," "be social," "meet people," "join youth organizations," "join good organizations," "join well known organizations," "don't play with other people," (bad); "don't go anyplace," (bad); "be a stay-at-home," (bad).

49. Social skills

"Not be a stick-in-the-mud at parties," "mix well with other people of our age," "being narrow-minded," "be good dancer," "give well-balanced talks," "talk with ease before groups," "play the piano—tunes everybody likes," "don't be a kill-joy," "learn how to dance."

50. Minding your own business; being nosey

51. Conceit; snobbishness; showing-off; modesty

"Smart alec," "participate in sports and get good, without getting the big head," "not having anything to do with others," "show off," "snub others," "bragging-boasting," "act smart."

52. Loyalty to other individuals; two-faced; "catty"

"Being able to be confided in," "talk about somebody behind their backs," "tattling," "gossiping," "be true to your friends."

53. "Parking"; "necking"; "mugging"

"Sit in the car and mug," "necking too much," "park and talk."

54. Marriage and "going steady"

"Getting married," (mentioned as a good thing); "settling down," "going steady," "getting married."

55. Sexual morality; "impure thoughts"

"Be clean in mind and soul," "go to bad movies," "be a good girl on dates," "tell dirty jokes," "visit houses of prostitution," "go to burlesque shows," "being intimate with boys," "read bad books."

56. Other sex behavior

"Don't chase boys," "write love notes," "dating," (bad); "not marrying at too young an age," "running around with a different boy every night of the week," "breaking up a couple who are going steady," "being nice on dates," "going on weekend parties with a mixed crowd," "treat girls respectfully," "having boy friends," (or girl friends); "having dates too much," "to tease girls," "be boy crazy."

57. Obedience and respect for government and community; loyalty to government

"Conserve on father's tires," "respect for country and flag," "don't do unpatriotic things."

57a. Keeping community and streets clean

58. Active work for government and community

"Join organizations helping in war work," "buy defense bonds," "help in victory gardens," "write to boys in service."

59. Miscellaneous

"Cook," "sew," "be grateful for what you have," "giggle," "don't be a sissy," "hitch-hike," "sew on buttons," "eat," "sleep," "making meals," "taking drugs," "don't play tricks," "don't play jokes," "borrowing," "go to the messenger class."

59a. Killing

59b. Dress appropriately

"Wear too much makeup," "dress cheap," "wearing slacks in school."

60. Aggressivity

"Roughhouse," "horseplay," "pushing in line," "making faces," "throw water on somebody," "pushing," "be rough," "cruelty," "hurt somebody," "throw stones," "always poking others," "bite," "kick."

61. Treatment of animals

"Ride horses correctly," "feed your pets," "kind to animals," "kill birds."

62. Self-control; self-denial; resist a strong temptation

"Think before you speak," "have control over emotions," "have work done before you play."

63.[1] Crying or complaining (with Midwest data, these responses are included in category 35)

64.[1] Physical injury to oneself (with Midwest data, these responses are

included in categories 32 or 59)

"Getting hurt," "break a leg," "be dead."

64a.[1] Give me something (with Midwest data, these responses are included in category 34)

64b.[1] So bad to me (with Midwest data, these responses are included in category 34)

65.[1] Rude (or kind) to old people (with Midwest data, these responses are included in category 34)

66.[1] Witchcraft, evil thoughts

APPENDIX C-2

MORAL IDEOLOGY TEST: "SURROGATE" CATEGORIES

1. Relatives ("family"; "home")

1a.[1] Uncle (with Midwest data, these responses are included in category 1)

2. Father
3. Mother
4. Parents ("guardian")
5. Adults ("most parents"; "parents of the other child")
6. Some parents ("some elders"; "some adults"; "gossipers")
7. Age-mates ("boys and girls"; "children"; "pupils"; "teammates"; "young people"; "fellow-workers")

7a. Individual children's names

8. Friends ("some friends"; "my best friend"; "my friend")
9. Other sex ("boy friend"; "girl friend"; "sweetheart")
10. Same sex ("the other boys"; "the rest of the girls")
11. Teachers ("school board"; "superintendent"; "principal"; "janitor"; "coach"; "music teacher"; "school patrol"; "school nurse")
12. Church ("congregation"; "Christians"; "church members"; "Sunday School teachers")
13. Clergy ("the preacher"; "minister")
14. Everybody ("people"; "others"; "community"; "country"; "public"; "the government"; "neighbors"; "people around you")

14a.[1] Nobody (with Midwest data, these responses are included in category 14)

14b.[1] White people

14c.[1] Uncle Sam (with Midwest data, these responses are included in category 14)

15. Representatives of government and law ("police"; "the court"; "laws")
16. Self ("my conscience"; "myself")
17. Recipient of the act; the person involved; (this category is used only when "recipient" or "person-involved" is explicitly stated. For example, "walking across neighbor's lawn—the neighbor would disapprove"; but not "be nice to your friends—friends would praise you.")

1. These categories were added for the Indian data.

18. Deity
19. Employer
20. Miscellaneous

    "Doctor," "soldiers," "scout-master"

21.[1] Animals, birds, pets

22.[1] Grandmother or grandfather (with Midwest data, these responses are included in category 1)

APPENDIX C-3

TABLE 44

THEMES OF MORAL IDEOLOGY FOR EACH TRIBAL GROUP: BY AGE AND SEX

(PERCENTAGE FREQUENCIES)

	PAPAGO									HOPI								
	Boys				Girls				Total Av.	Boys				Girls				Total Av.
	B[a]	C	D	Av.	B	C	D	Av.		B	C	D	Av.	B	C	D	Av.	
No. of responses	109	82	114	...	105	100	118	...	...	100	101	137	...	95	235	173	...	...
Major themes:																		
Self-achievement	8	15	19	14	9	16	11	12	13	20	15	22	19	11	11	14	12	15
Self-restraint	15	11	16	14	5	15	14	11	13	15	9	4	9	10	6	2	6	8
Personal virtues	9	10	17	12	8	15	15	13	12	14	9	12	12	12	11	11	11	11
Authority	4	10	7	7	12	5	13	10	8	9	7	12	9	11	10	10	10	10
Regard for others	29	26	31	29	31	18	20	23	26	28	46	34	36	42	37	35	38	37
Service	36	33	18	29	36	12	31	27	28	28	21	25	25	25	27	30	27	26
Sex	...	...	1	...	...	1	3	1	1	...	...	...	...	...	1	2	1	1
Subsidiary themes:																		
Family	39	38	18	31	45	43	28	38	35	25	24	20	23	37	30	28	32	27
School	1	2	5	3	5	2	3	3	3	7	2	7	5	3	5	5	4	5
Church	...	...	...	...	2	...	1	1	...	...	...	1	...	...	...	1	...	...
Community	...	...	1	...	...	...	...	...	...	...	...	1	1	...	...	1	...	...
Property	19	20	22	23	12	10	10	11	17	16	21	23	20	25	15	13	18	19
Work	44	44	30	39	40	54	38	44	42	38	30	33	34	31	31	28	30	32
Stealing	13	13	18	15	10	9	10	10	12	9	16	18	14	19	11	11	14	14
Drinking	3	2	4	3	1	...	4	2	3	...	...	1	...	...	...	1	...	...
Bad language	1	1	...	1	...	1	2	1	1	...	...	1	...	...	...	...	...	...
Aggressive toward peers	7	1	4	4	1	1	...	1	2	9	16	5	10	3	8	6	6	8

a. Indians: B = 8-10 years; C = 11-13 years; D = 14-18 years. Midwest: B = 10 years; C = 11-13 years; D = 14-18 years.

TABLE 44-Continued

	ZUNI									ZIA								
	Boys				Girls				Total Av.	Boys				Girls				Total Av.
	B	C	D	Av.	B	C	D	Av.		B	C	D	Av.	B	C	D	Av.	
No. of responses	72	72	122	...	78	100	62	...	...	66	40	31	...	35	23	39	...	...
Major themes:																		
Self-achievement	7	25	26	19	9	10	18	12	16	14	20	3	12	26	9	5	13	13
Self-restraint	10	...	12	7	4	8	3	5	6	11	5	13	10	14	4	15	11	10
Personal virtues	1	10	13	8	5	14	11	10	9	12	5	6	8	23	13	13	16	12
Authority	7	6	14	9	6	10	15	10	10	3	...	19	8	6	4	11	7	7
Regard for others	25	28	22	25	35	22	13	23	24	42	38	48	43	20	35	51	35	39
Service	47	40	23	37	45	38	32	38	38	36	30	13	26	37	44	15	32	29
Sex	...	1	1	1	...	3	11	5	3	...	...	...	...	...	...	...	...	...
Subsidiary themes:																		
Family	54	42	26	41	58	46	40	48	44	41	33	6	27	47	52	15	38	32
School	1	3	7	4	4	4	8	5	5	...	...	6	2	3	...	5	3	2
Church	...	...	...	...	...	...	...	...	...	...	...	3	1	3	...	...	1	1
Community	...	...	5	2	...	1	...	0	1	...	...	6	2	...	...	5	2	2
Property	14	21	11	15	13	14	6	11	13	8	13	23	14	9	13	15	12	13
Work	53	58	39	50	50	38	37	42	46	47	45	3	32	57	44	13	38	35
Stealing	8	18	9	12	6	7	2	5	8	8	10	16	11	3	8	15	9	10
Drinking	...	...	5	2	...	...	...	...	1	...	...	3	1	...	...	...	...	1
Bad language	...	...	...	...	...	...	...	...	...	8	...	3	4	6	4	3	4	4
Aggressive toward peers	8	7	6	7	6	5	...	4	5	10	15	10	12	...	8	18	9	10

TABLE 44-Continued

	NAVAHO MOUNTAIN									SHIPROCK								
	Boys				Girls				Total Av.	Boys				Girls				Total Av.
	B	C	D	Av.	B	C	D	Av.		B	C	D	Av.	B	C	D	Av.	
No. of responses	50	48	64	...	28	31	50	...	...	62	98	42	...	79	62	66	...	...
Major themes:																		
Self-achievement	64	63	34	54	32	42	48	40	47	23	26	25	22	23	20	21	23	...
Self-restraint	2	10	9	7	14	6	10	10	9	19	21	21	21	14	3	8	8	14
Personal virtues	50	35	25	37	21	13	16	17	27	21	19	17	19	15	19	8	14	17
Authority	2	2	2	2	...	3	2	2	2	8	8	5	7	1	8	15	8	8
Regard for others	18	13	23	18	14	16	8	13	15	24	25	31	27	24	24	23	24	25
Service	10	13	16	13	18	6	6	10	11	23	17	10	17	35	40	23	33	25
Sex	...	2	8	3	...	3	18	7	5	...	...	...	...	...	2	10	4	2
Subsidiary themes:																		
Family	10	13	...	8	21	10	8	13	10	27	20	12	20	35	44	29	36	28
School	...	2	6	3	...	3	...	1	2	5	6	2	4	1	2	5	3	3
Church	...	...	...	...	...	...	...	...	...	...	...	...	...	...	...	...	...	...
Community	...	...	2	1	...	...	...	...	...	...	...	...	...	...	...	...	...	...
Property	10	8	14	10	7	10	2	6	9	13	14	17	15	10	11	9	10	12
Work	70	59	30	53	43	32	54	43	48	42	37	31	37	52	58	29	46	41
Stealing	10	8	13	10	4	10	2	5	8	6	13	12	11	5	11	9	9	10
Drinking	...	...	2	1	...	...	...	...	...	...	...	...	...	...	...	...	...	...
Bad language	...	...	...	...	...	...	...	...	...	...	...	...	...	...	...	...	...	...
Aggressive toward peers	6	4	3	4	7	16	...	8	6	10	8	12	10	10	10	6	9	9

TABLE 44 - Continued

	SIOUX									MIDWEST								
	Boys				Girls				Total Av.	Boys				Girls				Total Av.
	B	C	D	Av.	B	C	D	Av.		B	C	D	Av.	B	C	D	Av.	
No. of responses	107	72	135	...	96	101	132	...	398	398	1667	3268	...	587	2179	4339	...	...
Major themes:																		
Self-achievement	6	13	16	11	5	5	9	6	9	4	8	15	8	6	7	12	8	8
Self-restraint	10	13	7	10	7	8	14	10	10	31	23	32	29	21	17	31	23	26
Personal virtues	3	6	12	7	5	5	5	5	6	7	11	20	13	8	10	19	13	13
Authority	8	8	12	10	22	16	20	19	14	15	21	14	17	25	30	15	23	20
Regard for others	51	47	36	45	38	36	26	33	39	32	28	20	27	27	30	20	26	26
Service	24	17	24	22	18	25	20	21	21	21	16	7	14	18	17	8	14	14
Sex	...	1	...	1	2	4	8	5	3	...	1	2	1	...	1	3	1	1
Subsidiary themes:																		
Family	20	8	13	14	27	19	16	21	17	17	15	6	13	20	17	8	15	14
School	5	6	7	6	9	6	13	9	8	8	11	8	9	16	11	7	11	10
Church	...	...	...	...	1	4	2	2	1	1	2	2	1	2	2	3	2	2
Community	3	1	4	3	...	...	2	1	2	5	7	4	5	5	5	3	4	5
Property	30	24	22	25	14	19	12	15	20	12	8	7	9	9	6	4	6	8
Work	22	14	21	19	19	18	14	17	18	15	9	9	11	12	9	6	9	10
Stealing	20	17	19	19	8	16	11	12	15	2	2	2	2	1	2	2	2	2
Drinking	...	1	5	2	...	...	7	2	2	...	1	4	2	1	1	4	2	2
Bad language	2	1	...	1	2	1	...	1	1	2	2	3	2	2	2	3	2	2
Aggressive toward peers	13	14	9	12	17	11	7	11	12	12	9	3	8	7	7	2	5	6

APPENDIX C-4

TABLE 45

MORAL SURROGATES FOR EACH TRIBAL GROUP, BY AGE AND SEX, BY PRAISERS AND BLAMERS (PERCENTAGE FREQUENCIES)

PAPAGO

	BOYS								GIRLS								Total Praisers	Total Blamers	Total Boys	Total Girls	Total Average[a]
	Praisers				Blamers				Praisers				Blamers								
	B[c]	C	D	Av.[b]	B	C	D	Av.	B	C	D	Av.	B	C	D	Av.					
No. of responses	57	42	54	...	53	40	59	...	54	49	59	...	46	49	63	...	315	310	305	320	625
Family: 1, 1a, 2, 3, 4, 22	79	95	63	79	64	75	51	63	87	92	61	80	76	80	51	69	80	66	71	74	73
Father: 2	25	26	24	25	30	28	10	23	11	18	9	13	28	16	6	17	19	20	24	15	19
Mother: 3	35	26	13	25	21	13	12	15	63	59	29	50	39	35	18	30	38	23	20	40	30
Grandparents: 22	7	10	2	6	4	8	...	4	2	2	5	3	...	10	2	4	5	4	5	4	2
Elders: 5, 6	2	...	...	1	8	...	2	3	...	...	2	1	4	...	2	2	1	3	2	1	2
Age-mates: 7, 8, 9, 10	5	...	2	2	9	5	5	7	...	2	3	2	4	8	16	10	2	8	5	6	5
Teacher: 11	2	2	6	3	...	...	5	2	9	6	3	6	2	4	5	4	5	3	3	5	4
Clergy: 13	...	...	...	...	...	...	...	...	...	...	...	...	...	...	...	...	...	...	...	...	...
Everybody: 14, 14c	2	2	6	3	9	18	15	14	4	...	15	6	7	8	11	9	5	11	9	8	8
Govt.: 15	...	...	2	1	...	...	5	2	...	...	...	...	2	...	...	1	1	1	1	...	1
Self: 16	2	...	2	1	...	...	2	1	...	...	...	...	4	...	3	2	1	2	1	1	1
Recipient: 17	5	...	13	6	9	3	12	8	...	...	12	4	...	...	8	3	7	5	7	3	5
Deity: 18	...	...	6	2	...	...	2	1	...	...	2	1	...	...	2	1	1	1	1	1	1

a. Average of total boys and total girls.
b. Apparent errors in "average" columns are the results of rounding.
c. B = 8-10 years; C = 11-13 years; D = 14-18 years.

TABLE 45-Continued

H O P I

	BOYS								GIRLS								Total Praisers	Total Blamers	Total Boys	Total Girls	Total Average
	Praisers				Blamers				Praisers				Blamers								
	B	C	D	Av.	B	C	D	Av.	B	C	D	Av.	B	C	D	Av.					
No. of responses	50	49	77	...	45	50	61	...	49	111	86	...	44	118	87	...	422	405	332	495	827
Family: 1, 1a, 2, 3, 4, 22	66	51	55	57	36	36	23	32	67	60	47	58	57	42	43	47	58	39	44	53	49
Father: 2	26	12	17	18	9	14	10	11	6	6	4	5	7	5	1	4	12	8	15	5	10
Mother: 3	24	18	17	20	9	14	2	8	33	26	31	30	25	25	31	27	25	18	14	29	21
Grandparents: 22	8	6	1	5	...	...	...	...	2	2	...	1	5	...	...	2	3	1	3	1	2
Elders: 5, 6	8	10	7	8	9	12	5	9	...	4	2	2	...	6	5	4	5	6	8	3	6
Age-mates: 7, 8, 9, 10	4	18	...	8	11	22	10	14	14	7	6	9	11	17	7	12	8	13	11	11	11
Teacher: 11	4	...	9	4	13	6	10	10	2	6	7	5	5	6	6	5	5	8	7	5	6
Clergy: 13	...	2	...	1	...	...	...	...	...	...	...	...	...	...	...	...	...	...	...	...	...
Everybody: 14, 14c	10	18	14	14	...	14	18	11	8	13	22	14	9	12	25	15	14	13	13	15	14
Govt.: 15	...	...	1	...	...	2	3	2	...	...	...	...	...	...	...	...	...	1	1	...	1
Self: 16	...	...	...	...	4	...	2	2	...	3	...	1	...	2	1	1	1	2	1	1	1
Recipient: 17	6	...	12	6	11	6	28	15	8	8	13	10	7	14	12	11	8	13	11	10	11
Deity: 18	...	...	...	...	...	...	...	...	...	...	1	...	...	...	...	...	...	...	...	...	...

TABLE 45-Continued

ZUNI

	BOYS								GIRLS								Total Praisers	Total Blamers	Total Boys	Total Girls	Total Average
	Praisers				Blamers				Praisers				Blamers								
	B	C	D	Av.	B	C	D	Av.	B	C	D	Av.	B	C	D	Av.					
No. of responses	36	36	59	...	36	36	56	...	39	47	34	...	37	47	28	...	251	240	259	232	491
Family: 1, 1a, 2, 3, 4, 22	81	81	76	79	83	70	73	75	72	83	76	78	68	49	82	66	78	79	77	72	75
Father: 2	36	31	41	36	42	39	38	39	8	11	6	8	8	15	11	11	22	25	38	10	24
Mother: 3	22	28	10	20	28	8	13	16	49	43	35	42	41	58	36	45	31	30	18	43	31
Grandparents: 22	14	...	3	6	3	...	2	2	3	...	6	3	5	6	...	4	4	3	4	3	4
Elders: 5, 6	3	...	2	2	8	...	2	3	...	...	...	...	3	2	...	2	1	3	3	1	2
Age-mates: 7, 8, 9, 10	6	3	3	4	...	...	2	1	13	4	...	6	3	...	...	1	5	1	2	3	3
Teacher: 11	3	8	10	7	3	6	7	5	13	9	21	14	24	9	18	17	11	11	6	16	11
Clergy: 13	...	...	...	...	...	...	...	...	...	...	...	...	...	...	...	...	...	...	...	...	...
Everybody: 14, 14c	...	...	3	1	6	3	5	5	...	4	3	2	...	...	...	...	2	2	3	1	2
Govt.: 15	...	3	2	2	...	...	...	...	...	...	...	...	...	...	...	...	1	...	1	...	...
Self: 16	3	3	...	2	...	...	...	...	...	...	...	...	3	...	...	1	1	1	1	1	1
Recipient: 17	6	3	2	3	...	17	11	9	...	...	...	...	...	6	...	2	2	6	6	1	4
Deity: 18	...	...	...	...	...	...	...	...	...	...	...	...	...	...	...	...	...	...	...	...	...

TABLE 45-Continued

ZIA

	BOYS								GIRLS								Total Praisers	Total Blamers	Total Boys	Total Girls	Total Average
	Praisers				Blamers				Praisers				Blamers								
	B	C	D	Av.	B	C	D	Av.	B	C	D	Av.	B	C	D	Av.					
No. of responses	32	23	14	...	32	17	15	...	18	12	17	...	17	11	19	...	116	111	133	94	227
Family: 1, 1a, 2, 3, 4, 22	78	74	43	65	53	35	...	30	83	75	35	65	65	64	11	46	65	38	47	56	51
Father: 2	28	31	...	20	19	29	...	16	...	...	...	...	...	...	...	...	10	8	18	...	9
Mother: 3	44	31	7	27	28	6	...	11	83	75	24	61	53	64	5	41	44	26	19	51	35
Grandparents: 22	3	4	...	3	3	...	...	1	...	...	...	...	...	...	...	...	1	1	2	...	1
Elders: 5, 6	16	...	14	10	22	12	7	14	...	8	...	3	6	18	11	12	6	13	12	7	10
Age-mates: 7, 8, 9, 10	...	...	...	...	3	6	13	7	...	...	...	...	...	...	...	...	...	4	4	...	2
Teacher: 11	...	4	14	6	...	12	...	4	6	...	...	2	...	...	11	4	4	4	5	3	4
Clergy: 13	...	...	...	...	...	...	...	...	...	...	...	...	...	...	...	...	...	...	...	...	...
Everybody: 14, 14c	...	17	7	8	16	18	7	13	6	8	6	7	12	18	11	4	7	13	11	10	11
Govt.: 15	...	...	...	...	...	...	...	...	...	...	...	...	...	...	...	...	...	...	...	...	...
Self: 16	...	...	...	...	...	...	7	2	...	...	6	2	...	...	5	2	1	2	1	2	2
Recipient: 17	3	...	7	3	6	...	20	9	...	8	47	18	...	...	42	14	11	11	6	16	11
Deity: 18	...	...	14	5	...	...	...	...	...	...	...	...	...	...	...	...	2	...	2	...	1

291

TABLE 45-Continued

NAVAHO MOUNTAIN

	BOYS								GIRLS								Total Praisers	Total Blamers	Total Boys	Total Girls	Total Average
	Praisers				Blamers				Praisers				Blamers								
	B	C	D	Av.	B	C	D	Av.	B	C	D	Av.	B	C	D	Av.					
No. of responses	39	36	45	...	34	38	43	...	22	23	42	...	18	19	34	...	207	186	235	158	393
Family: 1, 1a, 2, 3, 4, 22	85	78	62	75	88	89	44	74	100	87	98	95	78	63	68	70	85	72	74	82	78
Father: 2	8	8	16	11	...	3	2	2	9	4	14	9	17	...	3	7	10	4	6	8	7
Mother: 3	15	14	...	10	12	5	7	8	27	9	26	21	6	11	9	8	15	8	9	15	12
Grandparents: 22	18	11	4	11	21	13	2	12	23	26	19	23	6	11	...	5	17	9	12	14	13
Elders: 5, 6	...	3	...	1	...	...	2	1	...	...	...	...	...	...	...	...	1	...	1	...	1
Age-mates: 7, 8, 9, 10	...	3	7	3	...	...	5	2	...	...	...	...	...	5	...	2	2	2	2	1	2
Teacher: 11	5	3	7	5	3	3	14	7	...	9	...	3	11	21	...	11	4	9	6	7	6
Clergy: 13	...	...	...	...	...	...	...	...	...	...	...	...	...	...	...	...	...	...	...	...	...
Everybody: 14, 14c	8	14	16	12	6	16	26	16	...	...	2	...	6	11	27	14	7	15	14	8	11
Govt.: 15	...	...	...	...	...	...	...	...	...	...	...	...	...	...	...	...	...	...	...	...	...
Self: 16	3	...	...	1	...	...	2	1	...	4	...	2	...	...	...	...	1	...	1	1	1
Recipient: 17	...	...	4	2	3	5	7	5	...	...	...	...	6	...	6	4	1	5	3	2	3
Deity: 18	...	...	...	...	...	...	...	...	...	...	...	...	...	...	...	...	...	...	...	...	...

292

TABLE 45-Continued

SHIPROCK

	BOYS								GIRLS								Total Praisers	Total Blamers	Total Boys	Total Girls	Total Average
	Praisers				Blamers				Praisers				Blamers								
	B	C	D	Av.	B	C	D	Av.	B	C	D	Av.	B	C	D	Av.					
No. of responses	52	87	28	...	44	72	28	...	59	44	57	...	52	46	50	...	327	302	311	318	629
Family: 1, 1a, 2, 3, 4, 22	67	70	54	64	66	72	64	67	90	80	61	77	90	74	66	77	70	72	67	77	71
Father: 2	8	2	...	3	...	...	...	...	2	2	...	1	...	...	...	...	2	...	2	1	1
Mother: 3	6	1	4	4	7	...	4	4	10	9	4	8	6	4	8	6	6	5	4	7	5
Grandparents: 22	8	14	...	7	7	10	7	8	14	20	2	12	10	13	...	8	10	8	8	10	9
Elders: 5, 6	4	1	7	3	9	1	11	7	...	5	2	2	2	2	4	3	3	5	5	2	4
Age-mates: 7, 8, 9, 10	15	7	...	7	2	7	4	4	3	2	5	4	4	7	6	5	6	5	6	5	5
Teacher: 11	8	9	14	10	9	7	11	9	7	2	11	7	...	4	14	6	9	8	10	6	8
Clergy: 13	...	...	...	...	...	...	...	...	...	...	...	...	...	...	...	...	...	...	...	...	...
Everybody: 14, 14c	4	9	18	10	7	10	4	7	...	9	12	7	2	9	10	7	9	7	9	7	8
Govt.: 15	...	...	...	...	4	...	...	1	...	...	...	...	...	...	...	...	...	1	1	...	...
Self: 16	2	...	...	1	...	...	...	...	...	...	...	...	...	...	...	...	...	...	...	...	...
Recipient: 17	...	...	4	1	2	3	...	2	...	...	4	1	2	2	...	1	1	2	2	1	1
Deity: 18	...	...	...	...	...	...	...	...	...	...	...	...	...	...	...	...	...	...	...	...	...

TABLE 45-Continued

SIOUX

	BOYS								GIRLS								Total Praisers	Total Blamers	Total Boys	Total Girls	Total Average
	Praisers				Blamers				Praisers				Blamers								
	B	C	D	Av.	B	C	D	Av.	B	C	D	Av.	B	C	D	Av.					
No. of responses	54	31	68	...	50	36	68	...	48	45	64	...	47	48	66	...	310	315	307	318	625
Family: 1, 1a, 2, 3, 4, 22	37	35	34	35	26	33	25	28	50	42	42	45	66	44	38	49	40	39	32	47	39
Father: 2	6	13	7	9	4	14	6	8	8	9	2	6	6	6	3	5	8	7	8	6	7
Mother: 3	20	19	10	17	18	6	6	9	27	24	25	26	36	21	15	24	21	17	13	25	19
Grandparents: 22	...	...	...	...	...	...	...	...	4	2	...	2	2	4	...	2	1	1	...	2	1
Elders: 5, 6	4	13	6	8	14	8	3	8	2	2	...	1	...	2	3	2	5	5	8	2	5
Age-mates: 7, 8, 9, 10	19	23	...	14	12	14	2	9	4	...	14	6	4	...	15	7	10	8	11	6	9
Teacher: 11	7	3	16	9	8	3	13	9	20	9	16	15	17	6	17	13	12	11	9	14	12
Clergy: 13	...	...	2	1	...	...	...	...	...	...	2	1	...	...	...	...	1	...	...	...	...
Everybody: 14, 14c	9	13	18	13	4	8	19	11	6	20	16	14	6	21	12	13	14	12	12	14	13
Govt.: 15	4	...	2	2	4	8	3	5	...	...	...	...	...	...	...	...	1	3	3	...	2
Self: 16	...	...	2	1	...	...	2	1	...	...	...	...	...	...	2	1	...	1	1	...	...
Recipient: 17	7	13	10	10	18	8	29	19	6	18	6	10	2	25	11	13	10	16	14	11	13
Deity: 18	9	...	6	5	6	...	...	2	4	9	3	5	2	...	...	1	5	1	4	3	3

TABLE 45-Continued

MIDWEST

	BOYS				GIRLS				Total Average
	B	C	D	Total Boys	B	C	D	Total Girls	
No. of responses	393	1,578	3,752	5,723	590	2,220	5,807	8,617	14,340
Family: 1, 2, 3, 4	55	43	43	47	48	39	42	43	45
Father: 2	13	6	1	7	5	2	1	3	5
Mother: 3	26	13	3	14	26	16	4	15	15
Elders: 5, 6	1	2	1	1	2	2	2	2	1
Age-mates: 7, 8, 9, 10	12	4	11	10	3	6	16	8	9
Teacher: 11	11	17	15	14	24	18	14	18	16
Clergy: 13	...	1	1	1	...	...	1	...	1
Everybody: 14	5	13	18	12	9	20	18	16	14
Govt.: 15	7	6	2	5	3	4	1	3	4
Self: 16	2	3	5	3	1	3	3	3	3
Recipient: 17	5	5	2	4	4	5	2	3	4
Deity: 18	2	1	...	1	1	2	...	1	1
	PRAISERS								
Father: 2	12	6	1	7	6	2	1	3	
Mother: 3	31	15	3	16	28	17	5	17	
	BLAMERS								
Father: 2	14	5	1	7	4	2	1	2	
Mother: 3	24	10	3	13	23	15	3	14	

APPENDIX D-1

FREE DRAWINGS: CATEGORIES OF CONTENT

1. Landscape (including plants)

Sky	Mountains	Tree
Cloud	Hills	Woods
Sun	Rocks	Orchard
Moon	Arroyo	Grass
Stars	River	Shrubs
Snow	Pond	Cactus, yucca
Rain	Lake	Flower
Rainbow	Ocean	Flower garden
		Field

2. Dwellings (including household furnishings and equipment)

Pueblo	Bed	Pot, Pan	Piki Stone
Adobe	Chair	Bucket	Picture
Hogan	Stool	Basket	Icebox
Frame	Table	Blanket	Radio
Tipi	Bench	Clothes line, or rack	Clock
Tent	Cupboard	Water Barrel	Hammock
Village	Dresser	Fire	Wash tub
	Stove	Woodpile	Ironing board
	Curtain	Loom	Crib
	Dishes	Spindle	Lamp
	Bowl, Jar	Metate	

3. Human beings

White and Indian men, women, children, and babies

4. Other Structures and Miscellaneous Tools

Church	Pig pen	Telephone poles	Shovel
School	Shade, shelter	Gun	Light
Store	Ladder, steps	Saddle	Hammer
Hangar	Toilet	Whip	Rake
Gas station	Barn	Lasso	Hoe
Government Bldgs.	Windmill	Rope	Tractor
Garage	Water pump	Spear	Plow
Kiva	Hydrant	Sling shot	Reaper
Bread oven	Corral	Bow and arrow	Sled
Bird house	Fence	Club	Cactus stick
Dog house	Road, path	Axe	
Chicken house	Bridge		

5. Animals and Birds

Horse	Lion	Lizard	Owl
Dog	Wolf	Mouse, Rat	Eagle
Cow	Fox	Mole	Bluebird
Herd of Cattle	Snake	Chipmunk	Duck
Cat	Rabbit	Squirrel	Indeterminate
Sheep	Deer	Grasshopper	
Flock of sheep	Antelope	Horned toad	
Goat	Tiger	Spider	
Chicken	Buffalo	Elephant	
Burro, Mule	Coyote	Giraffe	
Pig	Bear	Porcupine	
	Zebra	Turtle	

6. Transportation

Wagon	Car	Bicycle, motorcycle
Cart	Train	Boat, row
Truck	Stagecoach	Boat, sail
Bus	Airplane	Boat, steam

7. War and Patriotism

Tank	Parachute	Patriotic symbols (U.S., Nazi, Japanese)
Jeep	Big guns	Flag
Battleship	Bomb	Bugle
Airplane	Tow target	

8. School Appurtenances

Christmas tree, etc. (ornaments, gifts)	Desk	Swing
	Flag	Slide
Book	Sign	Teeter totter, etc.
Pencil	Bell	Balls, bat, ball courts, etc.

9. Ceremonials

Dancers, costumes	Sand paintings	Nature symbols (sun, rain, clouds, mountains, etc.)
Dance mask	Altar designs	Bird and feather symbols
Rattle	Katcina	

10. Crafts

Pottery	Basketry	Miscellaneous designs
Weaving	Tipi designs	

APPENDIX D-2

FREE DRAWINGS: AGE DIFFERENCES IN CONTENT

As has been stated in chapter vii, there are a few age differences in the content of free drawings which appear to be common to all the groups in the Study.[1] While these differences lie principally in the categories of landscape, dwellings, and human figures, we shall summarize the data shown in Table 46, by discussing each category in turn.[2]

Landscape objects.—There is a general tendency for the frequency of landscape objects to increase with age. The 6-7-year-old group gives the lowest frequency of landscape objects without exception; and the 14-18 group gives the highest frequency of landscape objects. Third Mesa and Zuni show a substantial falling-off in the percentage of landscape objects from ages 11-13 to ages 14-18, where there is a sharp increase in drawings of ceremonial figures and objects and of articles of handicraft.

Dwellings.—From the point of view of statistical reliability, an approximate general rule with respect to drawings of dwellings is that the

1. We compared our age differences with those found in several studies made a generation or more ago and found very little in common with them. See M. Gallagher, "Children's Spontaneous Drawings," Northwestern Monthly, VIII (1897), 130-34 (drawings of white and Indian children in Nebraska); L. McDermott, "Favorite Drawings of Indian Children," Northwestern Monthly, VIII (1897), 134-37 (drawings from 17 widely separated Indian schools); L. M. Maitland, "What Children Draw To Please Themselves," Inland Educator, I (1895), 77-81 (drawings from white California children); P. B. Ballard, "What London Children Like To Draw," Journal of Experimental Pediatrics, I (1912), 185-97; see also R. W. Russell, "The Spontaneous and Instructed Drawings of Zuni Children," Journal of Comparative Psychology, XXXV (1943), 11-15.

2. In estimating the statistical significance of differences between the percentages shown in Table 46, it is necessary to know approximately how many items were counted for each group of children. This can be computed by reference to the second and third columns of the table. For comparisons of percentages from the various age groups, the numbers of items involved are usually in the neighborhood of 400 (10 children with 8 pictures averaging 5 items per picture). With this base, a difference of 5-7 per cent is reliable at the 5 per cent level of probability, provided that the percentages compared are larger than 6-10 per cent. There is further reason to be cautious in interpreting these percentage differences, as already indicated (see p. 170, n. 4).

TABLE 46

CONTENT OF FREE DRAWINGS FOR EACH TRIBAL GROUP: BY AGE

	No. of Children	No. of Drawings	Av. No. of Items per Drawing	Percentage of Items in the Various Categories: Landscape	Animals	Humans	Dwellings	Other Structures	Transportation	War and Patriotism	School	Crafts	Ceremonial
Hickiwan													
6-7	11	69	8.0	28	3	20	15	12	4	14	5	0	0
8-10	20	138	5.9	34	2	16	16	14	7	11	2	0	0
11-13	13	95	5.0	45	4	13	18	11	3	4	1	0	0
14-18	12	66	5.1	48	4	11	11	14	4	7	0	0	0
Topawa													
6-7	16	123	5.1	56	4	9	14	7	3	4	3	0	0
8-10	25	170	5.4	58	5	5	15	9	2	3	2	0	0
11-13	22	154	6.6	62	6	5	13	10	1	1	1	0	0
14-18	24	158	4.7	60	9	8	8	10	2	3	1	0	0
Total Papago													
6-7	27	192	6.7	39	3	15	14	10	4	10	4	0	0
8-10	35	308	5.8	46	4	11	15	11	4	7	2	0	0
11-13	45	249	5.8	54	5	8	16	11	2	2	1	0	0
14-18	36	224	4.9	54	6	10	10	12	3	5	1	0	0
Third Mesa													
6-7	18	143	3.1	31	2	8	41	10	0	1	3	0	5
8-10	22	175	5.2	58	5	4	18	10	1	2	0	0	1
11-13	29	217	5.2	54	8	5	16	10	1	0	2	0	4
14-18	14	109	2.2	34	7	1	13	9	0	4	1	3	27
First Mesa													
6-7	14	109	6.1	30	11	17	22	11	4	0	5	0	0
8-10	19	151	5.1	42	10	15	11	12	4	0	1	1	3
11-13	17	134	4.0	29	14	17	17	11	4	0	1	3	4
14-18	8	57	3.4	41	6	7	18	14	1	2	0	6	4

TABLE 46—Continued

	No. of Children	No. of Drawings	Av. No. of Items per Drawing	Percentage of Items in the Various Categories: Land-scape	Ani-mals	Humans	Dwell-ings	Other Struc-tures	Trans-porta-tion	War and Patri-otism	School	Crafts	Cere-monial
Total Hopi													
6-7	32	252	4.4	31	8	14	28	10	3	1	4	0	2
8-10	41	326	5.2	50	8	9	14	11	2	1	1	0	2
11-13	46	351	4.7	43	10	10	17	11	2	0	1	1	4
14-18	22	166	2.6	39	7	4	16	13	1	2	0	5	13
Zuni													
6-7	13	112	5.9	20	13	12	25	15	9	0	7	0	0
8-10	24	193	7.5	38	12	13	14	16	2	0	2	1	2
11-13	27	235	4.8	50	7	6	12	14	1	0	0	4	5
14-18	27	183	3.2	37	12	6	8	11	0	0	0	14	12
Zia													
6-7	11	84	5.4	20	37	9	17	5	6	0	0	0	6
8-10	17	132	8.2	30	26	15	15	11	1	0	0	1	2
11-13	12	89	5.4	27	16	15	21	15	2	0	0	0	2
14-18[a]	2	16	6.0	39	10	20	16	12	3	0	0	0	0
Kyle													
6-7	8	41	3.5	13	15	6	37	23	1	1	4	0	0
8-10	19	145	6.3	39	6	7	18	16	4	9	2	0	0
11-13	15	118	5.6	50	4	6	14	15	6	3	2	0	0
14-18	28	216	5.3	54	2	10	15	12	3	3	1	0	0
Pine Ridge													
6-7	5	35	3.5	32	3	9	25	9	6	12	4	0	0
8-10	12	100	4.7	37	2	17	16	6	3	8	10	0	0
11-13	8	70	4.9	33	4	14	12	9	2	21	4	0	0
14-18	9	72	5.1	45	9	9	15	7	1	2	12	0	0

a. There were only two children in this group.

TABLE 46—Continued

	No. of Children	No. of Drawings	Av. No. of Items per Drawing	Percentage of Items in the Various Categories: Land-scape	Ani-mals	Humans	Dwell-ings	Other Struc-tures	Trans-porta-tion	War and Patri-otism	School	Crafts	Cere-monial
Total Sioux													
6-7	13	76	3.5	22	9	8	31	16	3	6	4	0	0
8-10	31	245	5.6	38	5	11	17	11	4	9	6	0	0
11-13	23	188	5.4	42	4	9	13	12	4	11	3	0	0
14-18	37	288	5.2	49	6	9	15	9	2	3	7	0	0
Shiprock													
6-7	14	101	7.4	24	8	16	22	8	4	9	9	0	0
8-10	23	161	8.5	37	3	13	20	8	5	8	5	0	0
11-13	28	193	8.0	43	9	8	18	10	3	6	3	0	0
14-18	17	129	6.1	48	13	9	15	9	2	0	0	2	0
Ramah													
6-7	7	49	2.9	16	19	28	5	8	13	2	0	8	0
8-10	7	69	3.7	34	17	17	15	4	4	1	0	7	0
11-13	11	125	3.9	33	22	11	10	6	3	1	0	14	0
14-18	9	50	2.8	36	20	10	4	5	4	8	0	14	0
Navaho Mt.													
6-7	5	23	6.6	29	10	23	28	4	6	0	0	0	0
8-10	10	43	7.3	47	11	10	19	6	5	1	0	0	0
11-13	10	53	7.7	47	9	15	13	14	2	0	0	0	0
14-18	7	21	5.4	43	13	17	16	8	3	0	0	0	0
Total Navaho													
6-7	26	173	5.6	25	10	21	21	6	6	4	4	1	0
8-10	40	273	6.3	41	9	13	18	7	5	4	2	1	0
11-13	49	371	6.7	43	12	12	14	11	3	3	1	3	0
14-18	33	200	4.7	45	14	12	13	8	3	2	0	4	0

6-7-year-old group is quite high, with the other three age groups substantially below and approximately on a level. (While only 5 of 11 community groups show this pattern, the other 6 do not show a contrary pattern.)

Humans.—The general rule, statistically speaking, with respect to drawings of humans is an orderly decrease with increasing age. (Here again, while this pattern is followed in only 5 out of 11 communities, another 5 communities show no marked age trends one way or another, and only Zia shows an increase in humans with age.)

Animals.—There is no general rule with respect to drawings of animals. While Kyle and Zia show decreases with age, Third Mesa and Topawa show increases. There is a fairly constant level at Ramah, Navaho Mountain, Hickiwan, and Zuni.

Ceremonial.—In only 4 communities do ceremonial figures appear. The age trend is upward in 3—Zuni, Third Mesa, First Mesa—and downward in Zia. The reason for the upward trend seems clear. Older children become more aware of the significance of ceremonials and take more part in them. But the same thing is true in the experience of Zia children. The high degree of secrecy at Zia concerning tribal ceremonies may account for older Zia children ceasing to draw such pictures.

Crafts.—Children in 4 communities draw pictures of crafts, such as designs, pottery, and weaving. The tendency is to increase the frequency of such objects with age.

School.—There is a marked trend toward decrease of school appurtenances in the drawings with age. The one exception is Pine Ridge, with a 4-10-4-12 pattern that is idiosyncratic.

Transportation.—The trend is downward with age in the frequency of objects of transportation. Six communities show this trend, while the other 5 show slight and irregular changes with age.

War and Patriotism.—There are no age trends. Shiprock and Hickiwan show decreases with age, but Pine Ridge, with the greatest frequency of such objects, shows a 12-8-21-2 pattern, while 5 other communities show low and irregular frequencies.

Other structures.—The rather miscellaneous category of "other structures, various utilities, and miscellaneous tools" draws a remarkably constant number of items in 7 of the communities, while the other 4 show no general trends.

APPENDIX E-1[a]

TABLE 47

RELATIONS BETWEEN EMOTIONAL RESPONSE AND MORAL IDEOLOGY TEST THEMES

Theme	Test	Rank-Order Correlation[b]																
		B	C	D	E	F	G	H	I	J	K	L	M	N	O	P	Q	R
A. Individual achievement	ERT					-.64	-.83					-.73						-.79
B. Self-gratification	ERT							-.84	-.89		60	-.73			.68			
C. Work	ERT							.76	.69			.71			-.55			
D. Property and possessions	ERT																	
E. Discipline and authority of others	ERT					.79				-.70								
F. Smooth personal relations	ERT						.83			-.55	-.56						.55	.88
G. Aggression by others	ERT																	.82
H. Fear of supernatural	ERT								.95			.70			-.84			
I. Competence	MIT											.80			-.81			
J. Personal virtues	MIT												-.61				-.52	
K. Self-restraint	MIT																	
L. Work	MIT														-.78			

a. Interpretations based on these rank-order correlations should be undertaken with caution. The high correlation

TABLE 47—Continued

Theme	Test	B	C	D	E	F	G	H	I	J	K	L	M	N	O	P	Q	R
		Rank-Order Correlation[b]																
M. Property	MIT													.96			.72	
N. Stealing	MIT															.58	.71	
O. Relation to authority	MIT																.64	
P. Aggression toward peers	MIT																.71	
Q. Regard for others	MIT																	
R. Service	MIT																	

(.96) between "Property" (MIT) and "Stealing" (MIT), for example, is simply a reflection of the fact that the "Property" variable includes in it the "Stealing" variable. The more meaningful comparison is between "Property and possessions" (ERT) and "Property" (MIT); or between "Property and possessions" (ERT) and "Stealing" (MIT), where, in both cases, the relationships are insignificant.

To take another example: the correlation between "Self-gratification" (ERT) and "Self-restraint" (MIT) is positive (.60). This is not a contradictory finding, since "Self-restraint" included both good and bad behaviors and therefore deals with both self-restraint and self-indulgence. It can be inferred that children to whom self-gratification is important may see accompanying moral problems in this area of life—or, to put it another way, if it is important to gratify one's impulses, then it is also important to give attention to good and bad ways of doing so.

In interpreting any given correlation, the reader should refer back to earlier chapters, where each variable is described in terms of the types of responses it represents. He should also refer to Table 38 in chapter viii to see which societies contribute most to the correlation.

b. With only 8 groups to be ranked, a coefficient must be greater than .5 to be reliably different from zero. The coefficients not shown are all between +.5 and -.5.

APPENDIX E-2

TABLE 48

RELATIONS BETWEEN "PERSONS INVOLVED" AND MORAL SURROGATES

Person or Surrogate	Test	B	C	D	E	F	G	H	I	J	K	L	M	N	O	P	Q	R	S	T	U	V	W	X
		Rank-Order Correlations[a]																						
A. Family—pos.	ERT															-.55	-.66						.57	
B. Family—neg.	ERT			-.74				.51				-.61				-.54						.58	.65	
C. Family—total	ERT																	-.60						.59
D. Father—pos.	ERT									.52														
E. Father—neg.	ERT							.65					-.70	-.71										
F. Father—total	ERT																							
G. Mother—pos.	ERT															-.56								
H. Mother—neg.	ERT												-.80	-.52					.59			.64		
I. Mother—total	ERT														.71									.67
J. They, Somebody—pos.	ERT										.75												-.50	
K. They, Somebody—neg.	ERT																						-.58	
L. They, Somebody—total	ERT														-.73									
M. Family—praisers	MIT													.70		.69						-.82		
N. Family—blamers	MIT																					-.52		
O. Family—total	MIT																							
P. Father—praisers	MIT																.90			.64		-.79		
Q. Father—blamers	MIT																			.87		-.72		
R. Father—total	MIT																				.85			
S. Mother—praisers	MIT																			.55				
T. Mother—blamers	MIT																					-.53		
U. Mother—total	MIT																							
V. Everybody—praisers	MIT																							
W. Everybody—blamers	MIT																							
X. Everybody—total	MIT																							

a. With only 8 groups to be ranked, a coefficient must be greater than .5 to be reliably different from zero. The coefficients not shown are all between +.5 and -.5.

APPENDIX F

A COMPARISON OF UNITED STATES AND NEW ZEALAND CHILDREN ON EMOTIONAL RESPONSE AND MORAL IDEOLOGY

Introduction

During 1953-54 one of the authors was located in New Zealand as a Fulbright professor, and he took this occasion to collect data from children on the Emotional Response and Moral Ideology Tests.[1]

New Zealand is a British Dominion, slightly over a hundred years old, populated largely by people of English, Scotch, and Irish descent. (South Sea Island people, the Polynesian Maoris, make up about 7.5 per cent of New Zealand's present population, but Maori children are not included in the analysis to be reported here.) The white children of New Zealand and America can be regarded as biologically similar; and, assuming that the two groups of children are equivalent as far as biological potentials for health, vigor, intelligence, and temperament are concerned, such differences as we find between the two groups must be largely due to differences in the social environment.

New Zealand and the United States provide social environments, which, while somewhat different, are basically quite similar. New Zealand's population of 2,000,000 people is mainly divided between an urban group who live in four fairly large cities and a rural group who live on farms or in small towns. The four cities range in size from 100,000 to 300,000, and none of them is a metropolis in the American sense. They are almost without slums; 87 per cent of New Zealand families live in single-family houses; and almost every house has a flower and vegetable garden. The urban population is growing more rapidly than the rural population, just as it is in the United States. Observers agree that the tempo of life is slower in New Zealand than in the United States; there is a narrower range of socio-economic differences in New Zealand; family life is more tightly knit and the family occupies more of a

1. For a fuller report on the New Zealand studies see Robert J. Havighurst et al., Studies of Children and Society in New Zealand (Christchurch, N.Z.: Canterbury University College, Department of Education Publication, 1954).

person's life; and New Zealanders are not so competitive and individualistic as Americans.

The New Zealand Sample

Data have been secured from children in 14 New Zealand schools in three communities, as shown in Table 49.

Community A is a borough with its surrounding rural territory on the North Island. The urban part of this district contains about 5,000 people, and there are another 10,000 people in the rural villages and on the farms. This is one of the most prosperous dairy-farming and sheep-raising districts in New Zealand. Schools A, B, C, I, and K are situated in this community. The primary schools constitute all schools which are situated in, or contiguous to, the borough and include urban children as well as rural children who live close to the borough. School K is a comprehensive high school. Thus for community A we have a fairly good cross-section of rural and town children in the secondary school; and in the primary schools a good cross-section of town children, together with some rural children.

Community B is a village of about 500 population, with its surrounding rural territory of about 800 on the South Island. The district comprises a fairly good farm area, with mixed farms and sheep farms, two or three small sawmills, and the usual business and services of a rural village. School J is a combined primary school and district high school serving both farm and town children, with more children coming from farms than from the village.

Community C is the city of Christchurch, a city of about 180,000 population, including its suburbs. This is the largest city on the South Island and has a definitely urban character. Schools D, E, F, G, and H are primary and intermediate schools of Christchurch, selected so as to provide a fair cross-section of the socio-economic groups in the city. School L is a coeducational high school with substantial numbers of pupils in the homecraft and engineering forms, drawn largely from working-class homes. Schools M and N are boys' and girls' high schools which have an emphasis on preprofessional courses and which draw from middle-class professional and business homes, as well as from working-class homes.

While it would be inaccurate to say that the New Zealand children

TABLE 49

NEW ZEALAND SCHOOLS PARTICIPATING IN THE STUDY

School	Number of Pupils in Study	
	Boys	Girls
A Small-town primary	28	25
B Small-town primary	29	29
C Small-town primary	37	32
D City primary (predominantly working class)	16	15
E City primary (predominantly working class)	56	44
F City primary (predominantly professional)	32	36
G City primary (predominantly lower middle class)	45	42
H City intermediate (predominantly lower middle class)	64	59
I Small-town primary	50	40
J Rural-district primary and high school	93	89
K Small-town comprehensive high school	124	128
L City coeducational high school	158	143
M City boys' high school	159	...
N City girls' high school	...	204
Total for all schools	891	886

are representative of New Zealand as a whole, yet the three communities are typical of communities of their size, and the children are a fair cross-section of the children of these communities.

The Emotional Response and Moral Ideology Tests were given to school children from alternate classes, Standard 3 and Forms 1, 3, and 5. This corresponds with Grades IV, VI, VIII, and X of American schools. The New Zealand tests were given in August and September, 1953, which is toward the close of the school year.

The median ages of New Zealand school children in these classes, as of July 1, are given in years and months in the Annual Report of the Minister of Education for the year 1951, as:

Std. 3		F. 1		F. 3		F. 5	
Boys	Girls	Boys	Girls	Boys	Girls	Boys	Girls
10.1	9.10	12.2	11.11	14.1	13.10	16.0	15.10

For the Midwest children the age range was 10-17 for the Emotional Response Test and 10-18 for the Moral Ideology Test. The data from Midwest youth aged 17 and above on the Moral Ideology Test have been excluded from the comparison of American with New Zealand children. Age group B includes approximately equal numbers of 9- and 10-year-old New Zealanders but is practically limited to 10-year-old Americans. Age group C is quite similar in age for the New Zealanders and Americans. Age group D is similar in the two samples for the Moral Ideology Test, but for the Emotional Response Test it is slightly older, on the average, for Americans than for New Zealanders, since the American group includes 17-year-olds. Any data which are highly sensitive to age changes should, consequently, be interpreted carefully when dealing with age groups B and D.

The tests were given in very nearly identical ways in New Zealand and America. They were administered in school hours but in most cases not by a classroom teacher. They were administered by research persons who were not acquainted with the students and who assured them that their responses would be treated as confidential. In Community B in New Zealand the high-school students in two of the three schools were instructed to leave their names off the papers. In the opinion of the writer, this did not bring about any notable change in the responses of the boys and girls, but it did serve to make them feel more cordial toward the situation. In Community A the high-school tests were administered by the classroom teachers, and there was some resistance by students in a few classes, probably because of their attitudes toward their particular teachers. Resistance was shown by the fact that about a dozen pupils turned in blank papers.

Responsiveness on the Two Tests

The degree of responsiveness of the New Zealand and American children to the tests is shown in Tables 50 and 51. It is not likely that the differences in responsiveness were due to differences in the administration of the tests; the author was involved in administration of the tests to both groups; the tests were given in dozens of different rooms to various groups of children; and he does not believe that there was any systematic difference between New Zealand and America in the conditions under which the tests were given.

On both tests, New Zealand boys and girls did not differ much in their responsiveness, while American girls were more responsive than boys.

Moral Ideology

The American children were more responsive than New Zealand children on the Moral Ideology Test. Age trends showed a reversal between the two groups. New Zealand youth become steadily less responsive as they grow older, while American youth become more responsive as they grow older.

Emotional Response

In the Emotional Response Test, American girls, but not boys, were more responsive than New Zealand children. The order of responsiveness on the various emotions is similar for New Zealand and American children. There was a slight tendency for American children to mention persons in connection with emotional experiences more frequently than did the New Zealanders.

Reliability of the New Zealand Data

Moral Ideology

The same tests of reliability were made for the New Zealand as for the American data. In the case of the Moral Ideology Test, two judges independently categorized a set of 80 papers. There was only 5 per cent disagreement among the behavior categories, and 4 per cent disagreement among surrogate categories. When the behavior categories were combined into the themes, the disagreement practically vanished, becoming less than 1 per cent.

Emotional Response

In the case of the Emotional Response Test there was less agreement between judges, as had been true in the case of the American data. The categories for scoring this test are more finely drawn, and apparently the judge must use more of his own judgment in assigning a response to a category. Two judges independently scored 100 papers, representing both sexes and various ages, with disagreement as follows: Happiness, 20 per cent; Sadness, 9 per cent; Fear, 23 per cent; Anger, 23 per cent; Shame, 24 per cent; Best Thing, 20 per cent; Worst Thing, 13 per cent; and Persons Involved, 23 per cent. When the categories

TABLE 50

MORAL IDEOLOGY TEST: FREQUENCIES OF BEHAVIOR AND SURROGATE RESPONSES PER SUBJECT

	Age Group	No. of Subjects	Av. No. of Behavior Responses per Subject	Av. No. of Surrogate Responses per Subject
	New Zealand			
Boys	B[a]	159	17.1	16.4
	C	394	14.3	14.2
	D	324	12.7	12.1
	Total	877	14.7	14.2
Girls	B	174	16.9	17.0
	C	386	13.6	13.6
	D	326	11.7	11.1
	Total	886	14.1	13.9
Boys and girls		1,763	14.4	14.1
	United States			
Boys	B	27	14.8	14.6
	C	99	16.8	15.8
	D	106	17.7	19.7
	Total	232	16.4	16.7
Girls	B	34	17.3	17.4
	C	119	18.3	18.6
	D	132	18.8	24.6
	Total	285	18.1	20.2
Boys and girls		517	17.3	18.5

a. Age: B = 9-10 years old; C = 11-13; D = 14-16.

were grouped into the combined categories, the disagreements were reduced to: Happiness, 16; Sadness, 6; Fear, 14; Anger, 20; Shame, 16; Best Thing, 16; Worst Thing, 13.

Examination of the actual cases of disagreement indicated that they came from two main sources. Most frequent was a difference in the interpretation of a situation: e.g., when a boy says that he was ashamed "when I broke Mum's vase and said I didn't do it." This may be categorized either as unintentionally damaging property or as lying. The scorer is obliged to make a judgment of the psychological significance

TABLE 51

COMPARISON OF NEW ZEALAND AND AMERICAN CHILDREN IN RESPONSIVENESS TO THE EMOTIONAL RESPONSE TEST

Emotion	Av. No. of Responses per Person				Av. No. of "Persons Involved" per Response			
	New Zealand		Midwest		New Zealand		Midwest	
	Boys	Girls	Boys	Girls	Boys	Girls	Boys	Girls
Happiness	2.7	2.7	2.7	3.2	0.14	0.26	0.17	0.24
Sadness	2.3	2.5	2.0	2.6	.39	.54	.51	.53
Fear	2.1	2.3	2.0	2.5	.20	.25	.11	.20
Anger	2.1	2.2	2.2	2.4	.55	.62	.53	.61
Shame	1.7	1.8	1.6	2.2	.33	.43	.43	.51
Best Thing	0.85	0.84	1.1	1.1	.03	.07	.11	.20
Worst Thing	0.83	0.79	0.7	1.0	0.13	0.20	0.16	0.29
Total	12.6	13.1	12.3	15.0	...	...	...	...
Average	...	...	...	...	0.28	0.38	0.31	0.40
No. of responses	...	...	...	...	10,764	10,671	1,997	3,233
No. of "persons involved"	...	...	...	...	3,096	4,153	612	1,237
No. of subjects responding	891	838	159	209	...	...	...	...

of the incident to the child himself. A second source of disagreement, less frequently found, was obvious error by one or the other scorer.

The large percentage of disagreement as to "persons involved" was usually due to ambiguity in the child's response. When a 9-year-old girl wrote that she was angry "when Geoffrey hit me" and "when Geoffrey took my book," she may have been referring to a classmate or to a brother. The scorer had to make a choice between the two. Another source of disagreement arose when the judge did not note the "person involved" when it was implied by the designation of the behavior category — e.g., "I was afraid when the teacher made me stay after school," may be assigned to category 23 (school misdemeanor), without indicating

the teacher as a "person involved," or to category 25 (punishment), where the teacher must be indicated as the "person involved."

In spite of the relatively poor agreement of judges on the scoring of individual responses, they still achieve a very high degree of agreement on the scoring of the responses of a group of papers. The latter test of reliability was made by comparing the numbers of responses assigned by two judges to the various categories. When this was done for the scoring of the Anger responses on 100 papers, the results are shown in Table 52. (The reliability of scoring of Anger responses is reported in detail because disagreement was highest for Anger.)

The product-moment coefficient of correlation between the scores of the two judges is .95. The same test applied to the Happiness scores by the two judges gives a correlation coefficient of .98. For "persons involved" the correlation coefficient was .98. This indicates that the relative frequencies of the various categories are quite close when the scoring is done by two judges independently. One factor which operates to reduce the disagreements over a group of papers is a tendency for these disagreements to be compensatory. For example, category 18 of Happiness (Receiving presents or materials) and Category 15 (Birthday) are difficult to distinguish in a response such as "I was happy when I got a bicycle for my birthday." There may be considerable disagreement between judges on the scoring of specific responses; yet on 100 papers the two judges came out with identical totals on category 15 and differed by only one response on category 18.

Consequently (as was noted in the earlier section of this monograph on the reliability of scoring of the Emotional Response Test), it appears that the scoring of the Emotional Response Test is fairly reliable for groups, even though it is not sufficiently reliable on any individual paper.

Results—Moral Ideology

Comparison of Behavior Themes

The New Zealand data on behavior were organized into themes, just as the Midwest data were, and Table 53 shows how the two groups compare on the themes of moral ideology.[2]

It is clear that there are some major differences between the two groups of children. The American children are much higher on themes

2. See chap. iv, Sec. 2, of this monograph for a description of the themes.

TABLE 52

EMOTIONAL RESPONSE TEST: COMPARISON OF SCORING OF ANGER RESPONSES BY TWO JUDGES ON A SAMPLE OF 100 PAPERS

Category No.	No. of Responses Assigned to This Category by: Judge A	Judge B
1	41	43
2	1	2
3	8	5
4	3	3
5	4	7
6	30	25
7	1	5
8	2	1
10	12	9
11	11	9
12	27	26
13	6	3
14	11	13
15	7	4
17	15	18
18	2	5
19	11	11
20	9	9
21	14	19
22	17	12
24 (misc.)	1	6

of Restraint-Indulgence, Personal Virtues, and Relations to Authority, while the New Zealand children are much higher on Service and Family, and slightly higher on Regard for Others. Possibly these differences may be summarized by saying that the American children seem to be more overtly concerned with the conduct of the individual in the more personal or individualistic aspects of life—with such matters as smoking, drinking, swearing, gambling; and on the positive side with thrift, neatness, and regular hours. The New Zealand children, on the other hand, are more overtly concerned with their obligations and relations to other people.

Other major differences occur on the Property and Work themes, where New Zealand children mention these themes more frequently than do the American children.

Most of these differences between the two groups of children are due

TABLE 53

THEMES OF MORAL IDEOLOGY: COMPARISON OF NEW ZEALAND AND AMERICAN CHILDREN

(PERCENTAGE FREQUENCIES)

Theme	New Zealand[a] Boys B	C	D	Av.	Girls B	C	D	Av.	Boys + Girls Av.	United States[a] Boys B	C	D	Av.	Girls B	C	D	Av.	Boys + Girls Av.
Competence	5	7	10	7	5	7	10	7	7	4	8	13	9	6	7	12	8	8
Self-restraint, indulgence	15	17	21	18	17	15	16	16	17	31	23	34	30	21	17	32	23	26
Personal virtues	7	7	8	7	8	11	13	11	9	7	12	18	13	8	10	19	13	13
Relation to authority	12	12	14	13	14	14	16	15	14	15	21	14	17	25	30	16	24	20
Regard for others	33	33	27	31	32	31	24	29	30	32	28	21	27	27	30	21	26	27
Service	35	30	25	30	31	28	24	28	29	20	16	8	15	18	17	8	14	14
Sex	0	0.2	1.3	0.5	0.3	0.4	1.5	0.7	0.6	0	1	2	1	0	1	3	1	1
Family	38	28	22	30	30	26	23	26	28	17	15	6	13	20	17	9	15	14
School	6	6	6	6	8	7	6	7	6	8	11	7	9	16	11	7	11	10
Church	0.5	1.2	1.9	1.2	1.1	1.5	3	1.9	1.6	1	2	2	1	2	2	3	2	2
Community	1.0	2	3	2	0.8	1.0	1.4	1.1	1.6	5	7	5	6	5	5	3	4	5
Property	20	19	15	18	15	11	7	11	14	12	8	8	10	9	6	4	6	8
Work	.31	23	17	24	24	18	13	18	21	15	9	8	11	12	9	7	9	10
Stealing	4	6	5	5	4	4	4	4	5	2	2	3	2	1	2	2	2	2
Drinking	0.3	0.5	1.5	0.8	0	0.2	1.3	0.5	0.7	0	1	3	1	0	1	4	2	2
Bad language	1.3	1.6	1.4	1.4	1.7	1.3	1.5	1.5	1.5	2	2	3	2	2	2	3	2	2
Aggression to peers	6	5	3	5	8	6	3	6	5	12	9	3	8	7	7	2	5	6
Total no. of responses	2,707	5,653	4,038	12,398	2,940	5,427	3,779	11,986	24,384	398	1,667	3,268	5,333	587	2,179	4,399	7,105	12,488

a. New Zealand: B = 9-10-year-olds; C = 11-13; D = 14-16. United States: B = 10-year-olds; C = 11-13; D = 14-16.

to differences in a few key categories — categories which enter into the themes. Table 54 lists those categories in which the difference between American and New Zealand children is statistically reliable.[3] It will be seen from Table 54 that New Zealand children mention "work around the home" more than twice as often as do American children (this category appears both in the Family theme and in the Work theme). They also mention items involving property more frequently than do American children—"stealing" and "care of property."

American children mention playing games and having a good time—"amusements"—as good things to do much more frequently than do the New Zealand children. American children are also more concerned over conformity to school expectations and over respect and active support of government and community—although the latter may reflect the fact that the American data were collected in wartime, when children were more preoccupied with collecting scrap, buying war stamps, and so on.

Sex Differences in Behavior Themes

Most of the sex differences are the same in the two groups, as seen in Table 53, but there are a few interesting divergences. In relation to the theme Personal Virtues, New Zealand girls mention this more frequently than boys, while there is no sex difference among the Americans. Aggression toward Peers is mentioned more frequently by American boys than girls, but this difference is not found in New Zealand children. With respect to Family, New Zealand boys give a slightly higher number of mentions than girls do, while this sex difference is reversed among American children. This divergence is a reflection of the fact that New Zealand boys give very high frequencies to the category, Work at Home, which is included in this theme. In general, there are fewer sex differences in the New Zealand data than in the American.

3. Determining whether a difference between two percentages is statistically reliable is a problem treated in most books on elementary statistics. But the usual procedures are not valid for percentages that are less than 10. For this purpose we have used the chart given in Appendix 9 of Wilfrid J. Dixon and Frank J. Massey, Jr., An Introduction to Statistical Analysis (New York: McGraw-Hill Book Co., 1951), pp. 191-96. This chart allows us to decide whether differences between two small percentages are reliable, provided that the number of responses is large enough so that Np is greater than 5, where N is the number of responses and p is the proportion we are concerned with. For instance, when the proportion is .01, N must be 500 or more. Since most of our N's are over 1,000, we can deal with percentages as small as 0.5.

TABLE 54

PRINCIPAL DIFFERENCES BETWEEN NEW ZEALAND AND AMERICAN CHILDREN ON MORAL IDEOLOGY CATEGORIES

Category	Percentage Frequencies	
	New Zealand	United States
Amusements	2.1	5.8
Achievement in school	2.4	4.6
Industry; obedience and loyalty to employer	0.7	1.4
Good reputation; "right people"	0.3	1.4
Etiquette	1.8	1.1
Maturity; independence	1.3	0.3
Fighting	0.6	1.5
Sportsmanship	0.4	2.1
Dependability; responsibility	0.9	0.2
Stealing	4.7	2.0
Smoking	0.8	2.1
Drinking	0.7	1.5
Neatness; personal appearance	0.8	2.5
Keeping regular hours	0.6	1.3
Care of property	8.7	4.3
Thoughtfulness; kindness; tolerance	1.6	4.0
Regard for family; family solidarity	3.1	1.8
Respect and obedience to parents and elders	7.6	5.1
Work at home; help around the house	20.2	7.7
Conformity to school expectations and rules	5.0	6.9
Respect and obedience to teachers	1.3	3.1
Respect and obedience for government and community	0.9	2.1
Active work for government and community	0.6	2.9
Treatment of animals	3.3	1.1

Age Trends on Themes

Most of the age trends on themes are common to both groups of children (Table 53; but there are certain divergences. On the Restraint-Indulgence theme, which increases with age for New Zealand boys and shows no age trend for girls, the trend for American boys and girls is down from age B to C and then up sharply at age D. This suggests that, while New Zealand children are generally less preoccupied with this theme than American children, nevertheless it steadily increases in importance with New Zealand boys as they grow older. In American children, on the other hand, there is less continuity; and concern over restraint-indulgence (or, as we have described it in earlier sections of this monograph, a moral concern over the gratification of impulse life) is prominent among 10-year-olds and then again in adolescence (ages 14-16).

The Relation to Authority theme remains constant from age B to C for New Zealand youth and then goes up at D; for American boys and girls this goes up from age B to C and then sharply down at D, indicating that the American preadolescent (ages 11-13) has an intensified concern over his relations with authority figures which is not matched in the New Zealand preadolescent.

Comparison of Surrogate Responses

Table 55 shows the relative frequencies of mentions of various moral surrogates—praisers and blamers. It will be seen that the father alone is mentioned much more frequently both as a praiser and as a blamer by New Zealand boys and girls than by American boys and girls. The mother alone is also mentioned more frequently by New Zealanders, especially as a praiser. When the various forms of reference to family members are combined, New Zealand exceeds the United States, 52 to 45 per cent. This is a relatively small difference and indicates that the American youth make up to some extent for their lesser frequency of mention of father alone and of mother alone by a greater frequency of mention of both parents together.

American youth mention age-mates, teachers, and "everybody" more frequently than New Zealand youth do. The New Zealand youth mention the "recipient of the act" more frequently than do the American.

Sex Differences in Surrogate Responses

With only minor exceptions, the New Zealand and American children show the same over-all sex differences in surrogate responses.

Age Trends in Surrogate Responses

While there are certain differences in age trends between the New Zealand and American children (on the categories Teacher, Government, Recipient of the Act, Age-Mates), in general we are impressed more by the similarities and by the fact that the over-all pattern is much the same for the two groups.

One interesting difference, however, is that the downward trend of mentions of father alone and mother alone is much sharper from age C to D for American than for New Zealand youth. This may mean that the

New Zealand adolescent feels a more personal moral pressure from father or mother than does the American adolescent. The latter is more likely to lump father and mother together in the single expression "my parents" or "my folks."

Summary

In general, the surrogate responses bear out the behavior responses in stressing the family-centered nature of moral obligations and of reward-punishment relations in New Zealand, as compared with a greater stress felt by American children from school, peer group, and the community ("everybody") as sources of moral pressure. When the New Zealand youth mention a nonfamily person as praiser or blamer, they tend more than the American youth to mention the recipient of the act. Thus we get the impression that the New Zealand youth regard the praise and blame in their lives as coming mainly from persons who are closely and even intimately involved in and affected by their behavior—father, mother, and the person whom one helps or injures. For the American youth, on the other hand, praise and blame come from more generalized sources—from "parents" instead of father or mother, from friends and peers in general, and from "everybody."

Results—Emotional Response Test

As with the Moral Ideology data, in order to facilitate comparison of New Zealand and Midwest children, we have drawn up a set of tables showing the data on the Emotional Response Test from the two societies.

Tables 56 and 57 show the principal sources of the various emotions. To conserve on space, we have not shown the titles of the category combinations for each emotion but refer to them by Roman numerals (the reader should consult Appendixes B1-B8 for descriptions of the combinations). Tables 58 and 59 present the data on values and aversions by sex and age groups. The data on "persons involved" in emotion-arousing situations are summarized in Tables 60-64. In the following discussion of our results, we shall draw from all these tables.

First of all, we should keep in mind the fact that the New Zealand and American children are quite similar in their responses on the Emotional Response Test. For example, if the New Zealand data on values and aversions were placed in the series of such data for Midwest and the Indian tribes, the New Zealand data would usually fall adjacent

TABLE 55

MORAL SURROGATES: COMPARISON OF NEW ZEALAND AND AMERICAN CHILDREN

(PERCENTAGE FREQUENCIES)

Category	New Zealand									United States								
	Boys				Girls				Boys+ Girls	Boys				Girls				Boys + Girls
	B	C	D	Av.	B	C	D	Av.	Av.	B	C	D	Av.	B	C	D	Av.	Av.
Family	67	54	44	55	60	48	39	49	52	55	43	42	47	48	39	43	43	45
Father	22	15	11	16	14	8	4	9	12	13	6	1	7	5	2	1	3	5
Mother	30	20	10	20	27	19	11	19	20	26	13	3	14	26	16	6	16	15
Elders	1.5	1.1	1.4	1.3	1.3	2.2	1.9	1.8	1.6	1	2	1	1	2	2	1	2	1
Age-mates	3	3	4	3	3	4	6	5	4	12	6	7	8	7	8	13	9	9
Teacher	9	11	12	11	12	14	13	13	12	11	17	14	14	24	18	13	18	16
Clergy	0.3	0.8	1.9	1.0	0.4	0.7	1.5	0.9	1.0	0	1	1	1	0	0	1	1	1
Everybody	5	7	10	7	5	10	14	10	9	5	13	20	13	9	20	19	16	14
Govt.	4	9	8	7	5	5	5	5	6	7	6	2	5	3	4	1	3	4
Self	3	3	5	3	3	2	7	4	4	2	3	7	4	1	3	3	3	3
Recipient	6	11	11	9	8	12	12	11	10	5	5	2	4	4	5	2	4	4
Duty	0.6	0.4	0.7	0.6	1.4	1.2	1.1	1.2	0.9	2	1	0	1	1	2	1	1	1
Praiser																		
Father	24	18	14	18	14	9	5	9	14	12	6	1	7	6	2	1	3	5
Mother	33	25	13	24	32	22	14	23	23	31	15	3	16	28	17	7	17	17
Blamer																		
Father	21	13	7	14	14	7	3	8	11	14	5	1	7	4	2	1	2	4
Mother	25	16	8	16	22	16	6	15	15	24	10	2	12	23	15	5	14	13
Total no. of responses	2,607	5,606	3,925	12,148	2,957	5,256	3,618	11,831	23,979	393	1,578	2,092	4,063	590	2,220	3,248	6,058	10,121

a. New Zealand: B = 9-10-year-olds; C = 11-13; D = 14-16. United States: B = 10-year-olds; C = 11-13; D = 14-16.

to the Midwest data. The New Zealand and Midwest groups are much more alike than they are different when seen in relation to children of a non-Western culture. There are, however, a number of statistically reliable and practically significant differences between the New Zealand and Midwest data.

Discipline

As seen in Tables 58 and 59, New Zealand children find discipline and authority of others more troublesome than Midwest children do. (This is shown consistently in the responses on Sadness, Fear, Shame, and Worst Thing.) New Zealand children mention situations involving discipline and authority of others about twice as often as do American children. These test results might arise either from a greater frequency of punishment in the lives of New Zealand children or from a greater intensity of feeling about whatever punishment they receive. From general observation on child-rearing methods in home and school in the two societies, it appears that there is actually a greater frequency of punishment in the lives of New Zealand children.

Disappointment Due to Action of Others

Though American children express less emotion over being punished, they compensate by expressing more emotion over being disappointed by people who deny them things or are inconsiderate of them. They give about 50 per cent more responses of Sadness and Anger at having their wishes frustrated, usually by parents, though also by other people who can bring unpleasant pressure to bear on them (Tables 58 and 59: Sadness, IX; Anger, III, V). This might be thought of as another form of punishment or control—denial or withdrawal of privileges—which may be more prevalent in the lives of American children. Another possible explanation for this difference is that the American children may expect more privileges, such as going to the movies, staying out late at night, and visiting other children, and therefore they may feel deprivation of these privileges more keenly than New Zealand children, who may not expect so much.

Concern with Personal Health and Death

One of the few really striking differences between the two groups is the much greater frequency with which New Zealanders mention death of the self as the Worst Thing, along with the greater frequency of mention of illness or accident to one's self as a source of Sadness (Tables

TABLE 56

PRINCIPAL SOURCES OF THE VARIOUS EMOTIONS: COMPARISON OF NEW ZEALAND AND AMERICAN BOYS (PERCENTAGE FREQUENCIES)

	Happiness		Best Thing		Sadness		Fear		Anger		Shame		Worst Thing	
Combination No.	N.Z.	U.S.	N.Z.	U.S.	N.Z.	U.S.	N.Z.	U.S.	N.Z.	U.S.	N.Z.	U.S.	N.Z.	U.S.
I.	24.5	20.6	26.0	27.0	20.2	20.0	1.1	1.1	23.9	15.7	7.7	10.3	35.4	15.3
II.	11.0	12.5	57.4[a]	47.8[a]	13.1	12.5	12.4[c]	10.0	1.1	0.8	1.4	1.6	4.4	7.2
III.	...	...	3.6	5.1	18.3[b]	18.4[b]	48.1[c]	56.2[c]	8.7	14.6	0.1	...	19.8	10.9
IV.	19.5	28.7	0.7	3.3	5.2	2.5	20.2[c]	20.9[c]	0.6	0.6	14.6	6.6	1.0	...
V.	0.3	0.8	1.5	3.1	1.0	0.2	3.6	1.8	14.9	16.9	23.4	21.5	2.4	...
VI.	2.0	3.7	22.7[a]	6.0[a]	2.3	4.7	0.7	0.5	10.5	7.1	0.9	1.6	4.2	2.5
VII.	19.1	10.6	3.9	0.3	0.3	0.4	9.2	9.3	20.5	21.4	37.5	45.9	1.2	1.4
VIII.	3.5	3.2	3.4	2.4	1.5	1.0	7.0	2.5	3.0	3.7	1.0	...	8.6	1.4
IX.	3.6	3.4	0.6	6.8	18.7[d]	20.6[d]	5.9	8.9	2.5	4.2	0.7	...	9.0	18.7
X.	4.6	4.4	0.3	...	7.7[d]	14.9[d]	0.5	0.2	4.2	4.9	9.6	3.9	9.3	15.3
XI.	2.5	3.4	0.3	...	7.9	12.1	2.2	2.0	5.2	4.6	1.5	1.8	3.4	5.4
XII.	0.7	1.7	0.4	...	4.0	3.9	3.4	2.5	6.6	6.9	1.1	...	0.7	8.9
XIII.	10.7	12.0	0.2	...	1.5	0.6	1.3	1.4	0.4	1.1	0.8	1.8	0.1	1.7
XIV.	0.2	0.3	1.5	4.0	1.5	1.0	0.4	0.2	0.6	1.1	...	...	0.2	0.8
XV.	0.1	0.1	16.5[a]	28.3[a]	...	...	1.1	0.6	...	...	...	...	0.4	1.6
XVI.	0.8	...	...	...	0.5	...	1.2	0.5	...	...	...	...	0.1	...
XVII.	0.3	0.1	...	...	2.5	1.2	0.3	...	...	...	...	...	1.2	8.6
XVIII.	0.5	0.1	...	...	...	...	0.9	0.8	...	...	...	...	...	...
XIX.	0.6	...	...	...	0.7	0.8	1.4	0.8	...	...	...	...	...	...
XX.	1.1	1.3	...	...	10.1[b]	9.5[b]	...	...	...	...	...	...	...	...
XXI.	1.6	2.3	...	...	...	...	...	...	...	...	...	...	...	...
XXII.	1.6	0.5	...	...	...	...	...	...	...	...	...	...	...	...
Total no. of Responses	2,382	426	746	181	1,993	321	1,759	324	1,809	358	1,351	260	725	127

a. Combination II includes combinations VI and XV.
b. III includes XX.
c. III includes IV, but IV here stands for original categories 14 and 15, rather than 16-18.
d. IX includes X.

TABLE 57

PRINCIPAL SOURCES OF THE VARIOUS EMOTIONS: COMPARISON OF NEW ZEALAND AND AMERICAN GIRLS (PERCENTAGE FREQUENCIES)

	Happiness		Best Thing		Sadness		Fear		Anger		Shame		Worst Thing	
Combination No.	N.Z.	U.S.	N.Z.	U.S.	N.Z.	U.S.	N.Z.	U.S.	N.Z.	U.S.	N.Z.	U.S.	N.Z.	U.S.
I.	21.4	12.3	30.5	24.9	25.6	21.3	0.6	0.8	18.6	12.5	7.7	9.2	20.5	2.6
II.	9.9	11.3	53.5[a]	43.9[a]	15.3	9.7	15.0	18.5	1.5	1.1	1.1	1.6	9.2	15.5
III.	...	...	2.9	2.9	20.0[b]	15.8[b]	41.9[c]	45.8[c]	12.3	16.2	0.4	0.2	23.1	6.7
IV.	14.4	25.4	2.0	12.5	3.0	2.4	19.0[c]	13.7[c]	0.4	1.5	9.3	3.7	0.7	3.7
V.	0.8	0.6	4.5	5.0	0.3	0.3	7.3	8.2	18.4	25.1	23.4	21.1	1.1	0.7
VI.	1.3	0.8	30.3[a]	9.7[a]	1.6	1.6	0.8	1.0	9.7	7.7	0.8	0.4	6.2	2.5
VII.	16.1	14.2	3.5	1.4	0.5	0.4	7.5	3.7	26.1	21.2	40.0	50.0	1.3	2.9
VIII.	5.3	5.5	1.2	0.7	0.2	0.7	5.9	1.6	2.6	1.3	2.0	0.8	6.6	7.7
IX.	1.7	1.1	...	5.9	15.1[d]	24.2[d]	7.9	8.2	2.2	5.6	0.4	0.1	9.1	17.9
X.	12.1	15.8	0.9	...	5.5[d]	14.1[d]	0.8	1.0	4.1	2.1	10.9	3.3	11.3	16.2
XI.	4.6	3.1	...	...	3.5	4.7	2.0	4.1	3.8	2.7	1.1	2.4	8.1	8.4
XII.	1.4	1.0	0.3	...	7.6	10.0	3.3	2.6	4.2	3.9	1.1	0.1	0.9	5.7
XIII.	11.8	7.8	0.1	...	1.9	1.8	1.2	3.0	0.1	0.2	1.1	1.1	...	0.6
XIV.	0.7	0.5	0.6	9.5	1.6	2.8	0.5	0.3	1.2	0.6	...	...	0.2	0.6
XV.	0.1	0.4	7.5[a]	19.5[a]	0.1	0.3	0.8	0.6	...	...	...	...	0.6	0.5
XVI.	1.2	0.1	...	...	0.8	0.2	0.9	0.2	...	...	...	...	...	...
XVII.	...	...	...	...	2.2	0.1	1.2	0.1	...	...	...	...	0.4	11.6
XVIII.	1.0	0.9	...	...	...	1.0	0.8	1.1	...	...	...	...	...	...
XIX.	0.7	0.5	...	...	0.4	1.6	2.5	1.2	...	...	...	...	...	...
XX.	0.9	0.3	...	...	7.1[b]	3.1[b]	...	...	...	...	...	...	...	...
XXI.	1.1	1.0	...	...	...	...	...	...	...	...	...	...	...	...
XXII.	0.9	1.3	...	...	...	...	...	...	...	...	...	...	...	...
Total no. of Responses	2,264	671	694	244	2,034	560	1,838	534	1,757	518	1,439	478	650	228

a. Combination II includes combinations VI and XV.
b. III includes XX.
c. III includes IV, but IV here stands for original categories 14 and 15, rather than 16-18.
d. IX includes X.

TABLE 58

EMOTIONAL RESPONSE TEST: COMPARISON OF NEW ZEALAND AND AMERICAN BOYS ON VALUES AND AVERSIONS (PERCENTAGE FREQUENCIES)

	New Zealand					Midwest				
	B	C	D	Total	Av. No.	B	C	D	Total	Av. No.
Value										
Individual achievement	6.8	9.0	13.4	9.7	3,588	7.4	8.7	17.1	11.1	666
Property and possessions	13.7	16.2	11.9	13.9	3,347	16	19	10	14.9	623
Self-gratification	34.5	30.6	29.3	31.4	2,760	33	30	27	29.6	525
Smooth personal relations	13.8	11.6	12.4	12.6	3,588	10	12	14	12.2	666
Family-centeredness	1.3	4.1	4.8	3.4	1,284	4.5	2.8	3.6	3.6	245
Work	2.4	4.7	6.8	4.6	1,043	6.2	1.8	11.4	6.5	202
Aversion										
Aggression by others	6.3	7.2	6.9	6.8	2,546	7	10	8	8.2	463
Discipline and authority of others	11.2	7.0	5.3	7.8	2,546	3.6	3.0	5.4	4.0	463
Illness and danger of others	4.8	4.5	6.4	5.2	1,492	3.4	4.5	5.7	4.4	257
Death of others	10.1	15.8	21.9	15.9	906	10	18	21	16.2	149
Illness and accidents to self	15.5	13.7	7.8	12.3	906	15	9	5	9.4	149
Objective danger	50.1	48.6	45.4	48.1	586	67	50	52	56	108
Death of self	50.0	35.1	21.0	35.4	242	26	10	11	15.3	42

56 and 57: Worst Thing, I; Sadness, XX). While this finding is not easily interpreted (since feelings about death and illness have such complex causes), nevertheless one is tempted to guess from this evidence that New Zealand children, especially girls, are more likely to fantasy their own destruction than are American children.

Individual Achievement

The general theme of individual achievement (Tables 58 and 59) is

TABLE 59

EMOTIONAL RESPONSE TEST: COMPARISON OF NEW ZEALAND AND AMERICAN GIRLS ON VALUES AND AVERSIONS (PERCENTAGE FREQUENCIES)

	New Zealand					Midwest				
	B	C	D	Total	Av. No.	B	C	D	Total	Av. No.
Value										
Individual achievement	6.6	9.8	14.0	10.2	3,557	6.3	7.1	14.1	9.2	1,078
Property and possessions	10.3	10.5	7.1	9.3	3,341	10	15	8	10.9	1,002
Self-gratification	33.4	29.2	23.8	28.8	2,728	38	30	30	32.5	824
Smooth personal relations	15.9	11.8	14.6	14.1	3,557	13	13	16	13.9	1,078
Family-centeredness	5.4	9.8	11.7	9.0	1,203	13.7	17.1	7.0	12.6	381
Work	1.1	3.8	6.6	3.8	986	4.0	0.5	4.6	3.0	305
Aversion										
Aggression by others	9.1	7.0	9.5	8.5	2,573	9	7	8	8.1	773
Discipline and authority of others	11.7	5.7	3.8	7.1	2,573	4.8	4.4	2.4	3.9	773
Illness and danger of others	6.3	10.7	9.4	8.8	1,507	6.5	13.1	8.4	9.3	441
Death of others	14.0	23.7	27.2	21.6	895	13	22	24	19.5	263
Illness and accidents to self	16.9	8.6	7.4	11.0	895	3	4	4	3.8	263
Objective danger	47.1	45.0	33.7	41.9	613	61	39	38	46	179
Death of self	28.8	24.3	8.4	20.5	217	6	2	1	2.6	76

an important characteristic of the emotional responses of both groups and distinguishes them from the Indian societies. But the Midwest boys show a little more of this than do the New Zealand boys, owing to the relatively high frequency of this type of response among Midwest boys over 14. Somewhat related to this concept of individual achievement is that of Happiness at "being grown up" (Table 56: Happiness, XXI), where again the Midwest boys exceed the New Zealand boys.

TABLE 60

EMOTIONAL RESPONSE TEST: COMPARISON OF NEW ZEALAND AND AMERICAN CHILDREN ON PERSONS INVOLVED IN HAPPINESS (PERCENTAGE FREQUENCIES)

Category	New Zealand			Midwest		
	Boys	Girls	Total	Boys	Girls	Total
Family (except Fa., Mo., sibs)	17	30	23	25	33	29
Father	24	7	15	10	8	9
Mother	21	17	19	22	14	18
Sibs, same sex	6	13	10	12	10	11
Sibs, opp. sex	6	10	8	2	14	8
Total family	74	77	75	71	79	75
Peers, same sex	4	2	3	1	5	3
Peers, opp. sex	4	4	4	12	7	10
Peers in general	8	8	8	6	6	6
Teacher and school	6	5	5	8	2	5
Individual adult	2	2	2	. . .	. . .	. . .
They, somebody	2	2	2	2	3	3
Total outside family	26	23	24	29	23	27
No. of persons mentioned	355	627	982	73	158	231

Note: The percentages in the columns of this table will seldom add up to 100 because of rounding of numbers and exclusion of a few minor categories.

Relations with Family

It is generally said by observers that the New Zealand family is much more close-knit and self-sufficient than the American family. But the Emotional Response Test indicates that the American children may get as much pleasure from the family as do New Zealand children. On the Family-centeredness theme (Tables 58 and 59) there is very little difference between the two groups of boys, while the Midwest girls actually exceed the New Zealand girls. This theme represents responses mainly on Happiness and Best Thing and reflects pleasure in being with the family, in new additions to the family, and in the good fortune of the family.

TABLE 61

EMOTIONAL RESPONSE TEST: COMPARISON OF NEW ZEALAND AND AMERICAN CHILDREN ON PERSONS INVOLVED IN SADNESS (PERCENTAGE FREQUENCIES)

Category	New Zealand			Midwest		
	Boys	Girls	Total	Boys	Girls	Total
Family (except Fa., Mo., sibs)	36	39	38	39	42	41
Father	12	8	10	17	9	13
Mother	12	12	12	10	20	15
Sibs, same sex	9	6	7	11	5	8
Sibs, opp. sex	3	7	5	4	9	7
Total family	72	72	72	81	85	84
Peers, same sex	3	2	2	3	1	2
Peers, opp. sex	2	2	2	3	6	5
Peers in general	8	9	8	6	5	6
Teacher and school	7	6	6	3	2	3
Individual adult	6	6	6	. . .	. . .	. . .
They, somebody	2	1	1	1	2	2
Total outside family	29	26	25	16	16	18
No. of persons mentioned	778	1,137	1,915	164	297	361

The same conclusion is borne out by the equal frequencies of mention of family members as persons involved in Happiness situations (Table 60). While the New Zealand child may have an attitude of greater moral obligation to the family and greater respect for the authority of parents, yet the two groups of children seem to have approximately equal amounts of pleasurable experience in the family.

Property

Though there is not much difference between the two groups in the extent to which property and possessions are a major value (Tables 58 and 59), there is nevertheless a very interesting difference in the ways in which this theme occurs. The Midwest children give many more Happiness and Best Thing responses dealing with property (Tables 56 and 57: Happiness, IV; Best Thing, XV), but the New Zealanders give

Table 62

EMOTIONAL RESPONSE TEST: COMPARISON OF NEW ZEALAND AND AMERICAN CHILDREN ON PERSONS INVOLVED IN FEAR (PERCENTAGE FREQUENCIES)

Category	New Zealand			Midwest		
	Boys	Girls	Total	Boys	Girls	Total
Family (except Fa., Mo., sibs)	6	7	6	14	15	15
Father	13	6	9	6	8	7
Mother	7	14	10	11	21	16
Sibs, same sex	10	7	9	11	8	10
Sibs, opp. sex	2	11	7	0	15	8
Total family	38	45	41	42	67	56
Peers, same sex	10	1	6	29	4	17
Peers, opp. sex	1	7	4	0	4	2
Peers in general	2	2	2	3	1	2
Teacher and school	15	13	14	6	3	5
Strangers, drunks	8	14	11	3	9	6
Individual adult	8	4	6	...	...	...
They, somebody	8	7	8	17	12	15
Total outside family	52	48	51	58	33	47
No. of persons mentioned	363	468	831	35	106	141

many more Anger and Shame situations in which loss or damage to property is involved (Tables 56 and 57: Anger, I; Shame, IV). One might infer that American children find property easier to obtain and they enjoy its possession, while New Zealanders find it more difficult to obtain and begrudge its loss or damage.

Sex

There are very few responses dealing with relations with the opposite sex. This is probably due both to a taboo on discussion of this subject as well as a relative lack of interest in it by the younger children. It is mentioned with some frequency only in the 14-and-over age group. The Midwest boys mention Happiness over good relations with the opposite sex more than do the New Zealand boys, as well as Shame at bad

TABLE 63

EMOTIONAL RESPONSE TEST: COMPARISON OF NEW ZEALAND AND AMERICAN CHILDREN ON PERSONS INVOLVED IN ANGER (PERCENTAGE FREQUENCIES)

Category	New Zealand			Midwest		
	Boys	Girls	Total	Boys	Girls	Total
Family (except Fa., Mo., sibs)	2	4	3	3	9	6
Father	4	3	3	2	2	2
Mother	7	9	8	7	8	8
Sibs, same sex	24	19	22	12	21	17
Sibs, opp. sex	13	23	18	5	10	8
Total family	50	58	54	29	50	41
Peers, same sex	20	8	14	19	8	14
Peers, opp. sex	1	8	5	2	7	5
Peers in general	5	5	5	4	4	4
Teacher and school	7	7	7	9	5	7
Individual adult	1	1	1	...	...	...
They, somebody	13	10	12	39	26	33
Total outside family	47	39	44	73	50	63
No. of persons mentioned	996	1,085	2,081	189	317	506

behavior with the opposite sex (Table 56: Happiness, XII; Shame, VI). There is little difference between New Zealand and Midwest girls in this area. The same finding applies to mentions of peers of the opposite sex as persons involved in Happiness and Shame situations (Tables 60 and 64). A possible inference is that the American boys exhibit an earlier interest in girls than do New Zealand boys, while there is no comparable difference between the girls of the two societies.

Specific Categories

There are some minor categories in which there are interesting differences between New Zealand and Midwest children. For example, New Zealand youth mention travel much more frequently than do Midwest youth in their Happiness and Best Thing responses. It may be a "trip around the world" or a "trip to England" for Best Thing, and very

TABLE 64

EMOTIONAL RESPONSE TEST: COMPARISON OF NEW ZEALAND AND AMERICAN CHILDREN ON PERSONS INVOLVED IN SHAME (PERCENTAGE FREQUENCIES)

Category	New Zealand			Midwest		
	Boys	Girls	Total	Boys	Girls	Total
Family (except Fa., Mo., sibs)	5	9	7	9	10	9
Father	9	5	7	5	2	4
Mother	21	24	23	20	30	25
Sibs, same sex	11	10	10	2	11	7
Sibs, opp. sex	6	12	9	10	7	9
Total family	52	60	56	46	60	54
Peers, same sex	10	6	8	13	6	10
Peers, opp. sex	4	4	4	13	5	9
Peers in general	5	4	4	5	5	5
Teacher and school	10	14	12	9	10	10
Individual adult	5	2	4	...	...	...
They, somebody	6	8	7	17	17	17
Total outside family	40	38	39	57	43	51
No. of persons mentioned	457	625	1,082	111	244	355

often it is a vacation trip for Happiness. This probably reflects both a greater frequency of vacation trips in New Zealand (something that is quite noticeable to a visitor to the country) and a desire to see other parts of the world—a desire which might be expected in people who live on a relatively small island.

Another example is the difference in the frequency of mention of examinations as a source of Fear (Tables 56 and 56: Fear, XVII). While this is only mentioned 1.2 per cent of the time by New Zealand girls and 0.3 per cent by New Zealand boys, this is many times more frequent than the mentions by Midwest youth. This probably reflects the difference that school examinations play in the lives of children in the two countries. New Zealand youth must pass a national examination to get the "School Certificate," while for Midwest children, who can graduate from

high school simply by passing their courses, final examinations do not ʼlay such an important part in the outcome.

Relations with People

Father: As seen from Table 60, New Zealand boys mention the father on Happiness more than twice as often as do Midwest boys. Girls do not show a difference in this respect. On the other hand, Midwest boys mention the father more than New Zealand boys do on Sadness (Table 61). Thus it would appear that the father has a greater happiness-bringing (usually gift-giving) role in the lives of New Zealand boys. In general (Tables 60-64), it appears that New Zealand children see the father as more of an authority-figure than the Midwest children do and that the New Zealand father is also more positively related to his sons than is the Midwest father.

Mother: While Midwest girls mention the mother much more frequently than do New Zealand girls on Sadness,[4] on the whole it seems that there is not much difference between the two groups of children in their relations with their mothers, as reflected by these tests.

Siblings: There is considerable difference in the sibling relations of the New Zealand and American children as reflected on the tests. The most striking difference is in the persons involved in Anger situations (Table 63), where New Zealand boys mention siblings of both sexes twice as often as Midwest children do. New Zealand girls mention brothers in connection with Anger twice as often as Midwest girls do, but sisters slightly less often than Midwest girls.

Peers: In their relations with peers, Midwest boys and girls both mention peers of the opposite sex more frequently for Happiness than do New Zealanders. This probably reflects a greater frequency for the Midwest adolescents to become involved in boy-girl relationships.

Teachers: New Zealand children mention teachers much more frequently in Sadness, Fear, and Shame situations than do Midwest children. This probably reflects a greater frequency of punishment by teachers for New Zealand children or perhaps a greater intensity of punishment. It may reflect the greater prevalence in New Zealand schools

4. The meaning of this finding is ambiguous, as the girl may have been sad because of the mother's illness or because she had been punished by the mother.

of corporal punishment. "I was sad when I got the strap" or "I was afraid when I was going to get the strap" were common responses for New Zealand children. While corporal punishment is practiced in Midwest schools, it is probably not so frequent as in New Zealand schools.

The Community: People outside the family and school may be named as individual adults, as clergy, as police or other officers of government, or as a kind of impersonal "everybody, somebody, they." Midwest children mention the general and impersonal "everybody, somebody" much more frequently than the New Zealand children do, especially in Anger, Shame, and Fear situations. This may indicate a greater sensitivity to and contact with the human environment outside the home and school on the part of Midwest children. The New Zealand children sometimes mention individual adults outside the family by name in connection with Sadness, Fear, and Shame experiences, something that is almost never done by Midwest children. It may signify more of a tendency on the part of New Zealand children to think of people outside the immediate family as individuals, rather than to generalize about them as a group—a group which can exert moral or other pressures.

Comparison of Sex Differences

When one compares the responses from boys with those from girls in the two societies, two things at once become evident. First, most of the sex differences found in the Midwest data appear in the New Zealand data (while there are certain divergences, we have discussed the major ones in the sections above). Second, the degree of difference between boys and girls is usually less for New Zealand than for Midwest (this same tendency was seen in the Moral Ideology data). It is as if there were a greater difference between the lives of boys and girls in Midwest than in New Zealand.

Comparison of Age Trends

The age trends of values and aversions for New Zealand differ from those for Midwest on Smooth Personal Relations, Family-centeredness, Work, Discipline and Authority of Others, Illness and Accidents to Self, and Objective Danger. It would be a complex task to try to account for these differences between the two societies—a task that will not be attempted here. One of the most interesting problems would be that of explaining the difference in age trends on work as a value. The Midwest boys and girls go down from age B to C and then sharply up at age D.

By contrast, the New Zealand boys and girls show a regular increase with age. Apparently the New Zealand age group 11-13 has a much more pleasant experience with working and earning money and more interest in their future vocation than do Midwest boys and girls at this age.

Conclusions

The foregoing discussion of differences between New Zealand and Midwest children rests upon the fact of a common and similar foundation of moral ideology and emotion-arousing experience. The discussion has severe limits, due largely to the fact that we cannot accurately describe the very complex relations between the behavior of children, on the one hand, and their moral ideology and their memories of emotion-arousing situations, on the other hand. Still, we are probably on reasonably safe ground when we assume (1) that the stated moral ideology represents a set of moral pressures operating on the children and the reactions of the children to these pressures, and (2) that the responses on the Emotional Response Test reflect emotion-arousing experiences in combination of frequency, intensity, and recency.

It is on these assumptions that we have attempted to interpret the differences observed in the tests between New Zealand and Midwest youth. We have here data that are useful in studying the differences in "national character" or in "societal basic personality."

INDEX